Betty Crocker's
Buffets

Betty Crocker's
Buffets

Random House, Inc. New York

Plan a buffet! It's easily the most popular kind of party for today's space- and time-conscious hosts and hostesses. In *Betty Crocker's Buffets,* every step of your party plans is outlined and streamlined for you. Be relaxed and confident as you give parties that are a success in every way, with marvelous food, charming table settings and delighted guests.

Just pick from the sixty-seven Betty Crocker kitchen-tested menus for any occasion (breakfast, brunch, lunch, dinner or late supper), including ten special occasion menus for open houses, teas, cocktail parties and a wedding reception. Each is accompanied by its own timetable to make sure you are prepared down to the last detail when your first guest rings the doorbell.

The more than 270 recipes are for the kind of party food people love: appetizing, beautiful—often glamorous—and easy to prepare, to serve and to eat. Most recipes have detailed "do-ahead-of-party-time" directions with recommended storage, reheating or last-minute preparation information to ease your mind and leave you with more time for your guests.

The *Buffet Basics* section contains a wealth of ideas and tips for organizing your parties—from planning the menu to setting up a beverage service. Select from the three kinds of buffet service—true, seated or semi-buffet—and study the easy-to-follow diagrams for three kinds of buffet tables—the circular, the three-sided and the two-lined. Very important, too, are the explicit guidelines for assuring food safety, especially when you entertain large groups.

Here is everything you need to know about the art of entertaining graciously, imaginatively and with confidence at your buffet parties.

Betty Crocker

Editor, Lois Tlusty; Recipe Development Editor, Diana Gulden; Copy Editor, Judy Anderson; Copywriter, Elizabeth Lemmer; Food Styling Coordinator, Maria Rollandelli; Food Stylists, Camera Kitchen Home Economists; Art Director, Lynne Dolan; Prop Styling, Alice Meadows, Gail Bailey; Photographer, Steven Smith

Library of Congress Cataloging in Publication Data   Crocker, Betty. Betty Crocker's Buffets.

Includes index. 1. Buffets (Cookery). I Title.

TX738.5.C76   1984   642'.4   84-42536

Manufactured in the United States of America   24689753

ISBN 0-394-53592-8

Contents

Buffet Basics

LET'S GIVE A BUFFET PARTY

Whatever the occasion, the perfect way to entertain is with a buffet party. This is easily the most popular method of entertaining today. Guests enjoy the ease and freedom to serve themselves and to mingle in an atmosphere of warm hospitality and intimacy. They like the attention that places them rather than the table and the food in the limelight. And that is as it should be, for it is really the people who make any party.

For the host and hostess, the buffet party is popular for its practicality. In an era of shrinking living spaces, when most women work outside the home and the number of single-person households is growing rapidly, buffet service makes such good sense that a real "sitdown" party meal is now a rarity.

Whichever buffet service you select to use, the guests always serve themselves first and the host and hostess serve themselves last.

Buffet Service

There are basically three types of buffet service — true buffet, seated buffet and the semi-buffet. You can select the buffet service which best meets your needs as dictated by available space and the number of guests you wish to entertain.

True Buffet

The guests select food, beverage and silverware from the buffet table. They move to another room and sit wherever they are comfortable. Because the guests are usually eating with the plates or perhaps trays on their laps, it is best to serve food that can easily be eaten with a fork because cutting food with a knife can be difficult. Also, whenever possible, buttered rolls and bread should be on the buffet table. Small tables, supplied with coasters and ashtrays, placed near every few guests should be provided so beverage glasses and cups can be placed on them. After the main course, guests can leave their used dinner plates in a designated area and return to the buffet table for dessert or the host can remove the dinner plates and serve the dessert to the guests.

Seated Buffet

Only the food is placed on the buffet table. Guests serve themselves and then find places, at a table or tables set with glasses, silverware and napkins. Because guests are not balancing plates on their laps, the type of food served at this buffet is not limited to "fork food." Sometimes an appetizer or the salad course can be at the guests' place when they sit down or served at the table; then the guests go to the buffet table for the main course. After eating, the guests can remove their plates and return to the buffet for dessert. Or the dessert course can be served to the guests at the table.

Semi-Buffet

This buffet service can be performed one of two ways:

The guests can serve themselves from the buffet table and then be seated at a set table. The host or hostess then assists by serving each guest any accompaniments, such as a sauce or gravy, at the table.

Or, the host or hostess may fill each guest's plate from the buffet table and then serve the plates to the seated guests. This service is ideal if a roast is being served because each guest can be asked what cut of meat they prefer and the host can carve at the buffet table. Although buffet service is always considered informal, this type of service can lend itself to a more elegant meal.

Special Occasion Buffets

The open house, cocktail party or reception are some special occasions where buffet service is the only way to entertain a large number of guests. The party can be as casual as a cocktail party on a patio or lawn or as elegant as a wedding reception at home.

The Open House

This is a favorite way to entertain, especially at the holidays (see Holiday Open House menu, page 105). If you invite guests at stated, overlapping hours, you can entertain and exchange compliments of the season with many and more diversified people than on any other occasion and with less time and trouble.

If guests arrive within the time stated in your invitation — and written invitations are best so that they have a record of the time — they will usually depart after a half an hour or less, so that your entertaining space will never be overcrowded at any one time.

Mix and match close friends, business associates, office colleagues, church and club associates. Consider inviting whole families, including the children. Then serve something for everyone.

Paper party service and plastic glasses are acceptable at large open houses. Since the guests will stand for the most part, plenty of small paper cocktail napkins can substitute for plates and colorful toothpicks for forks. Keep food manageable in size and kind; replenish serving plates often. It is best to set out medium size platters and bowls rather than large ones and to replace them often. Large serving dishes can look empty or unappetizing after the first guests have served themselves.

No entertainment is required other than conversation, which will surely be general and animated enough to preclude even the need for soft music.

Of course, you need not wait for the holidays to entertain at an open house. The football season, for instance, is another welcome time for this pleasant and undemanding kind of party.

Receptions — Small and Large

A reception presupposes a guest or guests of honor — whether it is a wedding reception (see Wedding Reception menu, page 114), the recent recipient of an unusual award or title, a recently married couple or newcomers whom you wish to recognize and introduce to friends more formally than at an open house or cocktail party.

If you plan a reception in your home, you must enlist help both in preparations and serving arrangements. Unless it is a wedding reception, as host or hostess, you must remain with your honored guests to perform introductions through the entire event. This means you will not make trips to the kitchen, but will simply give instructions to your assigned assistants. While you should keep a watchful eye on the buffet table and offer food and drink to others, your primary attention will be given to your special guests.

As at other parties, refreshments may or may not include alcoholic beverages. Food will be somewhat more formal than at the open house, and plates and perhaps forks will be required. Small sandwiches, such as Watercress Triangles (page 115) made with both white and wheat breads, little cakes or a wedding cake plus nuts and mints are usual fare. Coffee, tea and punch accompany them.

The buffet table need not be covered with a long white cloth, although this is customary, and your decorations most likely will be a fresh floral centerpiece. Your best china, silver serving dishes, flatware and crystal are in order on this important occasion. Or, you can borrow from friends or rent the necessary dishes and equipment for a large reception.

For a large reception, see Buffets for Thirty or More on page 8 and follow the rules for Food Safety on page 13 scrupulously.

Teas

Afternoon teas are the perfect time to entertain guests, to introduce a guest of honor such as a visiting house guest or a new neighbor, or to wish a colleague good luck on a new career or job.

Plan to have your tea between 2:00 and 6:00 p.m. If it is a small, informal tea, the invitations can be done by telephone. For a more formal occasion, written invitations should be sent two weeks before. Specify the time, such as 2:30 p.m. to 3:30 p.m. to help control the flow of guests for a large tea.

Generally, most foods served at a tea are sweet. In addition, for the nonsweet eater, there are tea sandwiches or a sandwich loaf. Finger foods are ideal for a tea, however, small plates and a fork can be provided if a sandwich loaf is served. Salted mixed nuts add crunch and saltiness as a nice contrast to the sweets. Party mints add a decorative touch to the buffet table and serve as a refreshing finish.

The tea and coffee are placed at opposite ends of the buffet table. The tea or coffee server is placed on a tray along with the creamer and sugar. The cups and saucers are placed to the left of the tray within easy reach of the seated person who is pouring. Unless the food served requires silverware, only teaspoons are placed on the buffet table for the beverage.

Ask friends to do the "honors" of pouring — one person for each end of the table. You may want to ask four friends so they need to pour for only one-half hour and then can mingle with the guests. Chairs should be provided at each end of the table for the individual pouring so they can be seated. For a small tea, the hostess pours. Quantity recipes for tea and coffee are given on page 13. Remember, a refreshing punch or hot chocolate can replace the coffee.

Enlist extra help in the kitchen for a large tea to keep the tea and coffee servers filled, provide extra cups as needed and to replenish the food on the buffet table. For a small tea, no more than two foods need to be served and additional kitchen help should not be needed.

Cocktail Parties

Plenty of ice cubes, clean glasses and cocktail napkins are essential to a successful cocktail party. Since this is a stand-up affair, you can be as generous with your invitations as space and budget allow. Less intimate than a dinner party, the cocktail party is a vehicle for introducing and bringing together friends and business associates on an informal occasion.

Food is an essential part of the party for guests to nibble on while conversing with others. The buffet table can contain hot hors d'oeuvre, such as Greek Cheese Puffs (page 101), canapés, dips and dippers. Nuts and chips can be placed in several places throughout the room. Coffee in the kitchen or on a nearby table or cart is nice to have, or for a change of pace, offer hot bouillon in mugs from the kitchen range or a heat-proof container.

For a group of 18 or 20, it is wise to engage a bartender or ask a friend to fill in for the evening. For a really large group, plan on one bartender to serve guests. Smaller groups for "drinks" can be accommodated by host or hostess with the assistance of another guest. Also, be sure to have plenty of cocktail napkins, coasters and ashtrays placed throughout for your guests' convenience.

Let local customs help determine what you will need to stock your bar for the party. Have an ample supply of mixes, mineral water and club soda plus non-alcoholic beverages for the guests who prefer them. A general rule is to allow three cocktails per guest. Allow 2 liters of mix for every liter of liquor.

A reminder, you are responsible for your guests' safety when they leave your home, so be sure to provide transportation for anyone who may have consumed too much alcohol.

Buffets For Thirty Or More

There are special occasions for which special planning is required. These may be the open house, cocktail party, holiday or family reunion or wedding reception. At such times, it is important to think "big" and to plan in greater detail. Organization counts.

Inventory your kitchen work space, party room size, equipment and available oven, freezer and refrigerator storage capacity. Then borrow or rent what is needed, including heating devices for keeping foods safely and appetizingly hot.

Let lists be your guide. Make lists of the ingredients, special food items and beverages you plan to serve. To spread costs and labor, make several trips over a period of weeks to the market for staples. Then buy the fresh foods as close to party time as practical.

Except for really formal occasions, consider using disposable plates and paperware rather than planning to wash and dry dishes and glasses during the party to accommodate many guests.

Enlist competent help both for the kitchen and to replenish the buffet table, and make sure your assistants know what will be required of them and when.

Remember, if a recipe does not provide enough servings, it is better to prepare the recipe individually as many times as necessary.

When The Buffet Begins

Parties customarily, although not always, begin at the times suggested below. The open house and cocktail party invitation should state the time the party begins and ends and guests should not plan to stay longer.

Occasion	Time
Breakfast	Between 8 and 9:30 am
Coffee Party	At 10 am, 4 or 8 pm
Brunch	Between 10:30 am and 12 pm
Luncheon	At 12:30 or 1 pm
Open House	Between 3 and 5 pm
Teas	Between 2 and 6 pm
Cocktail Party	From 5 until 7 pm
Dinner	Between 6:30 and 8 pm Serve 45 minutes after guests arrive.
Reception	Anytime during the day or evening
Late Supper	Following an evening event after 10 pm.

Planning The Party

What your guests will appreciate most is you, your best food and most inviting and relaxing setting. For a successful party, careful planning and organizing is necessary.

A week or more before the party:
- ☐ Buy all staple foods and ingredients for dishes to be made ahead.
- ☐ Buy or freeze plenty of ice cubes.
- ☐ Do all possible food preparation for dishes that are to be frozen.
- ☐ Arrange or borrow or rent any party equipment you will need.
- ☐ Order the buffet table centerpiece, if any.
- ☐ Check all linens to be sure that they are immaculate and well pressed.

A few days before the party:
- ☐ Do all major house cleaning chores.
- ☐ Polish silverware.
- ☐ Have a dress rehearsal of the buffet table and guest seating arrangements.

The day before the party:
- ☐ Wash plates and glasses.
- ☐ Set up the buffet table and beverage service.

On the party day:
- ☐ Complete all food preparation.
- ☐ Give the house a once-over-lightly dusting.
- ☐ Clear a space for guests to leave their wraps.
- ☐ Clean the bathroom and put out fresh soap and guest towels.

Allow yourself an hour or two before your guests arrive to relax and make a last-minute check of the arrangement. Then, concentrate on enjoying your own party. And, after the party is over, make a record of the guests and the menu for future reference.

Entertaining On Your Own

If you live alone — and today a large and growing number of singles, both men and women, do — you need not always have to go it alone when you entertain.

Join forces with another single person; share your guest lists and friends. It may make for a more interesting mix of people at your parties and many new friends for everyone. Share your party equipment, share the planning, the preparation and the duties and pleasures of being a host or hostess. And even if you entertain by yourself, there are ways to simplify and make the event more gracious.

The Buffet Table

Before setting your buffet table, determine the number of guests and which buffet style you will be using — true, seated or semi-buffet. Then remember the key to success is to select a buffet table setting so the traffic flows smoothly and easily. The serving line should begin and end at a logical point to avoid congestion and confusion.

Whether you need one or two lines, the food should be placed in order so the guests can serve themselves without backtracking. Plates first, main course and vegetables next, then salad, condiments, bread and, if it is a true buffet, the silverware and napkins last. Each dish should be easy to reach and complete with serving pieces.

While the guests finish the main course, the hostess clears the buffet table and arranges the dessert, dessert plates and silverware on the buffet table or on a side table. Coffee can be served with dessert from the buffet or side table or both can be served in the family or living room. For a seated or semi-buffet, the dessert and coffee can be served to the guests at the table if it is more convenient.

After you have determined where your buffet table will be placed, plan your centerpiece. Arrange all the serving dishes on the buffet, each with its appropriate serving pieces, to estimate space requirements. The centerpiece should be of a size in proportion to the table but should not overwhelm the food, which is its principal attraction.

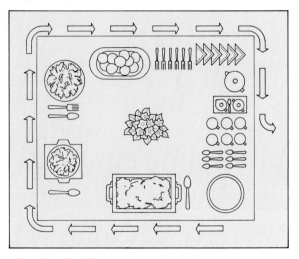

Circular Buffet

The buffet table is in the center of the room so the guests can help themselves from all sides whether the table is square, rectangular or round. The logical starting point begins with the plates and ends with the beverage service.

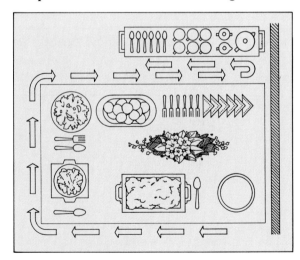

Three-sided Buffet

If space is limited, place the buffet table against a wall. The plates should be placed at the end of the table that makes the best traffic flow so guests can go directly to where they will be eating after serving themselves. The beverage service can be placed at the end of the table or at a small side table.

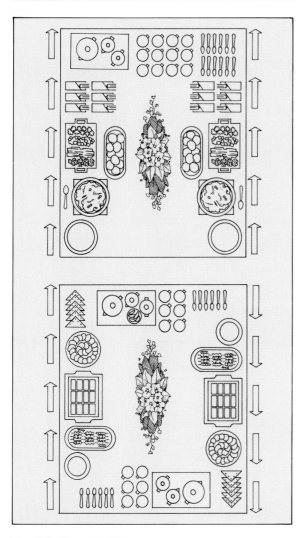

Double-line Buffet

Two serving lines are ideal for a large group because it makes service faster. Both lines should have the same arrangement of plates, food, silverware and napkins on both sides. For a tea or reception, it is convenient to have the lines go in opposite directions with tea service at one end and coffee at the other.

The buffet can be set up wherever it is most convenient — on a sideboard, the dining room table, a desk, two card tables placed together and covered with a cloth or even on the kitchen counter for a very informal potluck meal. The table is usually covered with a cloth or a fabric runner. However, polished wood surfaces can be left bare except for trivets and protective mats beneath the serving dishes.

Planning The Menu

Now that you know the number of guests to expect, choose a menu that fits your facilities, time requirements and expertise as a cook.

Choose foods that complement one another and contrast in texture, color, flavor, shape and size. Keep garnishes to a minimum. Above all, plan a menu that can be prepared almost entirely ahead of time. The menus in this book all stress do-ahead convenience and the recipes clearly indicate the point to which a dish can be prepared, then frozen or refrigerated until the day of the party. Information is included about times and methods for reheating or last minute preparation at serving time.

A reminder — the menus in this cookbook give the recommended number of servings; not the number of guests this will serve. For example, a menu for 12 servings may only be enough for 6 guests if each guest has 2 servings. Therefore, keep this in mind when planning your menu because you may want to prepare a recipe more than once.

When preparing food for a larger number of servings, it is better to prepare the recipe individually as many times as is necessary to have the correct number of servings. All the recipes in this cookbook can be easily prepared one or more times. It is not a good idea to double or multiply the recipe and prepare it in a larger container. Just because the other ingredients are increased does not necessarily mean that the seasonings are increased in equal portions. The result may be too highly seasoned. Also, the amount of liquid may need to be varied or the finished food may be too dry or too soupy.

It is easier to serve guests food at the right temperature if you use several containers, and before a hot dish on the buffet table gets cold or a cold dish loses its chill, replace it with a refill from the kitchen. If you plan to replenish the buffet table with hot food, stagger the heating times so the food will be fresh and hot for every refill. In this way, all the guests will have hot or cold food that is attractive whether they arrive at the table at the beginning or at the end of the buffet.

Beverage Service

Wine and Cocktails

Whether to serve cocktails or wine is the choice of the hosts, who are also responsible for the safe return home of their guests. If someone's sobriety is in question when the party ends, ask another person to drive, call a taxi or confiscate the guest's car keys, if necessary, and insist that the guest stay the night. Again, courteous attention to guests who don't drink alcohol decrees an alternate non-alcoholic beverage.

Refer to your wallet and local customs when you plan to serve cocktails. Vodka, gin, scotch, bourbon and whiskey are a few liquors that are popular in most areas of the United States. Be sure to have plenty of tonic, sweet mixes and sour-based mixes, club soda and cut-up fruit and vegetables to mix with the liquor. For mixed drinks, plan on 2 liters of non-alcoholic mix for each liter of liquor. Or you may just want to select one beverage, such as Sangria (page 94) and have pitchers of it available. You may also want to serve chilled beer such as domestic light, domestic premium or light and dark imports.

All glasses should be clean and sparkling but they do not need to be expensive. Wine or champagne should be served in a clear, tulip-shaped glass with a bowl about 2½ to 3½ inches in diameter. Mixed drink glasses range from tall for mixed drinks to short for "on the rocks." Beer glasses come in a variety of shapes but be sure the glass is chilled before pouring the beer.

Following is a chart to help you determine the amount of wine or liquor to purchase for the number of guests.

Liquor Bottle Sizes

Bottle Size	Ounces	Number of Servings
Fifth (⅘ quart)	25.6	10-16
Quart	32	12-20
Liter	33.8	12-20

Wine Bottle Sizes

Bottle Size	Ounces	Number of Servings
Split (¼ bottle)	6.4	1-2
Fifth (⅘ quart)	25.6	6-8
Quart	32	8-10
Liter (1 quart + ¼ cup)	33.8	8-10
Magnum	52	16
Jeroboam	104	24-32
Rehoboam	156	48

Punch

At a reception or tea, the punch can be placed on a small table near the buffet table or it can be placed at one end and both a coffee and tea server placed at the other end of the buffet table. For a lunch or dinner party, it is nice to have the punch ready when the guests arrive so they can enjoy it before the meal. The punch can be placed on a small side table so it does not have to be removed prior to setting the buffet table. It is a personal preference whether you serve an alcoholic punch or not.

Coffee and Tea

Beverage service, such as coffee and tea, can be placed on the buffet table after the silverware and napkins; or it can stand nearby on a sideboard, cart or small table. Guests serve themselves or are served by the hosts. Or, the beverage can be served in the family or living room after the meal. For a seated or semi-buffet, the beverage can be served at the set table. Coffee is accompanied by sugar and cream and tea by lemon slices as well. Sugar cubes are usually preferred for ease of serving.

The coffee and tea should be freshly brewed and of good quality. For a large group, prepare a tea concentrate to simplify service. Coffee can be made in a large kettle if you do not have a coffee urn or large coffee pot. The following are some recipes for quantity tea and coffee.

Coffee

Measure regular-grind coffee (see chart) in a clean cloth bag, filling only about ½ full to allow coffee to expand and water to circulate through grounds. Tie top of bag, leaving enough cord to fasten bag to handle of large container. Measure cold water into container and heat to full boil; reduce heat. Submerge bag of coffee in water. Brew, pushing bag up and down with wooden spoon for proper extraction, 6 to 8 minutes. Remove bag; keep coffee hot but do not allow it to boil.

Regular Grind Coffee	Water	Servings (¾ cup each)
2 cups	4 quarts	23
4 cups	8 quarts	46
9 cups	4½ gallons	100

Hot Tea

Prepare a concentrate by placing ¼ pound (1½ cups) loose tea in a large heat-proof container and pour 2½ quarts boiling water over tea; steep 5 minutes. Strain tea leaves. Mix 1 part concentrate to 3 parts boiling water and serve as needed. This concentrate will make about 50 servings of tea.

A Short Course In Food Safety

Finally, but really top priority, is food safety. While food safety is equally important whatever the number of guests, it is more difficult to guarantee freedom from food-borne illnesses when large quantities of food and numbers of people are involved.

General Food Safety Rules

1. Keep everything related to food clean.

2. Keep hot foods hot (about 140°) and cold foods cold (about 40° — refrigerator temperature).

☐ Begin with clean work surfaces, counters, equipment, cutting boards and utensils. For uncooked meat or poultry, use a separate hard plastic cutting board (less porous than wood) and wash immediately after using.

☐ Illness-causing bacteria thrive best at luke-warm or tepid temperatures — especially in these more perishable food categories:
   Meat and poultry (especially ground or chopped)
   Fish or seafood
   Eggs, cheese and milk products
   Sauces, gravies, mayonnaise
   Sandwich fillings, stuffings

☐ If refrigerator space is limited, borrow a shelf or two in a neighbor's refrigerator or store cold foods packed in ice in well-insulated coolers.

☐ Do not allow any hot or cold food to remain at room temperature for more than two hours. To keep cooked and reheated foods hot for a large party, serve them on electric hot trays or in chafing dishes, which may be electric or use alcohol, canned heat or butane gas as fuel supply. Candle-heated warmers are not sufficiently hot to assure hot food for safety.

☐ Cold foods, especially if they contain meat, fish and poultry or eggs, cream and salad mixtures, should be brought directly from the refrigerator to the buffet table in dishes they are to be served in, thus keeping them chilled longer. Serve them in medium-size quantities and replace as needed. On a hot day, serve cold foods over crushed ice to keep them chilled.

☐ If you carry perishable foods to another place or to a picnic outdoors, pack them in ice in a cooler; keep the cooler in a shady place and open it as infrequently as possible. Return leftover food to cooler on the return trip.

☐ Refrigerate leftovers from the buffet immediately. Remember, you cannot always detect spoilage from appearance, odor or taste. So discard any food that you know to have been exposed to room temperatures for too long a time. It is better to be safe than sorry!

Dinners

A Chinese Buffet

Menu

12 servings

Shrimp Toast*

Fried Wontons*

Hot Mustard*

Plum Sauce*

Chicken with Cashews*

Sweet-and-Sour Beef*

Steamed Rice

Oriental Fruit Bowl*

Tea

***Recipe included**

About 1 month before buffet:
☐ Prepare Fried Wontons; freeze.

1 week before:
☐ Prepare Sweet-and-Sour Beef; freeze.
☐ Prepare Plum Sauce; refrigerate.

1 day before:
☐ Prepare Shrimp Toast; refrigerate.

Several hours before serving:
☐ Prepare Oriental Fruit Bowl; refrigerate.
☐ Cut chicken into pieces for Chicken with Cashews; cover and refrigerate.
☐ Assemble ingredients for Chicken with Cashews.
☐ Prepare Hot Mustard; cover and refrigerate.

When guests arrive:
☐ Heat Fried Wontons and Shrimp Toast.
☐ Serve Fried Wontons, Shrimp Toast, Hot Mustard and Plum Sauce.

About 30 minutes before serving:
☐ Prepare Steamed Rice.
☐ Marinate chicken for Chicken with Cashews.
☐ Heat beef mixture and sauce for Sweet-and-Sour Beef.
☐ Prepare Tea.
☐ Cook Chicken with Cashews.

At dessert time:
☐ Serve Oriental Fruit Bowl.

A Chinese Buffet

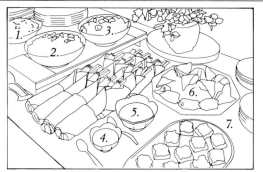

1. Steamed Rice, 2. Chicken with Cashews, 3. Sweet-and-Sour Beef, 4. Hot Mustard, 5. Plum Sauce, 6. Fried Wontons, 7. Shrimp Toast

Hot Mustard

Stir together ¼ cup dry mustard and 3 tablespoons plus 1½ teaspoons cold water until smooth. Let stand 5 minutes before serving. Cover and refrigerate any remaining mustard. ⅓ cup.

Plum Sauce

1 can (8¼ ounces) crushed pineapple in heavy
   syrup
⅓ cup sugar
½ cup water
½ cup vinegar
1 teaspoon soy sauce
1 tablespoon cornstarch
1 tablespoon cold water
½ cup plum sauce, plum jam or orange
   marmalade

Heat pineapple (with syrup), sugar, ½ cup water, the vinegar and soy sauce to boiling. Mix cornstarch and 1 tablespoon water; stir into pineapple mixture. Heat to boiling, stirring constantly. Cool to room temperature; stir in plum sauce. Cover and refrigerate no longer than 1 week. 2¼ cups.

Shrimp Toast

½ pound fresh or frozen raw shrimp, thawed
½ cup chopped green onions (with tops)
¼ cup all-purpose flour
¼ cup water
1 egg
1 tablespoon cornstarch
1 teaspoon salt
¼ teaspoon sugar
¼ teaspoon sesame oil
   Dash of white pepper
   Vegetable oil
5 slices white bread

Peel shrimp. Make a shallow cut lengthwise down back of each shrimp; wash out sand vein. Cut shrimp lengthwise into halves; cut crosswise into halves. Mix shrimp, onions, flour, water, egg, cornstarch, salt, sugar, sesame oil and white pepper.

Heat oil (1½ inches) in wok to 350°. Remove crusts from bread; cut each slice into 4 squares. Place 1 or 2 pieces shrimp with sauce on each bread square. Fry 5 squares at a time, turning frequently, until golden brown, about

2 minutes; drain. Cover and refrigerate no longer than 24 hours.

Heat uncovered in 400° oven until hot, 12 to 15 minutes; drain. 20 appetizers.

Fried Wontons

½ chicken breast (about ½ pound)
3 canned water chestnuts, finely chopped
2 tablespoons chopped green onions (with tops)
1 teaspoon vegetable oil
½ teaspoon cornstarch
½ teaspoon salt
½ teaspoon light soy sauce
   Dash of white pepper
½ pound wonton skins
1 egg, slightly beaten
   Vegetable oil

Remove skin and bones from chicken; finely chop chicken. Mix chicken, water chestnuts, onions, 1 teaspooon vegetable oil, the cornstarch, salt, soy sauce and white pepper.

Place ½ teaspoon chicken mixture in center of each wonton skin. (Cover remaining skins with dampened towel to keep them pliable.) Fold bottom corner of wonton skin over filling to opposite corner, forming a triangle. Brush right corner of triangle with egg. Bring corners together below filling; pinch left corner to right corner to seal. Repeat with remaining wonton skins. (Cover filled wontons with dampened towel or plastic wrap to prevent them from drying out.)

Heat oil (1½ inches) in wok to 350°. Fry 8 to 10 wontons at a time, turning 2 or 3 times, until golden brown, about 3 minutes; drain. Wrap, label and freeze no longer than 1 month.

Heat frozen wontons uncovered in 400° oven until hot, 10 to 12 minutes. 25 to 30 appetizers.

Chicken with Cashews

4 whole chicken breasts (about 4 pounds)
2 egg whites
2 teaspoons cornstarch
2 teaspoons soy sauce
  Dash of white pepper
1 large green pepper
2 medium onions
2 cans (8½ ounces each) sliced bamboo shoots,
  drained
2 tablespoons cornstarch
¼ cup soy sauce
2 tablespoons cold water
2 tablespoons vegetable oil
2 cups raw cashews
½ teaspoon salt
2 teaspoons finely chopped gingerroot
2 teaspoons vegetable oil
2 tablespoons Hoisin sauce
1 teaspoon finely chopped dried red pepper
¼ cup chicken broth
2 tablespoons chopped green onions (with tops)

Remove skin and bones from chicken; cut chicken into ¼-inch pieces. Mix egg whites, 2 teaspoons cornstarch, 2 teaspoons soy sauce and the white pepper in glass or plastic bowl; stir in chicken. Cover and refrigerate 20 minutes. Cut green pepper into ¾-inch pieces. Cut each onion into 8 pieces. Cut bamboo shoots into ½-inch pieces. Mix 2 tablespoons cornstarch, ¼ cup soy sauce and the water.

Heat wok until 1 or 2 drops of water bubble and skitter when sprinkled in wok. Add 2 tablespoons oil; rotate wok to coat side. Stir-fry cashews until light brown, about 1 minute. Remove cashews from wok; drain. Sprinkle with salt. Add chicken to wok; stir-fry until chicken turns white. Remove chicken from wok.

Add onion pieces and gingerroot to wok; stir-fry until gingerroot is light brown. Stir in bamboo shoots. Add 2 tablespoons oil; rotate wok to coat side. Add chicken, green pepper, Hoisin sauce and red pepper; stir-fry 1 minute. Stir in chicken broth; heat to boiling. Stir in cornstarch mixture; cook and stir until thickened, about 20 seconds. Stir in cashews and green onions.

Sweet-and-Sour Beef

1½ pounds beef flank steak
2 eggs, slightly beaten
2 tablespoons cornstarch
2 tablespoons vegetable oil
2 teaspoons salt
2 teaspoons soy sauce
½ teaspoon white pepper
2 medium carrots
  Vegetable oil
½ cup all-purpose flour
½ cup water
2 tablespoons cornstarch
1 tablespoon vegetable oil
½ teaspoon baking soda
2 cups sugar
1½ cups chicken broth
1½ cups white vinegar
2 tablespoons vegetable oil
1 tablespoon plus 1 teaspoon soy sauce
1 teaspoon salt
2 cloves garlic, finely chopped
½ cup cold water
⅓ cup cornstarch
2 cans (8¼ ounces each) pineapple chunks,
  drained
1 medium green pepper

Trim fat from beef; cut beef with grain into 2-inch strips. Cut strips across grain into ⅛-inch slices. Mix eggs, 2 tablespoons cornstarch, 2 tablespoons oil, 2 teaspoons salt, 2 teaspoons soy sauce and the white pepper in glass or plastic bowl; stir in beef. Cover and refrigerate 20 minutes. Cut carrots diagonally into thin slices. Place carrots in boiling water. Cover and cook 1 minute; drain. Immediately rinse under cold water; drain.

Heat oil (1½ inches) in wok to 350°. Mix flour, ½ cup water, 2 tablespoons cornstarch, 1 tablespoon oil and the baking soda. Stir beef slices into batter until well coated. Fry ⅛ of the slices at a time, turning 2 or 3 times, until light brown, about 2 minutes; drain. Wrap, label and freeze no longer than 1 week.

Heat sugar, chicken broth, vinegar, 2 tablespoons oil, 1 tablespoon plus 1 teaspoon soy sauce, 1 teaspoon salt and the garlic to boiling in 3-quart saucepan. Mix ½ cup water and ⅓ cup cornstarch; stir into sauce. Cook and stir until thickened, about 15 seconds. Stir in carrots and pineapple. Label and freeze no longer than 1 week.

Cut green pepper into 1-inch pieces. Dip container of sauce into very hot water just to loosen. Place frozen block in 3-quart saucepan. Cover tightly and heat, stirring occasionally, until thawed. Heat frozen beef uncovered in 400° oven until hot, about 20 minutes. Place beef on heated platter. Stir green pepper into sauce. Heat to boiling; pour over beef.

Oriental Fruit Bowl

2 *cans (11 ounces each) mandarin orange segments, drained*
1 *can (11 ounces) lychee nuts, drained*
1 *medium pineapple, cut into 1-inch pieces*
1 *honeydew melon, cut into 1-inch pieces*
1 *pint strawberries, cut into halves*

Toss all ingredients. Cover and refrigerate no longer than 12 hours.

Spoon fruit into serving bowl. Garnish with mint leaves if desired.

Oriental Fruit Bowl

An East Indian Buffet

Menu

8 servings

Tandoori-style Chicken*

Roasted Onions*

Cucumber-Tomato Salad*

Poppadums*

Mango Dessert*

Tea

*Recipe included

2 days before buffet:
- ☐ Prepare Poppadums; store at room temperature.

1 day before:
- ☐ Marinate chicken for Tandoori-style Chicken; refrigerate.
- ☐ Prepare vegetables and yogurt mixture for Cucumber-Tomato Salad; refrigerate.

Several hours before serving:
- ☐ Prepare mangoes and mango purée for Mango Dessert; cover and refrigerate.

About 1 hour before:
- ☐ Bake Tandoori-style Chicken.
- ☐ Bake Roasted Onions.

At serving time:
- ☐ Complete Cucumber-Tomato Salad.

At dessert time:
- ☐ Prepare Tea.
- ☐ Complete Mango Dessert.

Tandoori-style Chicken

4 whole chicken breasts (about 4 pounds)
1/2 teaspoon water
1/4 teaspoon dry mustard
1 cup unflavored yogurt
1/4 cup lemon juice
1 1/2 teaspoons salt
1 1/2 teaspoons paprika
1/2 teaspoon ground cardamom
1/4 teaspoon ground ginger
1/4 teaspoon ground cumin
1/4 teaspoon dried crushed red pepper
1/4 teaspoon pepper
1 clove garlic, crushed
1/4 cup water

Remove skin and bones from chicken breasts; cut chicken into halves. Place chicken in large glass or plastic bowl. Mix 1/2 teaspoon water and the mustard in 1-quart bowl; stir in yogurt, lemon juice, salt, paprika, cardamom, ginger, cumin, red pepper, pepper and garlic. Pour over chicken; turn to coat well with marinade. Cover and refrigerate at least 12 hours but no longer than 24 hours.

Remove chicken from marinade; place chicken in greased rectangular baking dish, 13×9×2 inches. Bake uncovered in 375° oven until done, about 45 minutes. Garnish with lemon slices if desired.

Roasted Onions

Place 8 medium onions (with skins) directly on middle oven rack. Bake in 375° oven until onions are tender, 25 to 30 minutes. Remove skins; place onions upright in serving dish. Score top of each onion. Garnish with parsley if desired.

Poppadums

Prepare 1 package (4 ounces) poppadums* as directed. Cover loosely and store at room temperature no longer than 48 hours.

*If poppadums are not available, substitute large crisp, unsalted crackers.

Cucumber-Tomato Salad

2 *medium cucumbers*
2 *medium tomatoes, chopped*
2 *green onions (with tops), chopped*
1 *tablespoon snipped parsley*
1 *cup unflavored yogurt*
½ *teaspoon salt*
¼ *teaspoon ground cumin*

Cut cucumbers lengthwise into halves. Scoop out seeds and cut cucumbers into ½-inch pieces. Mix cucumbers, tomatoes, onions and parsley. Cover and refrigerate at least 4 hours but no longer than 24 hours. Mix yogurt, salt and cumin. Cover and refrigerate at least 4 hours but no longer than 24 hours.

Drain vegetables and fold into yogurt mixture. Garnish with additional chopped cucumbers and tomatoes if desired.

Mango Dessert

4 *mangoes (about 2 pounds)*
1 *cup chilled whipping cream*
¼ *cup powdered sugar*
1 *lime, cut into halves*

Cut 3 of the mangoes into pieces; cover and refrigerate no longer than 8 hours. Cut remaining mango into pieces and place in blender container. Cover and blend on high speed, stopping blender occasionally to scrape sides, until smooth, about 1 minute. Cover and refrigerate no longer than 8 hours.

Beat whipping cream and powdered sugar in chilled bowl until thick but not stiff. Fold in puréed mango. Squeeze juice from lime halves over mango pieces; spoon whipped cream on top. Garnish with lime slices if desired.

Boning Chicken Breast

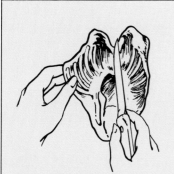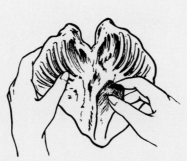

Cut through white gristle at neck end of chicken breast.

Bend back to pop keel bone; loosen keel and remove.

Cut rib cage through shoulder joint and remove. Cut wishbone from chicken.

A Mother's Day Buffet

Menu

8 servings

Coconut Chicken*

Chutney*

**Bulgur Wheat
(page 70)**

Whole Green Beans

Orange Salad*

Parkerhouse Rolls

Fruit Tart*

Coffee   Tea

***Recipe included**

Several days before buffet:
☐ Prepare Chutney; refrigerate.

1 day before:
☐ Prepare Fruit Tart; refrigerate.
☐ Prepare Lime-Honey Dressing for Orange Salad;
refrigerate.
☐ Prepare Coconut Chicken for baking; refrigerate.

Several hours before serving:
☐ Prepare oranges, onion and green pepper for
Orange Salad; cover and refrigerate.

About 1 hour before:
☐ Bake Coconut Chicken.
☐ Remove remaining Chutney from refrigerator; let
stand at room temperature.

About 30 minutes before:
☐ Complete Orange Salad; refrigerate.
☐ Cook Whole Green Beans.
☐ Prepare Bulgur Wheat.
☐ Heat Parkerhouse Rolls.
☐ Prepare Coffee and Tea.

Coconut Chicken

Chutney (page 24)
8 chicken breast halves (about 4 pounds)
1 teaspoon salt
¼ teaspoon ground coriander
¼ teaspoon ground cumin
2 cloves garlic, finely chopped
½ cup buttermilk or milk
2 cups flaked coconut
¼ cup margarine or butter, melted

Prepare Chutney. Remove skin and bones from chicken breasts. Flatten each chicken piece to ¼-inch thickness between waxed paper or plastic wrap. Mix salt, coriander, cumin and garlic; sprinkle about ¼ teaspoon on each chicken piece.

Place about 1 tablespoon Chutney on center of each chicken piece. Fold long sides over Chutney; fold ends up and secure with wooden picks. Dip chicken into buttermilk; coat evenly with coconut. Place chicken pieces, seam sides down, in greased rectangular pan, 13×9×2 inches. Cover and refrigerate no longer than 24 hours.

Pour margarine evenly over chicken. Cover and bake in 425° oven 30 minutes. Uncover and bake until chicken is done, about 15 minutes. Serve with remaining Chutney.

---

*Clockwise from top: Fruit Tart, Orange Salad and Coconut
Chicken*

Chutney

2½ cups chopped apples (about 2 apples)
1 cup cut-up dried apricots (about 4 ounces)
¾ cup packed brown sugar
½ cup vinegar
1 teaspoon ground ginger
½ teaspoon salt
½ teaspoon ground cinnamon
½ teaspoon ground cumin
¼ teaspoon ground coriander
¼ teaspoon ground cloves
⅛ teaspoon red pepper sauce
1 lemon, cut into thin slices and seeds removed
1 clove garlic, finely chopped

Mix all ingredients in 3-quart saucepan. Heat to boiling; reduce heat. Cook over low heat, stirring frequently, until thickened, about 1 hour. Cool slightly; cover and refrigerate no longer than 2 weeks. Serve at room temperature. About 2 cups.

Orange Salad

Lime-Honey Dressing (below)
5 medium oranges, pared and sliced
1 medium onion, thinly sliced
1 medium green pepper, cut into thin rings
Salad greens

Prepare Lime-Honey Dressing. Arrange orange slices, onion rings and green pepper rings on salad greens. Drizzle Lime-Honey Dressing over salad.

Lime-Honey Dressing

¼ cup vegetable oil
¼ teaspoon grated lime peel
3 tablespoons lime juice
3 tablespoons honey
½ teaspoon dry mustard
¼ teaspoon seasoned salt
¼ teaspoon paprika
Dash of white pepper

Shake all ingredients in tightly covered container; refrigerate at least 2 hours. Shake before using.

Fruit Tart

1 cup buttermilk baking mix
2 tablespoons sugar
1 tablespoon margarine or butter, softened
2 packages (3 ounces each) cream cheese, softened
¼ cup sugar
¼ cup dairy sour cream
1 kiwi fruit, thinly sliced
1 cup seedless green grape halves
⅓ cup sugar
2 teaspoons cornstarch
⅓ cup water
2 drops yellow food color
1 drop green food color
1 to 2 teaspoons lemon juice

Heat oven to 400°. Mix baking mix, 2 tablespoons sugar, the margarine and 1 package cream cheese until dough forms a ball. Press into ungreased springform pan, 9 × 3 inches. Bake until light brown, 10 to 12 minutes; cool.

Beat 1 package cream cheese, ¼ cup sugar and the sour cream on low speed until smooth. Spread over baked layer. Arrange kiwi and grapes on cream cheese mixture.

Mix ⅓ cup sugar and the cornstarch in 1-quart saucepan. Gradually stir in water. Heat to boiling, stirring constantly. Boil and stir 1 minute. Stir in food colors and lemon juice. Cool 2 to 3 minutes; carefully spread over fruit. Refrigerate at least 2 hours but no longer than 24 hours. Refrigerate any remaining dessert.

OTHER BETTY CROCKER RECIPES

Some foods suggested in the menus do not include recipes because they can be purchased readily or easily prepared following package directions. However, some of these recipes appear in other Betty Crocker cookbooks and a listing is given at the end of the Index (page 192) for your convenience.

Arroz con Pollo and Avocado-Pineapple Salad

A Caribbean Buffet

Menu

12 servings

Cola Punch*

Surullitos*

Plantain Chips*

Arroz con Pollo*

Avocado-Pineapple Salad*

Crusty Bread

Sweet Potato Cake*

Coffee   Tea

***Recipe included**

Several weeks before buffet:
- ☐ Bake Sweet Potato Cake; freeze.

2 days before:
- ☐ Prepare Surullitos and Plantain Chips; store at room temperature.
- ☐ Prepare Sweet-and-Sour Onion Dressing for Avocado-Pineapple salad; refrigerate.

1 day before:
- ☐ Prepare Arroz con Pollo for baking; refrigerate.
- ☐ Prepare Coconut Cream for Sweet Potato Cake; refrigerate.

About 6 hours before serving:
- ☐ Remove Sweet Potato Cake from freezer; let stand at room temperature.

About 1 hour 30 minutes before:
- ☐ Prepare Avocado-Pineapple Salad; refrigerate until serving.
- ☐ Bake Arroz con Pollo.

When guests arrive:
- ☐ Heat Surullitos. Prepare Cola Punch. Serve Surullitos and Plantain Chips with Cola Punch.

About 15 minutes before serving:
- ☐ Add peas to Arroz con Pollo.
- ☐ Prepare Coffee and Tea.
- ☐ Arrange Crusty Bread in serving container.

At dessert time:
- ☐ Serve Sweet Potato Cake with Coconut Cream.

Cola Punch

3 cups rum
1/2 cup lime juice
  Ice
2 quarts cola carbonated beverage, chilled
  Lime slices

Pour rum and lime juice over ice in punch bowl. Add cola; stir. Garnish with lime slices. 24 servings (about 1/2 cup each).

Surullitos

1 1/2 cups water
  1 teaspoon salt
  1 cup yellow cornmeal
  1 cup shredded Gouda or Cheddar cheese
      (4 ounces)
    Vegetable oil

Heat water and salt to boiling in 1-quart saucepan. Gradually stir in cornmeal. Cook over medium heat, stirring constantly, until mixture thickens and pulls from side of pan; remove from heat. Stir in cheese; cool.

Shape mixture by teaspoonfuls into sticks, 3 × 1/2 inch. (Dip hands in cold water to help prevent dough from sticking to hands.)

Heat oil (2 inches) to 350°. Fry several sticks at a time, turning once, until golden brown, about 5 minutes; drain. Cover and store at room temperature no longer than 48 hours.

Heat uncovered in 350° oven until hot, about 10 minutes. About 2 1/2 dozen sticks.

Plantain Chips

    Vegetable oil
4 green plantains
1 teaspoon salt

Heat oil (2 inches) to 350°. Remove peel from plantains; cut plantains into 1/8-inch slices. Fry in hot oil until golden brown, about 2 minutes; drain. Sprinkle with salt. Wrap in aluminum foil and store at room temperature no longer than 48 hours. About 5 cups chips.

Arroz con Pollo

  2 cups uncooked regular rice
  4 cups water
  1 tablespoon instant chicken bouillon
  1 teaspoon salt
  1 teaspoon dried oregano leaves
  1 teaspoon ground cumin
  1 teaspoon ground turmeric
  2 cloves garlic, crushed
  2 jars (2 ounces each) sliced pimientos, drained
1 1/2 teaspoons salt
  1 teaspoon paprika
1/2 teaspoon pepper
  3 2 1/2- to 3-pound broiler-fryer chickens,
      cut up
    Olive or vegetable oil
  1 package (10 ounces) frozen green peas

Heat rice, water, chicken bouillon (dry), 1 teaspoon salt, the oregano, cumin, turmeric and garlic to boiling, stirring once or twice; reduce heat. Cover and simmer 14 minutes (do not lift cover or stir). Remove from heat; fluff rice lightly with fork. Cover and let steam 5 to 10 minutes. Divide rice between 2 ungreased rectangular baking dishes, 13 × 9 × 2 inches. Stir 1 jar pimientos into rice in each dish.

Mix 1 1/2 teaspoons salt, the paprika and pepper; sprinkle over chicken. Heat oil (1/4 inch) in 12-inch skillet. Cook several pieces of chicken at a time in oil over medium heat until brown, 15 to 20 minutes. Place chicken on rice mixture. Cover and refrigerate no longer than 24 hours.

Bake chicken covered in 350° oven until chicken is done and rice is hot, about 1 hour. Rinse peas under running cold water to separate. Sprinkle half of the peas over chicken and rice mixture in each dish. Cover and let stand until peas are hot, 10 to 15 minutes.

Avocado-Pineapple Salad

Sweet-and-Sour Onion Dressing (below)
3 avocados
1 pineapple, cut into wedge-shaped pieces, about
   2½ × 1 inch

Prepare Sweet-and-Sour Onion Dressing. Cut avocados into ¼-inch slices. (To prevent avocados from discoloring, sprinkle with fruit protector or lemon juice.) Arrange avocados and pineapple on lettuce leaves if desired; drizzle dressing over top.

Sweet-and-Sour Onion Dressing

¼ cup vegetable oil
2 tablespoons lime juice
2 tablespoons white wine vinegar
1 tablespoon water
2 teaspoons sugar
½ teaspoon salt
¼ cup finely chopped onion

Shake all ingredients in tightly covered container. Refrigerate at least 1 hour but no longer than 48 hours.

Sweet Potato Cake

2 cups all-purpose flour
2 cups sugar
1 cup chopped nuts
1 cup vegetable oil
2 teaspoons baking soda
2 teaspoons ground cinnamon
1 teaspoon baking powder
1 teaspoon ground nutmeg
1 teaspoon vanilla
½ teaspoon salt
4 eggs
1 can (18 ounces) vacuum-pack sweet
   potatoes, drained, or 2 cups cooked sweet
   potatoes
   Coconut Cream (right)
1 cup toasted flaked coconut

Heat oven to 350°. Grease and flour 12-cup bundt cake pan or tube pan, 10 × 4 inches.

Beat all ingredients except Coconut Cream and coconut in large bowl on low speed, scraping bowl constantly, 30 seconds. Beat on medium speed, scraping bowl occasionally, 3 minutes. Pour into pan.

Bake until wooden pick inserted in center comes out clean, 1 hour to 1 hour 10 minutes. Cool 10 minutes; remove from pan. Cool completely. Freeze uncovered 1 hour. Wrap, label and freeze no longer than 1 month.

Prepare Coconut Cream. About 6 hours before serving, remove cake from freezer; thaw in wrapper at room temperature 45 minutes. Remove wrapper carefully; thaw cake at room temperature. Serve with Coconut Cream and toasted coconut.

Coconut Cream

2 tablespoons cornstarch
¼ teaspoon salt
⅔ cup milk
1 can (15 ounces) coconut cream
2 egg yolks, slightly beaten
2 tablespoons light rum
2 tablespoons margarine or butter
1 teaspoon vanilla

Mix cornstarch and salt in 2-quart saucepan. Stir in milk and coconut cream gradually. Cook over medium heat, stirring constantly, until mixture thickens and boils. Boil and stir 1 minute. Stir at least half of the hot mixture gradually into egg yolks. Blend into hot mixture in saucepan. Boil and stir 1 minute; remove from heat. Stir in remaining ingredients. Cover and refrigerate until cold, at least 2 hours but no longer than 24 hours.

Fruited Coleslaw, Blueberry Muffin, Picnic Chicken, Curried Rice Salad and Assorted Relishes

A Family Reunion Picnic

Menu

12 servings

Picnic Chicken*

Curried Rice Salad*

Fruited Coleslaw*

Assorted Relishes

Blueberry Muffins

Brownies*

Assorted Beverages

***Recipe included**

Several weeks before buffet:
- [ ] Bake Brownies; freeze.

1 day before:
- [ ] Bake Picnic Chicken; refrigerate.
- [ ] Prepare Curried Dressing and rice mixture for Curried Rice Salad; refrigerate.
- [ ] Prepare Fruited Coleslaw; refrigerate.

About 30 minutes before serving:
- [ ] Remove Brownies from freezer.

At serving time:
- [ ] Arrange Assorted Relishes in serving container.
- [ ] Arrange Blueberry Muffins in serving container.
- [ ] Complete Curried Rice Salad.
- [ ] Arrange Brownies in serving container.

Picnic Chicken

3 2½- to 3-pound broiler-fryer chickens, cut up
2 teaspoons onion salt
½ teaspoon pepper
1 cup margarine or butter, melted
9 cups corn flake cereal, crushed (about 3 cups)

Sprinkle chicken with onion salt and pepper. Dip chicken into margarine, then roll in cereal crumbs. Place chicken, skin sides up, in 2 un- greased jelly roll pans, 15½ × 10½ × 1 inch. Drizzle any remaining margarine over chicken. Bake uncovered in 350° oven until thickest parts are done, 1¼ to 1½ hours. Remove chicken from pans. Cover and refrigerate at least 6 hours but no longer than 24 hours. (After serving, refrigerate or return to cooler any remaining pieces of chicken.)

Curried Rice Salad

Curried Dressing (below)
4 *cups cold cooked rice*
2 *stalks celery, thinly sliced (about 1 cup)*
1 *small onion, chopped (about 1/4 cup)*
1/2 *cup sliced pimiento-stuffed olives*
1/3 *cup toasted slivered almonds*

Prepared Curried Dressing. Cover and refrigerate at least 4 hours but no longer than 24 hours. Mix rice, celery, onion and olives. Cover and refrigerate no longer than 24 hours.

Toss rice mixture with dressing until evenly coated. Spoon onto lettuce leaves if desired. Sprinkle with almonds.

Curried Dressing

1 *carton (8 ounces) unflavored yogurt (about 3/4 cup)*
1 *to 1 1/2 teaspoons curry powder*
1/2 *teaspoon salt*
1/4 *teaspoon ground allspice*
1/4 *teaspoon ground turmeric*

Mix all ingredients.

Fruited Coleslaw  *Very good*

1 *medium head green cabbage (about 1 1/2 pounds), coarsely shredded*
3 *cups miniature marshmallows*
1 *cup golden raisins*
1 *can (15 1/2 ounces) crushed pineapple, drained (reserve 1 tablespoon syrup)*
1 *can (11 ounces) mandarin orange segments, drained*
3/4 *cup salad dressing*
3 *tablespoons lemon juice*
1/2 *teaspoon salt*

Mix all ingredients. Cover and refrigerate at least 1 hour but no longer than 24 hours.

used cranberry raisins instead of golden

Brownies

2/3 *cup shortening*
4 *ounces unsweetened chocolate*
2 *cups sugar*
4 *eggs*
1 *teaspoon vanilla*
1 1/4 *cups all-purpose flour*
1 *cup chopped nuts*
1 *teaspoon baking powder*
1 *teaspoon salt*
Chocolate Icing (below)

Heat oven to 350°. Heat shortening and chocolate in 2-quart saucepan over low heat, stirring constantly, until melted; remove from heat. Mix in sugar, eggs and vanilla. Stir in remaining ingredients except Chocolate Icing. Spread chocolate mixture in greased rectangular pan, 13 × 9 × 2 inches.

Bake until brownies begin to pull away from sides of pan, about 30 minutes (do not overbake); cool slightly. Prepare Chocolate Icing; spread over brownies. Cool completely or until icing is firm. Cut into bars, about 2 × 1 1/2 inches. Wrap, label and freeze no longer than 2 months.

Remove brownies from freezer and unwrap. Arrange brownies on serving plate; let stand uncovered at room temperature until thawed, about 30 minutes.

Chocolate Icing

3 *tablespoons shortening*
3 *ounces unsweetened chocolate*
2 *cups powdered sugar*
1/4 *teaspoon salt*
1/3 *cup milk*
1 *teaspoon vanilla*

Heat shortening and chocolate in 2-quart saucepan over low heat, stirring constantly, until melted. Stir in remaining ingredients; beat until smooth. Place pan of icing in bowl of ice and water; continue beating until of spreading consistency.

A Thanksgiving Dinner Buffet

Menu

12 servings

Turkey Breast with Stuffed Apples*

Mashed Potatoes

Fall Vegetable Medley*

Layered Gelatin Salad*

Whole Wheat Rolls

Pumpkin Cheesecake*

Coffee   Tea

***Recipe included**

---

3 days before buffet:
- ☐ Bake Pumpkin Cheesecake; refrigerate. Prepare walnuts for Pumpkin Cheesecake; store at room temperature.
- ☐ Prepare Layered Gelatin Salad; refrigerate.

2 days before:
- ☐ Cook carrots for Fall Vegetable Medley; refrigerate.

1 day before:
- ☐ Prepare Stuffed Apples for Turkey Breast with Stuffed Apples; refrigerate.

About 3 hours before serving:
- ☐ Roast Turkey Breast with Stuffed Apples.

About 30 minutes before:
- ☐ Prepare Mashed Potatoes.
- ☐ Complete Layered Gelatin Salad; refrigerate until serving time.
- ☐ Heat Whole Wheat Rolls.
- ☐ Complete Fall Vegetable Medley.
- ☐ Complete Pumpkin Cheesecake; refrigerate.
- ☐ Prepare Coffee and Tea.

Turkey Breast with Stuffed Apples

Stuffed Apples (page 31)
4½- to 5-pound turkey breast
¼ cup margarine or butter
¼ cup apple juice or cider
½ teaspoon salt
½ teaspoon paprika
1 clove garlic, crushed
2 teaspoons cornstarch
2 tablespoons cold water

Prepare Stuffed Apples. Remove keel and breast bone from turkey breast. Place turkey, skin side up, on rack in large shallow roasting pan. Insert meat thermometer so tip is in thickest part of meat. Roast uncovered in 325° oven 1 hour.

Heat margarine and apple juice until margarine is melted. Stir in salt, paprika and garlic. Brush turkey with margarine mixture. Roast 30 minutes. Place apples on rack around turkey; stir margarine mixture and brush turkey. Roast until thermometer registers 185° and apples are tender, about 1 hour. (If apples are done before thermometer registers 185°, remove apples from oven and place in rectangular pan, 13 × 9 × 2 inches; cover with aluminum foil to keep warm.) Remove turkey and apples; keep warm.

Pour drippings into measuring cup; skim off any excess fat. Add enough water to drippings to measure 1 cup. Heat drippings to boiling in

1-quart saucepan. Mix cornstarch and cold water; stir into drippings. Boil and stir 1 minute. Serve with turkey.

Stuffed Apples

12 *large baking apples*
 1 *large stalk celery, chopped (about ¾ cup)*
 1 *medium onion, chopped (about ½ cup)*
 3 *cups sage and onion stuffing mix*
⅓ *cup margarine or butter, melted*
½ *cup apple juice or cider*

Cut a ½-inch slice from top of each apple; core apple, being careful not to cut through to bottom. Remove centers of apples, leaving about a ¼-inch wall. Chop enough removed apple to measure ¾ cup. Mix chopped apple with remaining ingredients, stirring until all liquid is absorbed. Divide apple mixture among apples. Cover and refrigerate no longer than 24 hours.

Fall Vegetable Medley

 4 *medium carrots, cut crosswise into halves, then into ⅜-inch strips*
 2 *medium onions, thinly sliced*
⅓ *cup margarine or butter*
 1 *medium head green cabbage (about 1 pound), shredded (about 5 cups)*
 2 *medium green peppers, cut into thin strips*
1½ *teaspoons salt*
¼ *teaspoon pepper*

Heat 1 inch salted water (½ teaspoon salt to 1 cup water) to boiling. Add carrots. Heat to boiling; reduce heat. Cover and simmer until tender, about 10 minutes; drain. Cover and refrigerate no longer than 48 hours.

Cook and stir onions in margarine in 12-inch skillet or 4-quart Dutch oven over medium heat until almost tender, about 5 minutes. Stir in carrots and remaining ingredients. Cover and cook, stirring occasionally, until vegetables are just tender, about 10 minutes.

Preparing Stuffed Apples

Cut ½-inch slice from top of apple; core apple, being careful not to cut through to bottom.

Remove center of apple, leaving about a ¼-inch wall. Spoon apple mixture into apple.

Layered Gelatin Salad

1 cup boiling water
1 package (3 ounces) raspberry-flavored gelatin
1 package (10 ounces) frozen raspberries
1 cup boiling water
1 package (3 ounces) orange-flavored gelatin
1 package (8 ounces) cream cheese, softened
1 can (11 ounces) mandarin orange segments, undrained
1 cup boiling water
1 package (3 ounces) lime-flavored gelatin
1 can (8¼ ounces) crushed pineapple in syrup, undrained

Pour 1 cup boiling water on raspberry-flavored gelatin in 2-quart bowl; stir until gelatin is dissolved. Stir in frozen raspberries. Refrigerate until thickened slightly but not set. Pour into 8-cup mold, 12 individual molds or square pan, 9 × 9 × 2 inches. Refrigerate until almost firm.

Pour 1 cup boiling water on orange-flavored gelatin; stir until gelatin is dissolved. Gradually stir gelatin mixture into cream cheese. Refrigerate until thickened slightly but not set. Stir in orange segments; pour evenly over raspberry layer. Refrigerate until almost firm.

Pour 1 cup boiling water on lime-flavored gelatin in 2-quart bowl; stir until gelatin is dissolved. Stir in pineapple. Refrigerate until thickened slightly but not set. Pour evenly over orange layer. Refrigerate until firm. Cover and store no longer than 3 days.

Unmold on salad greens if desired, or cut into serving pieces and serve on salad greens.

Pumpkin Cheesecake

1¼ cups gingersnap cookie crumbs (about twenty 2-inch cookies)
¼ cup margarine or butter, melted
3 packages (8 ounces each) cream cheese, softened
1 cup sugar
1 teaspoon ground cinnamon
1 teaspoon ground ginger
½ teaspoon ground cloves
1 can (16 ounces) pumpkin
4 eggs
2 tablespoons sugar
12 walnut halves
¾ cup chilled whipping cream

Heat oven to 350°. Mix cookie crumbs and margarine. Press in bottom of springform pan, 9 × 3 inches. Bake 10 minutes; cool.

Reduce oven temperature to 300°. Beat cream cheese, 1 cup sugar, the cinnamon, ginger and cloves in 4-quart bowl on medium speed until smooth and fluffy. Add pumpkin. Beat in eggs, one at a time on low speed. Pour over crumb mixture. Bake until center is firm, about 1¼ hours. Cool to room temperature. Cover and refrigerate at least 3 hours but no longer than 3 days.

Cook and stir 2 tablespoons sugar and the walnuts over medium heat until sugar is melted and nuts are coated. Immediately spread on a dinner plate or aluminum foil; cool. Carefully break nuts apart to separate if necessary. Cover tightly and store at room temperature no longer than 3 days.

Loosen cheesecake from side of pan; remove side. Beat whipping cream in chilled 1½-quart bowl until stiff. Spread whipped cream over top of cheesecake; arrange walnuts on top.

Pumpkin Cheesecake and Turkey Breast with Stuffed Apples

Turkey Breast with Vegetables and Cucumber-Fruit Salad

A Welcome Home Buffet

Menu

12 servings

Avocado Soup*

Turkey Breast with Vegetables*

Cucumber-Fruit Salad*

Rye Dinner Rolls

Brazil Nut Torte*

Coffee   Tea

*Recipe included

1 day before buffet:
- ☐ Bake layers for Brazil Nut Torte; store at room temperature.
- ☐ Prepare Avocado Soup; refrigerate.

Several hours before serving:
- ☐ Complete Brazil Nut Torte; refrigerate.
- ☐ Prepare Cucumber-Fruit Salad; refrigerate.

About 2 hours 30 minutes before:
- ☐ Roast Turkey Breast with Vegetables.

About 1 hour 30 minutes before:
- ☐ Brush turkey and vegetables with margarine mixture.

About 1 hour before:
- ☐ Brush turkey and vegetables with remaining margarine mixture.

About 20 minutes before:
- ☐ Prepare Coffee and Tea.
- ☐ Arrange Rye Dinner Rolls in serving container.
- ☐ Serve Avocado Soup.

At serving time:
- ☐ Complete Cucumber-Fruit Salad.
- ☐ Complete Turkey Breast with Vegetables.

Avocado Soup

3 large ripe avocados, cut up
2 cans (10¾ ounces each) condensed chicken broth
1½ cups milk
3 tablespoons lemon juice
2 cloves garlic, crushed
2 or 3 drops red pepper sauce
Dairy sour cream
Paprika

Place half of the avocados, 1 can chicken broth and ¾ cup milk in blender container. Cover and blend on medium speed until smooth, about 20 seconds. Repeat with remaining avocados, chicken broth and milk. Mix avocado mixture, lemon juice, garlic and pepper sauce. Cover and refrigerate at least 3 hours but no longer than 24 hours.

Stir before serving. Garnish with sour cream and paprika.

Turkey Breast with Vegetables

4½- to 5-pound turkey breast
12 medium potatoes
12 medium carrots, cut diagonally into 2-inch pieces
½ cup margarine or butter, melted
¼ cup dry white wine
1½ teaspoons dried rosemary leaves
1 teaspoon salt
1 teaspoon paprika
2 cloves garlic, crushed
2 teaspoons cornstarch
2 tablespoons cold water

Place turkey breast, skin side up, on rack in shallow roasting pan. Insert meat thermometer so tip is in thickest part of meat and does not touch bone. Cut potatoes crosswise into ¼-inch slices about ¾ of the way through. Place potatoes and carrots on rack around turkey. Mix margarine, wine, rosemary, salt, paprika and garlic. Brush vegetables with about ¼ of the margarine mixture. Roast uncovered in 325° oven 1 hour.

Brush turkey and vegetables with ½ of the remaining margarine mixture. Roast 30 minutes; brush with remaining margarine mixture. Roast until thermometer registers 185° and vegetables are tender, about 1 hour. Remove turkey and vegetables; keep warm.

Pour drippings into measuring cup; skim off any excess fat. Add enough water to drippings to measure 2 cups. Heat drippings to boiling in 1-quart saucepan. Mix cornstarch and cold water; stir into drippings. Boil and stir 1 minute. Serve with turkey. Sprinkle carrots with snipped parsley if desired.

Cucumber-Fruit Salad

2 tablespoons sesame seed
2 cans (20 ounces each) pineapple chunks in juice
3 medium cucumbers
½ cup vegetable oil
1 tablespoon honey
½ teaspoon salt
¼ teaspoon pepper
4 apples, cut into ½-inch pieces

Cook sesame seed over medium heat, stirring occasionally, until golden brown, about 4 minutes; store at room temperature. Drain pineapple; reserve ½ cup juice. Cut cucumbers lengthwise into fourths; remove seeds. Cut cucumbers crosswise into thin slices. Mix reserved pineapple juice, the oil, honey, salt and pepper. Toss with cucumbers, pineapple and apples. Cover and refrigerate, stirring occasionally, at least 4 hours but no longer than 8 hours.

Drain fruit mixture; toss with sesame seed. Serve on lettuce leaves if desired.

Brazil Nut Torte

6 *eggs, separated*
½ *cup sugar*
2 *tablespoons vegetable oil*
1 *tablespoon brandy*
½ *cup sugar*
¼ *cup all-purpose flour*
1¼ *teaspoons baking powder*
1 *teaspoon instant coffee*
½ *teaspoon ground cinnamon*
½ *teaspoon ground cloves*
1 *cup fine graham cracker crumbs (about 12 squares)*
1 *cup finely chopped Brazil nuts*
1½ *cups chilled whipping cream*
¼ *cup sugar*
2 *teaspoons instant coffee*

Heat oven to 350°. Line bottoms of 2 round pans, 8 or 9 × 1½ inches, with aluminum foil. Beat egg whites in large bowl until foamy. Beat in ½ cup sugar, 1 tablespoon at a time; continue beating until stiff and glossy.

Beat egg yolks, oil and brandy in small bowl on low speed until blended. Add ½ cup sugar, the flour, baking powder, 1 teaspoon instant coffee, the cinnamon and cloves. Beat on medium speed 1 minute. Fold egg yolk mixture into egg whites. Fold in cracker crumbs and nuts. Pour into pans.

Bake until top springs back when touched lightly in center, 30 to 35 minutes. Cool 10 minutes. Loosen edge with knife; invert pan and hit sharply on table. Remove foil; cool completely. Cover layers tightly and store at room temperature no longer than 24 hours.

Beat whipping cream, ¼ cup sugar and 2 teaspoons instant coffee in chilled bowl until stiff. Fill layers and frost side and top of cake with whipped cream. To decorate cake, frost side and top of cake with thin layer of whipped cream; place remaining whipped cream in decorating bag with decorator tip; decorate top and side of cake. Garnish with Brazil nuts if desired. Refrigerate uncovered no longer than 8 hours.

Brazil Nut Torte

Beef with Yellow Rice, Garlic Tomato Slices and Sesame Green Beans

A Celebration Dinner

Menu

12 servings

Beef with Yellow Rice*

Sesame Green Beans*

Garlic Tomato Slices*

Hard Rolls

Layered Fruit Dessert*

Coffee   Tea

***Recipe included**

1 day before buffet:
- ☐ Prepare Garlic Tomato Slices: refrigerate.
- ☐ Prepare sesame seed for Sesame Green Beans; store at room temperature.
- ☐ Prepare Layered Fruit Dessert; refrigerate.

About 3 hours before serving:
- ☐ Roast beef for Beef with Yellow Rice.

About 30 minutes before:
- ☐ Cook rice for Beef with Yellow Rice.
- ☐ Prepare Coffee and Tea.

About 15 minutes before:
- ☐ Prepare Sesame Green Beans.
- ☐ Arrange Garlic Tomato Slices in serving container.
- ☐ Complete Beef with Yellow Rice.
- ☐ Arrange Hard Rolls in serving container.

Beef with Yellow Rice

4- pound tip, heel of round or rolled
    rump roast
2⅓ cups uncooked regular rice
4⅔ cups water
2 teaspoons salt
1 teaspoon ground turmeric
¼ teaspoon red pepper sauce
½ cup snipped parsley

Place beef, fat side up, on rack in shallow roasting pan. Insert meat thermometer so tip is in center of thickest part of beef and does not rest in fat. Roast uncovered in 325° oven until thermometer registers 160°, about 3 hours.

About 30 minutes before beef is done, heat rice, water, salt, turmeric and pepper sauce to boiling, stirring once or twice; reduce heat. Cover and simmer 14 minutes (do not lift cover or stir). Remove from heat; fluff rice lightly with fork. Cover and let steam 5 to 10 minutes. Stir parsley into rice. Cut beef into ¼-inch slices. Serve beef with rice. Garnish with sliced green onions if desired.

Sesame Green Beans

2 tablespoons sesame seed
3 packages (9 ounces each) frozen cut green
    beans*
¼ cup margarine or butter, melted
½ teaspoon salt
¼ teaspoon pepper

Cook and stir sesame seed over medium heat until golden brown, 3 to 5 minutes. Cool; store at room temperature.

Cook green beans as directed on package in 3-quart saucepan; drain. Toss beans with sesame seed, margarine, salt and pepper.

*2 pounds fresh green beans cut into 1-inch pieces, cooked and drained, can be substituted for the frozen cut green beans.

Garlic Tomato Slices

4 medium tomatoes, cut into ¼-inch slices
¼ cup olive or vegetable oil
2 tablespoons red wine vinegar
⅛ teaspoon salt
3 drops red pepper sauce
2 large cloves garlic, finely chopped

Place tomatoes in glass or plastic dish. Shake remaining ingredients in tightly covered container; pour over tomatoes. Cover and refrigerate at least 3 hours but no longer than 24 hours. Serve on lettuce leaves if desired.

Layered Fruit Dessert

1 package (about 3 ounces) vanilla regular
    pudding and pie filling
1 cup chilled whipping cream
1 teaspoon almond extract
1 white angel food cake, torn into 1-inch pieces
    (about 9 cups)
1 pint strawberries, sliced
2 bananas, sliced
2 kiwi fruit, thinly sliced

Prepare pudding and pie filling as directed on package; cool. Beat whipping cream and almond extract in chilled 1-quart bowl until stiff. Fold pudding into whipped cream.

Place half of the cake pieces in 3-quart glass bowl; top with half of the strawberries, bananas and kiwi. Spread with half of the pudding mixture; repeat with remaining cake pieces, fruit and pudding mixture. Cover and refrigerate at least 8 hours but no longer than 24 hours. Garnish with additional strawberries and kiwi if desired.

A New Year's Eve Buffet

You may prefer a more quiet celebration of auld lang syne to the more traditional large party. If so, plan an elegant dinner at home to welcome in the new year. Serve your guests from a buffet table where you carve and serve the Peppered Beef Roast, and seat guests at a set dining table or small tables.

Menu

8 servings

Peppered Beef Roast*

Potato Ring with Brussels Sprouts*

Grapefruit-Orange Salad*

Rye Dinner Rolls

Holiday Ice-cream Balls*

Coffee   Tea

***Recipe included**

1 week before buffet:
- ☐ Prepare fruit mixture for Holiday Ice-cream Balls; refrigerate.

1 day before:
- ☐ Prepare ice-cream balls for Holiday Ice-cream Balls.
- ☐ Prepare potato mixture for Potato Ring with Brussels Sprouts; refrigerate.
- ☐ Pare and section grapefruit for Grapefruit-Orange Salad; refrigerate.
- ☐ Press pepper into beef roast; refrigerate.

About 1 hour 45 minutes before serving:
- ☐ Roast Peppered Beef Roast.

About 30 minutes before:
- ☐ Bake potato mixture ring.
- ☐ Prepare Horseradish Sauce; cover and refrigerate.
- ☐ Complete Grapefruit-Orange Salad.
- ☐ Cook Brussels sprouts; complete Potato Ring with Brussels Sprouts.
- ☐ Heat Rye Dinner Rolls.
- ☐ Prepare Coffee and Tea.

At dessert time:
- ☐ Complete Holiday Ice-cream Balls.

Peppered Beef Roast

3- pound beef eye of the round roast, 3 to 3½ inches in diameter
2 tablespoons black peppercorns, cracked
  Horseradish Sauce (below)

Roll beef roast in cracked pepper; press pepper into beef with heels of hands. Cover and refrigerate no longer than 24 hours.

Heat oven to 425°. Place beef on rack in shallow roasting pan. Insert meat thermometer in thickest part of beef. Roast uncovered in 425° oven to desired doneness, 140° for rare, 160° for medium or about 1 hour 30 minutes. Prepare Horseradish Sauce. Garnish beef with watercress if desired, and serve with sauce.

Horseradish Sauce

¾ cup chilled whipping cream
3 tablespoons prepared horseradish
½ teaspoon dry mustard
¼ teaspoon salt

Beat all ingredients in chilled bowl until stiff.

Potato Ring with Brussels Sprouts

1 *package (5 ounces) mashed potato mix*
1/2 *cup shredded Cheddar cheese (2 ounces)*
1 *tablespoon prepared mustard*
   Margarine or butter, softened
2 *tablespoons dry bread crumbs or wheat germ*
2 *packages (8 ounces each) frozen baby*
   Brussels sprouts*
2 *tablespoons margarine or butter*
2 *teaspoons lemon juice*
1/2 *teaspoon salt*

Prepare mashed potato mix as directed on package for 8 servings except — stir in cheese and mustard with fork after liquid is absorbed.

Brush 4-cup ring mold with margarine; sprinkle with bread crumbs. Press potato mixture in mold. Cover and refrigerate no longer than 24 hours. Bake uncovered in 425° oven until hot and golden brown, 25 to 30 minutes.

Cook Brussels sprouts as directed on package; drain. Toss sprouts with 2 tablespoons margarine, the lemon juice and salt. Unmold potato ring on heatproof serving plate. Fill center of ring with Brussels sprouts; place remaining sprouts around outside of ring.

*2¼ pounds fresh Brussels sprouts, cooked and drained, can be substituted for the frozen baby Brussels sprouts.

Grapefruit-Orange Salad

2 *grapefruits, pared and sectioned*
1/2 *cup mayonnaise or salad dressing*
1 *teaspoon instant minced onion*
1/2 *teaspoon celery seed*
   Dash of salt
4 *cups bite-size pieces lettuce*
1/2 *cup chopped celery*
2 *cans (11 ounces each) mandarin orange*
   segments, drained
   Pomegranate seeds or chopped pimiento

Cut grapefruit sections into halves. Cover and refrigerate no longer than 24 hours.

Drain grapefruit; reserve 1 tablespoon juice. Mix mayonnaise, onion, celery seed, salt and reserved grapefruit juice. Toss mayonnaise mixture with grapefruit, lettuce, celery and orange segments. Sprinkle salad with pomegranate seeds.

Holiday Ice-cream Balls

1 *cup cut-up fruitcake mix*
1/4 *cup rum*
1 *quart vanilla ice cream*
1 *cup toasted coconut*

Mix fruitcake mix and rum. Cover and refrigerate at least 24 hours but no longer than 1 week.

Scoop ice cream into 8 servings. Roll each in toasted coconut and place on chilled cookie sheet. Cover loosely and freeze no longer than 24 hours.

Spoon about 1 tablespoon of the fruitcake mixture over each ice-cream ball.

NOTE: To toast coconut, heat oven to 350°. Spread coconut evenly in ungreased shallow pan. Toast, stirring frequently, until golden brown, about 8 minutes.

Peppered Roast Beef, Horseradish Sauce, Potato Ring with Brussels Sprouts, and Grapefruit-Orange Salad

Clockwise from top: Party Potato Salad, Marinated Bean Salad, Beef Brisket Barbecue and Assorted Sandwich Rolls

A July 4th Barbecue

Menu

12 servings

Beef Brisket Barbecue*

Party Potato Salad*

Marinated Bean Salad*

Assorted Sandwich Rolls

**Rum-plugged
Watermelon***

Iced Tea   Lemonade

*Recipe included

1 day before buffet:
- ☐ Prepare potato mixture and eggs for Party Potato Salad; refrigerate.
- ☐ Prepare Marinated Bean Salad; refrigerate.

About 8 hours before serving:
- ☐ Prepare Rum-plugged Watermelon; refrigerate.
- ☐ Prepare Iced Tea and Lemonade; refrigerate.

About 2 hours before:
- ☐ Start coals for Beef Brisket Barbecue; grill beef.

At serving time:
- ☐ Complete Party Potato Salad.
- ☐ Complete Marinated Bean Salad.
- ☐ Serve Assorted Sandwich Rolls with Beef Brisket Barbecue.

Beef Brisket Barbecue

4- to 5-pound well-trimmed beef boneless brisket
1½ teaspoons salt
½ cup catsup
¼ cup vinegar
½ cup finely chopped onion
1 tablespoon Worcestershire sauce
1½ teaspoons liquid smoke
¼ teaspoon pepper
1 bay leaf, finely crushed

Rub surface of beef with salt. Place on 20 × 15-inch piece of heavy-duty aluminum foil. Stir together remaining ingredients; pour over beef. Wrap securely in foil. Grill 5 inches from medium coals, turning once, until tender, about 1½ hours.

Cut thin diagonal slices across the grain at an angle from two or three "faces" of beef. Spoon any remaining juices in aluminum foil over sliced beef if desired.

NOTE: Beef Brisket Barbecue can be baked in the oven. After rubbing surface of beef with salt, place in ungreased rectangular pan, 13 × 9 × 2 inches. Stir together remaining ingredients; pour over beef. Cover and bake in 325° oven until tender, about 3 hours.

Party Potato Salad

2 teaspoons celery seed
3 tablespoons vinegar
7 cooked large potatoes, cut into ¾-inch pieces
1½ cups salad dressing
2 tablespoons salt
1 teaspoon dry mustard
½ teaspoon pepper
1½ cups chopped celery (about 4 stalks)
¼ cup chopped green onions (with tops)
1 cup sliced radishes
6 hard-cooked eggs, chopped
1 large cucumber, chopped

Soak celery seed in vinegar 30 minutes. Place potatoes in large bowl. Mix salad dressing, salt, celery seed-vinegar mixture, mustard and pepper; toss gently with potatoes. Cover and refrigerate at least 4 hours but no longer than 24 hours.

Add celery, onions, sliced radishes, eggs and chopped cucumber; toss gently. Spoon mixture into serving bowl; garnish with radish roses and cucumber slices if desired.

Marinated Bean Salad

1 can (16 ounces) cut green beans, drained*
1 can (15½ ounces) garbanzo beans, drained
1 can (15 ounces) red kidney beans, drained
3 medium tomatoes, chopped (about 1½ cups)
1 hot pepper, seeded and finely chopped
1 small green pepper, chopped (about ½ cup)
¾ cup chopped onion
⅓ cup sliced green onions (with tops)
1 bottle (8 ounces) herb and garlic French dressing
Lettuce leaves

Mix all ingredients except lettuce. Cover and refrigerate, stirring occasionally, at least 3 hours but no longer than 24 hours.

Remove bean mixture to lettuce-lined salad bowl with slotted spoon.

*1 pound fresh green beans cut into 1-inch pieces, cooked and drained, can be substituted for the canned green beans.

Rum-plugged Watermelon

Cut hole 3 inches square and 3 inches deep in center of 1 ripe watermelon (about 10 pounds); pour in ¾ cup rum. Trim pink flesh from plug, leaving ½-inch rind; replace plug in watermelon. Refrigerate, plugged side up, until rum permeates watermelon, about 8 hours.

A Wedding Rehearsal Dinner

For such a special occasion, serve a spectacular dessert — Flambéed Peaches. Flaming desserts are easier to prepare than they look. Start with a hot mixture and 80-proof liquor. Also to be safe, use a long match when lighting the heated liquor. The alcohol burns off but the flavor remains. Dim the lights, bring in the peach mixture and brandy and entertain your guests by creating this exciting dessert.

Menu

10 servings

Beef en Gelée*

Marinated Vegetables*

Wild Rice Casserole*

French Bread

Flambéed Peaches*

Coffee   Tea

*Recipe included

2 days before buffet:
☐ Bake beef roast for Beef en Gelée; refrigerate.

1 day before:
☐ Arrange beef slices on platters; cover beef with gelatin mixture. Refrigerate.
☐ Prepare Marinated Vegetables; refrigerate.
☐ Prepare Wild Rice Casserole; refrigerate.
☐ Scoop ice cream for Flambéed Peaches; freeze.

Several hours before serving:
☐ Prepare peaches for Flambéed Peaches; refrigerate.

30 minutes before:
☐ Bake Wild Rice Casserole.
☐ Heat French Bread.
☐ Arrange Marinated Vegetables around Beef en Gelée.
☐ Prepare Coffee and Tea.

At dessert time:
☐ Prepare Flambéed Peaches.

Beef en Gelée

3- pound beef rolled rump roast
2 tablespoons vegetable oil
½ cup water
1 teaspoon salt
¼ teaspoon pepper
1 envelope unflavored gelatin
2 tablespoons cold water
1 teaspoon instant beef bouillon
1 cup dry red wine
   Marinated Vegetables (page 45)

Cook beef in oil in Dutch oven over medium heat until brown on all sides; drain. Add ½ cup water; sprinkle beef with salt and pepper. Cover and bake in 325° oven until tender, about 1½ hours; cool slightly. Cover and refrigerate beef and broth separately at least 8 hours but no longer than 24 hours.

Sprinkle gelatin on 2 tablespoons water in saucepan to soften; stir in bouillon (dry) and wine. Heat over medium heat, stirring constantly, until gelatin is dissolved; remove from heat. Skim fat from broth; add enough cold water to broth to measure 1 cup. Stir into gelatin mixture. Place saucepan with gelatin mixture in bowl of ice and water; stir until mixture begins to thicken, 5 to 10 minutes.

Remove string from beef; trim fat. Cut beef into very thin slices; arrange on two large platters. Pour about ¼ cup gelatin mixture evenly over beef on each platter. Pour any remaining gelatin mixture into loaf dish, 9 × 5 × 3 inches. Cover and refrigerate beef and gelatin mixture no longer than 24 hours. Prepare Marinated Vegetables.

Arrange vegetables around beef on each platter. Cut gelatin mixture in loaf dish into small diamonds or squares; arrange around beef or serve separately.

Marinated Vegetables

16 medium carrots (about 2½ pounds)
 2 pounds green beans*
 2 cans (16 ounces each) whole onions, drained
1⅓ cups olive or vegetable oil
 ⅔ cup red wine vinegar
 2 teaspoons salt
 ¼ teaspoon pepper
 4 cloves garlic, finely chopped

Cut carrots into 2-inch pieces, rounding edges to resemble baby carrots if desired. Cover and cook carrots and beans in 1 inch boiling salted water (½ teaspoon salt to 1 cup water) in separate saucepans until tender, beans 15 to 20 minutes, carrots 20 to 25 minutes; drain.

Arrange cooked vegetables and the onions in separate shallow glass dishes. Shake remaining ingredients in tightly covered container; pour over vegetables and onions. Cover and refrigerate, spooning marinade over vegetables occasionally, at least 2 hours but no longer than 24 hours.

*3 packages (9 ounces each) frozen cut green beans, cooked and drained, can be substituted for the fresh green beans.

Wild Rice Casserole

16 ounces mushrooms, sliced
 ¼ cup margarine or butter
 2 packages (6 ounces each) long grain and wild rice
 ¼ cup snipped parsley

Cook mushrooms, stirring occasionally, in margarine until tender; drain. Cook rice as directed on package; stir in mushrooms. Spoon into ungreased 2-quart casserole. Cover and refrigerate no longer than 24 hours.

Bake in 350° oven until hot, 30 to 35 minutes. Sprinkle with parsley.

Flambéed Peaches

1½ quarts vanilla ice cream
 8 large peaches or 2 cans (28 ounces each) sliced peaches, drained
 ⅓ cup sugar
 1 cup water
 ½ cup apricot jam
 2 teaspoons lemon juice
 ½ cup brandy

Scoop ice cream into 10 servings and place on chilled cookie sheet. Freeze uncovered no longer than 24 hours. Cut peaches into thin slices. (To prevent peaches from discoloring, sprinkle with fruit protector or lemon juice.) Cover and refrigerate no longer than 4 hours.

Heat sugar, water and jam to boiling in 10-inch skillet; reduce heat. Simmer until mixture is syrupy, about 5 minutes; stir in peaches. Cook over low heat until hot, 1 to 3 minutes. Stir in lemon juice. Heat brandy; pour over peaches and light with match to flame. Place ice-cream balls in 10 individual dishes. Stir peaches gently; spoon over ice cream.

NOTE: Guests may enjoy seeing flaming peach sauce prepared at the table. Assemble all ingredients and utensils needed on a large serving tray. Mix sugar, water and jam in chafing dish. Simmer over direct heat until syrupy, 5 to 10 minutes; stir in peaches. Cook until hot, 3 to 5 minutes. Continue as directed.

A Hungarian-Style Dinner

One of the most famous and delicious of Hungarian desserts is the Apple Strudel. The Individual Apple Strudels for this menu have been simplified by using commercially prepared phyllo for the thinly rolled strudel dough. Phyllo leaves, which are paper-thin sheets of pastry, are available frozen in most supermarkets. The individual strudels are easy to serve for a buffet because there is no need for cutting and serving.

Menu

8 servings

Hungarian Goulash*

Buttered Noodles

Sweet-Sour Red Cabbage*

Cucumber Sticks

Individual Apple Strudels*

Coffee   Tea

***Recipe included**

2 days before buffet:
- ☐ Prepare Sweet-Sour Red Cabbage; refrigerate.

1 day before:
- ☐ Prepare Hungarian Goulash; refrigerate.
- ☐ Prepare Individual Apple Strudels for baking; refrigerate.

About 40 minutes before serving:
- ☐ Bake Individual Apple Strudels.

About 20 minutes before:
- ☐ Prepare Coffee and Tea.
- ☐ Prepare Buttered Noodles.
- ☐ Heat Hungarian Goulash.
- ☐ Heat Sweet-Sour Red Cabbage.
- ☐ Arrange Cucumber Sticks in serving container.

At dessert time:
- ☐ Complete Individual Apple Strudels.

Hungarian Goulash

2 tablespoons vegetable oil
2 pounds beef boneless chuck, tip or round, cut
    into ¾-inch cubes
2 tablespoons all-purpose flour
1 cup water
1 tablespoon paprika
1½ teaspoons salt
1 teaspoon caraway seed
½ teaspoon instant beef bouillon
¼ teaspoon pepper
3 medium onions, chopped (about 1½ cups)
2 cloves garlic, crushed
1 can (14½ ounces) whole tomatoes,
    undrained
2 green peppers, cut into 1-inch pieces

Heat oil in 4-quart Dutch oven. Toss beef with flour. Cook and stir beef in hot oil until brown, about 10 minutes. Add water, paprika, salt caraway seed, bouillon (dry), pepper, onions, garlic and tomatoes; break up tomatoes with fork. Heat to boiling; reduce heat. Cover and simmer until beef is tender, about 1½ hours. Add green peppers. Cover and simmer until tender, 8 to 10 minutes. Cover and refrigerate no longer than 24 hours.

Heat over medium heat, stirring occasionally, until hot, about 15 minutes.

Sweet-Sour Red Cabbage

8 slices bacon
½ cup packed brown sugar
¼ cup all-purpose flour
1 teaspoon salt
¼ teaspoon pepper
12 cups shredded red or green cabbage (1 large head)
1 cup water
½ cup vinegar
1 medium onion, sliced

Fry bacon in 12-inch skillet until crisp. Remove bacon; crumble and reserve. Pour off all but 2 tablespoons bacon fat. Stir brown sugar, flour, salt and pepper into bacon fat until smooth. Stir in remaining ingredients. Heat to boiling; reduce heat. Cover and simmer, stirring occasionally, until cabbage is tender, 25 to 30 minutes. Stir in bacon. Cover and refrigerate no longer than 48 hours.

Heat over medium heat, stirring occasionally until hot, about 15 minutes.

Individual Apple Strudels

3 cups chopped apples (about 3 medium)
½ cup granulated sugar
¼ cup finely chopped walnuts
¼ cup raisins
¼ cup dry bread crumbs
.1 tablespoon lemon juice
1 teaspoon ground cinnamon
8 frozen phyllo leaves, thawed
¼ cup margarine or butter, melted
   Powered sugar
   Whipped cream

Mix apples, granulated sugar, walnuts, raisins, bread crumbs, lemon juice and cinnamon. Fold 1 phyllo leaf in half crosswise; brush with margarine. (Keep remaining phyllo leaves covered with a dampened towel to prevent them from drying out.) Place ½ cup of the apple mixture in center of phyllo leaf 1 inch

from one narrow end of leaf. Fold sides of phyllo toward center, overlapping sides. Roll up, beginning at filling end. Place on ungreased cookie sheet; brush with margarine. Repeat with remaining phyllo leaves and apple mixture. Cover and refrigerate no longer than 24 hours.

Bake in 375° oven until golden brown, 30 to 35 minutes; cool. Sprinkle with powdered sugar. Serve with whipped cream.

Forming Individual Apple Strudels

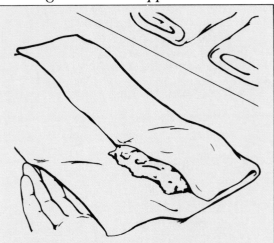

Place apple mixture in center of phyllo leaf 1 inch from narrow end; fold sides to center, overlapping sides.

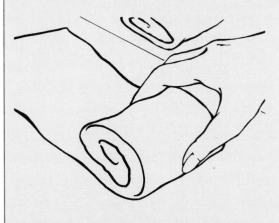

Roll up loosely, beginning at filling end. Place on ungreased cookie sheet.

A Promotion Celebration Buffet

Menu

8 servings

Beef Burgundy*

Rice

Broccoli Spears

Tangy Tomato Aspic*

Popovers*

Frozen Lime Pie*

Coffee   Tea

***Recipe included**

Several days before buffet:
☐ Prepare Frozen Lime Pie; freeze.

1 day before:
☐ Prepare Beef Burgundy; refrigerate.
☐ Prepare Tangy Tomato Aspic; refrigerate.

About 1 hour before serving:
☐ Bake Popovers.
☐ Unmold Tangy Tomato Aspic; refrigerate.

About 30 minutes before:
☐ Cook Rice.
☐ Heat Beef Burgundy.
☐ Cook Broccoli Spears.
☐ Prepare Coffee and Tea.

Beef Burgundy

4 pounds boneless round steak, 1 inch thick
¼ cup shortening
5 large onions, sliced
1 pound mushrooms, sliced
3 tablespoons all-purpose flour
2 teaspoons salt
¼ teaspoon dried marjoram leaves
¼ teaspoon dried thyme leaves
¼ teaspoon pepper
2 cups dry red wine
1 cup beef bouillon

Cut beef into 1-inch cubes. Cook and stir beef in shortening in 4-quart Dutch oven until brown. Remove beef; reserve. Cook and stir onions and mushrooms in Dutch oven until onions are tender, adding shortening if necessary. Remove vegetables; cover and refrigerate. Mix beef, flour, salt, marjoram, thyme and pepper in Dutch oven. Stir in wine and bouillon. Heat to boiling; reduce heat. Cover and simmer until beef is tender, about 1½ hours (liquid should just cover beef). If necessary, add more wine and bouillon (2 parts wine to 1 part bouillon). Cover and refrigerate no longer than 24 hours.

Add vegetables to beef in Dutch oven. Heat stirring occasionally, until hot, about 15 minutes.

Popovers

4 eggs
2 cups all-purpose flour
2 cups milk
1 teaspoon salt

Heat oven to 450°. Generously grease twelve 6-ounce custard cups. Beat eggs slightly; beat in remaining ingredients just until smooth (do not overbeat). Fill cups about ½ full. Place cups in jelly roll pan, 15½ × 10½ × 1 inch. Bake 25 minutes. Decrease oven temperature to 350°. Bake until deep golden brown, about 15 minutes longer. Immediately remove from cups; serve hot. 12 popovers.

Tangy Tomato Aspic

1¼ cups boiling water
 1 package (3 ounces) lemon-flavored gelatin
 1 can (8 ounces) tomato sauce
 ½ teaspoon salt
 1 tablespoon plus 1½ teaspoons vinegar
 ⅛ teaspoon onion powder
 ⅛ teaspoon red pepper sauce
   Dash of ground cloves
 2 cups chopped celery
   Lettuce leaves
   Mayonnaise or salad dresing

Pour boiling water on gelatin in bowl; stir until gelatin is dissolved. Stir in tomato sauce, salt, vinegar, onion powder, pepper sauce and cloves. Refrigerate until slightly thickened but not set. Stir in celery. Pour into 4-cup mold or 8 individual molds. Refrigerate until firm, about 4 hours. Cover and refrigerate no longer than 24 hours. Unmold on lettuce leaves. Serve with mayonnaise.

Frozen Lime Pie

   Meringue Pie Shell (right)
 4 egg yolks
 ½ cup sugar
 ¼ teaspoon salt
 ⅓ cup lime juice

 2 or 3 drops green food color
 1 cup chilled whipping cream
 1 tablespoon grated lime peel

Bake Meringue Pie Shell. Beat egg yolks in small bowl until light and lemon colored. Mix sugar, salt, lime juice and eggs yolks in saucepan. Cook over medium heat, stirring constantly, until mixture thickens, about 5 minutes. Cool; stir in food color.

Beat whipping cream in chilled 1-quart bowl until stiff. Fold in lime mixture and lime peel. Spoon into meringue shell. Freeze uncovered 1½ hours or wrap, label and freeze no longer than 1 month.

Cut frozen pie with knife that has been dipped in hot water (wipe knife after cutting each slice); serve immediately.

Meringue Pie Shell

Heat oven to 275°. Lightly grease pie plate, 9 × 1¼ inches. Beat 4 egg whites and ¼ teaspoon cream of tartar in large bowl until foamy. Beat in ½ cup sugar, 1 tablespoon at a time; continue beating until stiff and glossy. Do not underbeat. Spoon into pie plate, pressing meringue against bottom and side.

Bake 1 hour. Turn off oven; leave meringue in oven with door closed 1 hour. Remove meringue from oven; cool away from draft.

Frozen Lime Pie

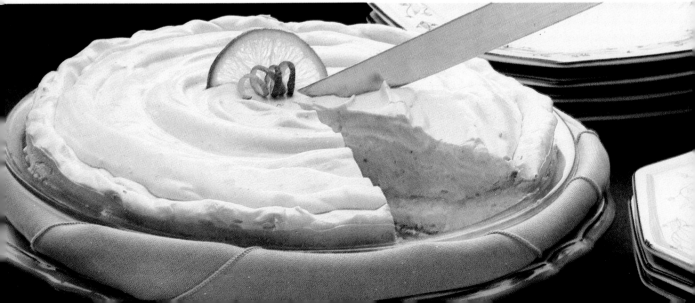

An Irish Dinner

Several weeks before buffet:
□ Prepare Pickled Beets; refrigerate.

Several hours before serving:
□ Bake Soda Bread.

About 4 hours before:
□ Cook Corned Beef Dinner.

About 30 minutes before:
□ Cook Buttered New Potatoes.
□ Prepare coffee for Irish Coffee

At dessert time:
□ Complete Irish Coffee; serve with Ladyfingers.

Corned Beef Dinner

5- *pound well-trimmed corned beef boneless brisket*
2 *cloves garlic, crushed*
1 *medium onion, cut into fourths*
1 *medium head green cabbage, cut into 10 wedges*

Place beef, garlic and onion in 4-quart Dutch oven; cover with water. Heat to boiling; reduce heat. Cover and simmer until beef is tender, 3½ hours. Remove beef to warm platter. Skim fat from liquid. Add cabbage. Simmer uncovered until tender, 15 to 20 minutes. Cut thin diagonal slices across the grain at an angle from two or three "faces" of beef.

Soda Bread

3 *tablespoons margarine or butter, softened*
2½ *cups all-purpose flour*
2 *tablespoons sugar*
1 *teaspoon baking soda*
1 *teaspoon baking powder*
½ *teaspoon salt*
⅓ *cup raisins*
¾ *cup buttermilk*

Cut margarine into flour, sugar, baking soda, baking powder and salt until mixture resembles fine crumbs. Stir in raisins and enough buttermilk to make a soft dough. Turn onto lightly floured surface; knead until smooth, 1 to 2 minutes. Shape into round loaf, about 6½ inches in diameter. Place on greased cookie sheet. Cut an X about ¼ through loaf with floured knife.

Bake in 375° oven until golden brown, 35 to 45 minutes. 1 loaf.

Irish Coffee

1 *cup chilled whipping cream*
¼ *cup powdered sugar*
1 *teaspoon vanilla*
10 *ounces (1¼ cups) Irish whiskey or brandy*
10 *teaspoons granulated sugar*
8 *cups hot coffee*

Beat whipping cream, powdered sugar and vanilla in chilled bowl until stiff. Add 1 ounce (2 tablespoons) whiskey and 1 teaspoon granulated sugar to each mug; stir. Pour hot coffee into each mug; top with whipped cream. Serve immediately.

Clockwise from top: Greek Salad, Pasticcio, Hummus and Pita Wedges

A Greek Buffet

Borrow a menu from Greece for a different dinner party. Pasticcio, an economical Greek dish made with ground beef and macaroni, can be prepared a day ahead and heated just before the party. Feta cheese, a salty, soft white cheese made from goat's milk, adds an interesting flavor and texture to the salad. The rich honey and walnut Baklava completes the meal. If you are unable to find the Turkish-style substitute strong regular coffee.

Menu

12 servings

Pasticcio*

Greek Salad*

Hummus*

Pita Wedges

Baklava*

Middle Eastern coffee*

***Recipe included**

Several days before buffet:
- ☐ Prepare Baklava; refrigerate.

1 day before:
- ☐ Prepare Pasticcio; refrigerate.
- ☐ Prepare romaine for Greek Salad; refrigerate.
- ☐ Prepare Hummus; refrigerate.

About 2 hours before serving:
- ☐ Remove Baklava from refrigerator; let stand at room temperature.

About 1 hour before:
- ☐ Bake Pasticcio.
- ☐ Remove Hummus from refrigerator; let stand at room temperature.

At serving time:
- ☐ Complete Greek Salad.
- ☐ Serve Hummus with Pita Wedges.

At dessert time:
- ☐ Prepare Middle Eastern Coffee; serve with Baklava.

Pasticcio

14 ounces uncooked elbow macaroni (about
    4 cups)
1½ pounds ground beef
1 medium onion, chopped (about ½ cup)
2 cans (15 ounces each) tomato sauce
1½ teaspoons salt
1½ cups grated Parmesan or Romano cheese
    (6 ounces)
¼ teaspoon ground cinnamon
2 cups milk
⅓ cup margarine or butter
3 eggs, beaten
¼ teaspoon ground nutmeg

Cook macaroni as directed on package; drain. Cook and stir ground beef and onion in 10-inch skillet until beef is light brown; drain. Stir in tomato sauce and salt. Spread half of the macaroni in greased rectangular baking dish, 13 × 9 × 2 inches; cover with beef mixture. Mix ½ cup of the cheese and the cinnamon; sprinkle over beef mixture. Cover beef mixture with remaining macaroni.

Heat milk and margarine in 2-quart saucepan, stirring constantly, until margarine is melted; remove from heat. Stir at least half of the milk mixture gradually into beaten eggs. Blend into milk mixture in saucepan; pour over macaroni. Sprinkle with remaining 1 cup cheese. Cover and refrigerate no longer than 24 hours.

Bake uncovered in 325° oven until brown and center is set, about 50 minutes. Sprinkle with nutmeg. Garnish with parsley if desired.

Greek Salad

2 bunches romaine, torn into bite-size pieces
    (about 12 cups)
¾ cup crumbled feta or blue cheese
½ cup bottled oil and vinegar dressing
½ teaspoon dried oregano leaves
24 pitted ripe olives
3 medium tomatoes, cut into wedges.

Place romaine in plastic bag. Fasten bag and refrigerate no longer than 24 hours.

Add remaining ingredients to bag. Fasten bag securely and shake until well coated.

NOTE: To crumble blue cheese, freeze first (it is easier to handle and remains in separate pieces). After crumbling, wrap and freeze. Separate into pieces before adding to salad.

Hummus

1 can (15½ ounces) garbanzo beans, drained
    (reserve liquid)
½ cup sesame seed
1 clove garlic, cut into halves
3 tablespoons lemon juice
1 teaspoon salt
    Snipped parsley
9 pita breads, cut into fourths

Place reserved bean liquid, the sesame seed and garlic in blender container. Cover and blend on high speed until mixed. Add beans, lemon juice and salt. Cover and blend on high speed, scraping sides of blender if necessary, until of uniform consistency. Cover and refrigerate no longer than 24 hours.

Remove from refrigerator; let stand at room temperature 1 hour before serving. Garnish with parsley. Serve with pita wedges.

Baklava

Honey Syrup (right)
4 *cups finely chopped walnuts, almonds, pecans*
  or combination of nuts (1 pound shelled)
2 *teaspoons ground cinnamon*
1 *teaspoon ground nutmeg*
½ *teaspoon ground cloves*
1 *pound margarine or butter, melted*
1 *package (16 ounces) frozen phyllo leaves,*
  thawed

Prepare Honey Syrup; cool. Mix nuts, cinnamon, nutmeg and cloves. Brush bottom and sides of jelly roll pan, 15½ × 10½ × 1 inch, with some of the margarine. Unfold phyllo leaves. Gently separate 1 leaf; place in pan, folding edges over to fit pan if necessary. (Keep remaining phyllo leaves covered with a dampened towel to prevent them from drying out.) Brush lightly with margarine; repeat 7 times. Sprinkle 2 cups of the nut mixture evenly over top. Layer more phyllo leaves in pan, brushing each leaf with margarine. Sprinkle remaining nut mixture over top. Layer remaining phyllo leaves over nuts, brushing each leaf with margarine.

With sharp knife, cut pastry in pan ½ inch deep into 6 lengthwise strips, about 1¾ inches wide. Make diagonal cuts across strips ½ inch deep and about 2 inches wide. Pour remaining margarine over top.

Bake in 350° oven until golden brown, 1 to 1¼ hours. Remove to wire rack. Pour Honey Syrup over pastry top; cool. Cut along scored lines to bottom. Cover and refrigerate no longer than 2 weeks.

Remove from refrigerator at least 2 hours before serving; let stand at room temperature. About 42 pieces.

Honey Syrup

2 *cups sugar*
2 *cups water*
3 *tablespoons lemon juice*
3- *inch stick cinnamon*
6 *whole cloves*
½ *cup honey*

Heat all ingredients except honey to boiling in 3-quart saucepan, stirring until sugar is dissolved. Boil 5 minutes or until candy thermometer registers 220°; remove from heat. Discard cinnamon and cloves; stir in honey.

Middle Eastern Coffee

4 *cups water*
⅓ *cup sugar*
3- *inch stick cinnamon*
½ *cup Turkish-style coffee*

Heat water to boiling in 3-quart saucepan; stir in sugar and cinnamon. Heat to boiling; remove from heat. Stir in coffee. Heat coffee mixture until it foams; immediately remove from heat and stir. Repeat once; return to heat. When coffee foams the third time, it is ready to serve. Do not stir. Spoon some foam into each cup; ladle coffee over foam.

Scoring Baklava

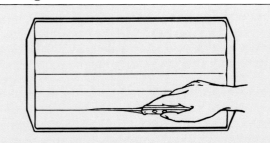

Cut pastry ½ inch deep into 6 lengthwise strips, about 1¾ inches wide.

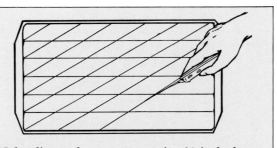

Make diagonal cuts across strips ½ inch deep and about 2 inches wide to form diamonds.

A Father's Day Buffet

Menu

8 servings

Spinach Meat Roll*

Lemony Potatoes*

Cranberry-Fruit Mold*

Vegetable Relish Tray

Hard Rolls

Apricot Brandy Pound Cake*

Coffee   Tea

*Recipe included

3 days before buffet:
- ☐ Prepare Cranberry-Fruit Mold; refrigerate.

1 day before:
- ☐ Prepare Spinach Meat Roll for baking; refrigerate.
- ☐ Prepare Lemony Potatoes for baking; refrigerate.
- ☐ Bake Apricot Brandy Pound Cake; store at room temperature.
- ☐ Prepare vegetables for Vegetable Relish Tray; cover and refrigerate.

About 1 hour 45 minutes before serving:
- ☐ Bake Spinach Meat Roll.

About 1 hour before:
- ☐ Bake Lemony Potatoes.
- ☐ Unmold Cranberry-Fruit Mold; refrigerate.

About 20 minutes before:
- ☐ Prepare Coffee and Tea.
- ☐ Arrange Hard Rolls in serving container.

At dessert time:
- ☐ Complete Apricot Brandy Pound Cake.

Spinach Meat Roll

1 package (10 ounces) frozen leaf spinach
2 pounds ground beef
¾ cup soft bread crumbs (about 1 slice)
¼ cup milk
¼ cup catsup
½ teaspoon salt
¼ teaspoon pepper
¼ teaspoon dried oregano leaves
2 eggs
½ teaspoon salt
1 package (2.5 ounces) sliced smoked ham
3 slices mozzarella cheese, cut diagonally into triangles

Rinse spinach under running cold water to separate; drain. Mix ground beef, bread crumbs, milk, catsup, ½ teaspoon salt, the pepper, oregano and eggs. Pat beef mixture into rectangle, 12 × 10 inches, on 18 × 15-inch piece of aluminum foil. Arrange spinach evenly on beef mixture, leaving ½-inch margin. Sprinkle ½ teaspoon salt over spinach; arrange ham on spinach. Roll up carefully, beginning at narrow end and using foil to lift beef mixture. Press edges and ends of roll to seal. Place on rack in rectangular pan, 13 × 9 × 2 inches. Cover with plastic wrap and refrigerate no longer than 24 hours.

Bake uncovered in 350° oven 1½ hours. (Center of roll may be slightly pink because of ham.) Place cheese on roll in overlapping triangles. Bake just until cheese begins to melt, about 5 minutes longer.

Lemony Potatoes

8 large potatoes, cut into ½-inch cubes (about 8 cups)
⅓ cup margarine or butter, melted
¼ cup lemon juice
1 teaspoon salt
½ teaspoon ground nutmeg
¼ teaspoon coarsely ground pepper
1 small onion, chopped (about ¼ cup)

Heat 1 inch salted water (½ teaspoon salt to 1 cup water) to boiling. Add potatoes. Heat to boiling; reduce heat. Cover and simmer just until tender, about 12 minutes; drain. Mix remaining ingredients; toss with potatoes. Spoon into ungreased 1½-quart casserole. Cover and refrigerate no longer than 24 hours.

Bake covered in 350° oven until hot and bubbly, about 50 minutes.

Cranberry-Fruit Mold

¾ cup boiling water
1 package (3 ounces) raspberry-flavored gelatin
1 can (16 ounces) whole cranberry sauce
1 can (8 ounces) crushed pineapple in juice, undrained
1 cup seedless grapes
½ cup coarsely chopped nuts
  Salad greens

Pour boiling water on gelatin in large bowl; stir until gelatin is dissolved. Stir in cranberry sauce and pineapple. Refrigerate until thickened slightly but not set.

Stir in grapes and nuts. Pour into 5-cup mold or 8 individual molds. Refrigerate until firm, at least 4 hours. Cover and refrigerate no longer than 3 days.

Unmold on salad greens; serve with favorite fruit salad dressing if desired.

Apricot Brandy Pound Cake

3 cups all-purpose flour
3 cups sugar
1 cup margarine or butter, softened
1 cup dairy sour cream
½ cup apricot brandy or apricot nectar
1 teaspoon orange extract
1 teaspoon lemon extract
1 teaspoon almond extract
½ teaspoon salt
¼ teaspoon baking soda
6 eggs
1 jar (12 ounces) apricot preserves
3 tablespoons lemon juice
  Whipped cream

Heat oven to 325°. Grease and flour 12-cup bundt cake pan or tube pan, 10 × 4 inches. Beat all ingredients except preserves, lemon juice and whipped cream in large bowl on low speed, scraping bowl constantly, 30 seconds. Beat on high speed, scraping bowl occasionally, 2 minutes. Pour into pan.

Bake until wooden pick inserted in center comes out clean, about 1 hour 20 minutes. Cool 20 minutes; remove from pan and cool. Heat preserves and lemon juice over medium heat, stirring occasionally, until preserves are melted; cool slightly. Spoon about half of the preserves mixture over cake. Cover and store at room temperature no longer than 24 hours. Serve cake with remaining preserves mixture and whipped cream.

A Winter Evening Dinner

Warm your guests with hot, foamy Lemon Soup in front of the fire on a brisk, cold day. After the soup, invite them to serve themselves from the buffet table and enjoy the individual Beef and Wheat Molds. Mixed fruit and spicy cookies with hot coffee or tea will prepare your company for venturing out into the cold night air.

Menu

10 servings

Lemon Soup*

Beef and Wheat Molds*

Corn-Zucchini Skillet*

Tossed Green Salad*

Crusty Bread*

Mixed Fruit Bowl*

Sesame Triangles*

Coffee   Tea

***Recipe included**

1 month before buffet:
- ☐ Bake Sesame Triangles; freeze.

1 day before:
- ☐ Prepare Beef and Wheat Molds for baking; refrigerate. Prepare Tomato Sauce; refrigerate.
- ☐ Prepare Mixed Fruit Bowl; refrigerate.
- ☐ Prepare zucchini for Corn-Zucchini Skillet.

About 1 hour before serving:
- ☐ Bake Beef and Wheat Molds.

When guests arrive:
- ☐ Prepare Lemon Soup; serve.

About 30 minutes before:
- ☐ Arrange Sesame Triangles on serving plate; let stand at room temperature.
- ☐ Prepare Coffee and Tea.
- ☐ Prepare Corn-Zucchini Skillet.
- ☐ Heat Crusty Bread.
- ☐ Prepare Tossed Green Salad.

At dessert time:
- ☐ Serve Mixed Fruit Bowl with Sesame Triangles.

Lemon Soup

Lemon Soup

4 cans (10¾ ounces each) condensed chicken broth
3 cups water
¼ teaspoon salt
3 eggs, beaten
¼ cup lemon juice

Heat chicken broth, water and salt to boiling in 3-quart saucepan. Mix eggs and lemon juice. Stir about ½ cup of the hot broth into egg mixture; stir into broth mixture in saucepan. Cook and stir over low heat until slightly thickened, 3 to 4 minutes. (Do not boil or eggs will curdle.) Beat with hand beater until foamy; serve immediately.

Beef and Wheat Molds

1 pound ground beef
1 stalk celery, chopped (about ¼ cup)
1 small onion, chopped (about ¼ cup)
¾ cup uncooked cracked wheat (bulgur)
½ cup water
½ teaspoon salt
½ teaspoon dried dill weed
⅛ teaspoon pepper
1 can (10¾ ounces) condensed beef broth
1 can (4 ounces) mushroom stems and pieces,
    drained and coarsely chopped
2 eggs, slightly beaten
    Margarine or butter, softened
10 frozen phyllo sheets, thawed
½ cup margarine or butter, melted
    Tomato Sauce (right)

Cook and stir ground beef, celery and onion in 10-inch skillet until beef is brown; drain. Stir in wheat, water, salt, dill, pepper, beef broth and mushrooms. Heat to boiling; reduce heat. Cover and simmer until wheat is tender and liquid is absorbed, 20 to 25 minutes; cool slightly. Stir in eggs.

Brush ten 6-ounce custard cups or individual molds with softened margarine. Cut phyllo sheets lengthwise into halves; cut each half crosswise into three 5½-inch squares (see sketch). Keep phyllo covered with a dampened towel to prevent them from drying out.

Place 4 phyllo squares diagonally in cup, overlapping to fit side of cup; brush with melted margarine. Place about ½ cup beef mixture in cup; press down slightly. Fold 2 phyllo squares into fourths and place on filling; brush with melted margarine. Bring 4 overhanging corners up and over filling; brush with melted margarine. Repeat with remaining phyllo squares and beef mixture. Place in jelly roll pan, 15½ × 10½ × 1 inch; cover tightly with plastic wrap. Refrigerate no longer than 24 hours. Prepare Tomato Sauce.

Bake Beef and Wheat Molds uncovered in jelly roll pan in 350° oven until golden brown, 40 to 45 minutes; let stand 10 minutes. Re-move from custard cups. Heat Tomato Sauce, stirring occasionally; serve with beef molds.

Tomato Sauce

2 cloves garlic, crushed
1 medium onion, chopped (about ½ cup)
1 tablespoon olive or vegetable oil
½ cup water
1 teaspoon salt
1 teaspoon sugar
1 teaspoon dried basil leaves
¼ teaspoon pepper
1 can (16 ounces) whole tomatoes, undrained
1 can (15 ounces) tomato sauce

Cook and stir garlic and onion in oil in 3-quart saucepan until onion is tender. Stir in remaining ingredients. Heat to boiling; reduce heat. Simmer uncovered, stirring occasionally, until thickened, about 30 minutes. Cover and refrigerate no longer than 24 hours.

Assembling Beef and Wheat Molds

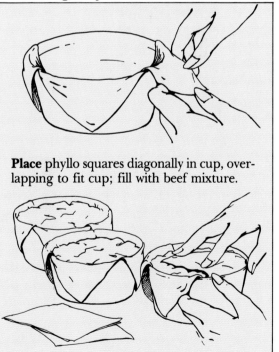

Place phyllo squares diagonally in cup, overlapping to fit cup; fill with beef mixture.

Top beef mixture with folded phyllo square. Bring sides over filling, overlapping corners.

Corn-Zucchini Skillet

4 medium zucchini
1/3 cup coarsely chopped walnuts
2 cloves garlic, crushed
2 tablespoons margarine or butter
1/4 cup sliced green onions (with tops)
1 teaspoon salt
1/4 teaspoon pepper
2 cans (16 ounces each) whole kernel corn, drained
1 jar (2 ounces) sliced pimientos, drained

Coarsely shred zucchini; cover with ice water and refrigerate no longer than 24 hours.

Drain zucchini. Cook and stir walnuts and garlic in margarine in 10-inch skillet over medium heat until walnuts are brown, about 10 minutes. Remove walnuts with slotted spoon and reserve. Add onions, zucchini, salt, pepper, corn and pimientos to skillet. Cook, stirring occasionally, until corn is hot, about 5 minutes; stir in reserved walnuts.

Mixed Fruit Bowl

1 package (8 ounces) mixed dried fruit*
2 cups water
4 bananas, thinly sliced
1 tablespoon lemon juice
4 ounces pitted dates, cut up (about 1 cup)
1 tablespoon finely shredded lemon peel
2 cups unsweetened whipped cream

Cut dried fruit into bite-size pieces. Heat dried fruit and water to boiling; reduce heat. Cover and simmer until tender, about 20 minutes; cool and drain.

Toss bananas with lemon juice. Layer half of the mixed fruit, bananas, dates, lemon peel

and whipped cream in 1½-quart glass bowl or 10 individual dishes; repeat. Cover and refrigerate at least 4 hours but no longer than 24 hours. Sprinkle with coconut if desired.

*1½ cups bite-size pieces dried apricots, apples, peaches or pears can be substituted for the mixed dried fruit.

Sesame Triangles

1/2 cup sesame seed
1 cup margarine or butter, softened
1 cup packed brown sugar
1 egg yolk
1 teaspoon vanilla
2 cups all-purpose flour
1/4 teaspoon salt
1 teaspoon ground nutmeg
1 egg white, slightly beaten

Cook and stir sesame seed over medium heat until golden brown; cool. Mix margarine, brown sugar, egg yolk and vanilla. Stir in flour, salt and nutmeg. Spread evenly in ungreased jelly roll pan, 15 × 10½ × 1 inch. Brush dough with egg white; sprinkle with sesame seed.

Bake in 275° oven until golden brown, about 1 hour; cool slightly. Cut into 2½-inch squares. Cut each square diagonally into halves; cool completely. Wrap, label and freeze no longer than 1 month.

Remove Sesame Triangles from freezer and unwrap. Arrange on serving plate and let stand at room temperature until thawed, at least 20 minutes. About 4 dozen triangles.

Chocolate-Apricot Cake

A Family Reunion Dinner

Menu

12 servings

Burgundy Meatballs*

Oven-steamed Rice*

Green Beans

Tossed Vegetable Salad*

Almond Flatbread*

Chocolate-Apricot Cake*

Coffee   Tea

***Recipe included**

2 days before buffet:
- ☐ Bake Almond Flatbread; store at room temperature.

1 day before:
- ☐ Prepare Burgundy Meatballs; refrigerate.
- ☐ Prepare Chocolate-Apricot Cake; cover and store at room temperature.
- ☐ Prepare vegetables for Tossed Vegetable Salad; cover and refrigerate.

About 45 minutes before serving:
- ☐ Bake Oven-steamed Rice.

About 20 minutes before:
- ☐ Cook Green Beans.
- ☐ Heat Burgundy Meatballs.
- ☐ Prepare Coffee and Tea.

At serving time:
- ☐ Complete Tossed Vegetable Salad.

Burgundy Meatballs

2 pounds ground beef
1 medium onion, chopped (about ½ cup)
½ cup water chestnuts, finely chopped
1 cup dry bread crumbs
½ cup milk
1 teaspoon salt
1 teaspoon Worcestershire sauce
⅛ teaspoon pepper
2 eggs
  Burgundy Sauce (below)
  Snipped parsley

Mix all ingredients except Burgundy Sauce and parsley. Shape mixture into 1-inch balls; place in ungreased jelly roll pan, 15½ × 10½ × 1 inch. Bake uncovered in 400° oven until done, about 10 minutes. Prepare Burgundy Sauce; stir meatballs into Burgundy Sauce. Cover and refrigerate no longer than 24 hours.

Heat meatball mixture to boiling; reduce heat. Cover and simmer just until meatballs are hot, about 10 minutes. Garnish with parsley.

Burgundy Sauce

⅓ cup cornstarch
½ cup cold water
2 cans (10½ ounces each) condensed beef broth
1 cup dry red wine
1 clove garlic, crushed

Mix cornstarch and water in 3-quart saucepan; stir in remaining ingredients gradually. Heat to boiling, stirring constantly. Boil and stir 1 minute.

Oven-steamed Rice

Mix 4 cups boiling water, 2 cups uncooked regular rice and 1½ teaspoons salt in ungreased 3-quart casserole. Cover and bake in 350° oven until rice is tender and liquid is absorbed, 25 to 30 minutes.

Tossed Vegetable Salad

1 head iceberg lettuce, torn into bite-size pieces (about 6 cups)
2 small bunches romaine, torn into bite-size pieces (about 6 cups)
16 radishes, sliced
2 medium cucumbers, sliced
8 green onions (with tops), sliced
1 can (6 ounces) pitted ripe olives, drained
½ cup bottled oil and vinegar salad dressing
½ cup crumbled blue or feta cheese

Divide lettuce, romaine, radishes, cucumbers, onions and olives between 2 large plastic bags. Fasten bags securely and refrigerate no longer than 24 hours.

Add ¼ cup salad dressing to each bag. Fasten bags securely and shake until all ingredients are coated. Sprinkle cheese on salad.

Almond Flatbread

¾ cup toasted whole almonds
1 cup all-purpose flour
¼ cup dairy sour cream
3 tablespoons milk
2 tablespoons margarine or butter, softened
1½ teaspoons sugar
½ teaspoon salt
¼ teaspoon baking soda

Heat oven to 400°. Finely chop almonds in blender or food processor, watching carefully, or finely chop almonds with knife. Mix all ingredients with fork. Shape mixture into 1-inch balls. Roll each ball into 4-inch circle with floured cloth-covered rolling pin on lightly floured cloth-covered board.

Bake on ungreased cookie sheet until golden brown, 6 to 8 minutes. Cover and store at room temperature no longer than 48 hours. About 2½ dozen rounds.

Chocolate-Apricot Cake

3 eggs
1 cup sugar
⅓ cup water
1 teaspoon vanilla
¾ cup all-purpose flour
¼ cup cocoa
1 teaspoon baking powder
¼ teaspoon salt
1 can (17 ounces) peeled whole apricots, drained
1 jar (12 ounces) apricot preserves
1 tablespoon lemon juice
   Chocolate Frosting (right)
¼ cup almond-flavored liqueur

Heat oven to 375°. Line jelly roll pan, 15½ × 10½ × 1 inch, with aluminum foil or waxed paper; grease generously. Beat eggs in small bowl on high speed until very thick and lemon colored, about 5 minutes. Pour eggs into large bowl. Beat in sugar gradually. Beat in water and vanilla on low speed. Add flour, cocoa, baking powder and salt gradually, beating just until batter is smooth. Pour into pan, spreading batter to corners.

Bake until wooden pick inserted in center comes out clean, 12 to 15 minutes. Immediately loosen cake from edges of pan; invert on towel sprinkled generously with cocoa. Carefully remove foil; cool cake.

Cut apricots into halves and remove pits. Drain halves, with cut sides down. Heat apricot preserves and lemon juice just to boiling. Prepare Chocolate Frosting.

Trim off stiff edges of cake if necessary. Cut cake crosswise into 3 equal pieces, about 10½ × 5 inches each. Place one piece on plate; sprinkle with 1 tablespoon liqueur. Spread about ⅓ cup frosting on cake to within ⅜ inch of edges. Spread with ⅓ cup of the apricot mixture. Place second cake piece on apricot mixture; sprinkle with 1 tablespoon liqueur. Spread with ⅓ cup frosting and ⅓ cup apricot mixture; top with remaining cake piece. Sprinkle cake with remaining liqueur. Arrange apricot halves, cut sides down, on cake. Spread remaining apricot mixture over apricots. Remove 1 cup frosting; reserve. Frost sides of cake with remaining frosting. Place reserved frosting in decorators' tube or bag fitted with decorating tip; pipe border around top and bottom edges of cake. Cover loosely and store at room temperature no longer than 24 hours.

Chocolate Frosting

½ cup margarine or butter, softened
3 ounces unsweetened melted chocolate (cool)
3 cups powdered sugar
1 teaspoon vanilla
1 teaspoon almond extract
   About 3 tablespoons milk

Mix margarine and chocolate. Stir in powdered sugar. Beat in remaining ingredients until frosting is of spreading consistency.

VERSATILE CHAFING DISH

A chafing dish is ideal for buffet service. It can be a simple but elegant serving dish—for main dishes such as Burgundy Meatballs (page 60), hot hors d'oeuvres or vegetables. Or, it can be a star performer when you want to prepare a main dish or dessert at the table.

Almost any food that is prepared in a skillet or saucepan can easily be prepared in a chafing dish if the heat source is suitable. Heat can be provided by canned fuel, an alcohol burner using denatured alcohol, a butane gas burner, electric heating unit or candle warmer. Be sure to read and follow the manufacturer's instructions before cooking in your chafing dish.

Because cooking in a chafing dish takes longer, most people prefer to cook the food in the kitchen and just serve it in the chafing dish to keep it warm. However, Peaches Flambée (page 45) may be the perfect recipe to prepare at the table in a chafing dish to entertain your guests.

An Italian Cold Buffet

Menu

12 servings

Veal with Tuna Sauce*

Pasta-Tomato Salad*

Marinated Eggplant*

Breadsticks

Ricotta Cheesecake*

Assorted Grapes

Espresso

*Recipe included

2 days before buffet:
  ☐ Prepare Ricotta Cheesecake; refrigerate.

1 day before:
  ☐ Prepare Veal with Tuna Sauce; refrigerate.
  ☐ Prepare Pasta-Tomato Salad; refrigerate.
  ☐ Prepare Marinated Eggplant; refrigerate.

Several hours before serving:
  ☐ Complete Ricotta Cheesecake; refrigerate.

About 30 minutes before:
  ☐ Prepare Espresso.

At serving time:
  ☐ Arrange Breadsticks in serving container.

At dessert time:
  ☐ Serve Ricotta Cheesecake and Assorted Grapes.

Veal with Tuna Sauce, Pasta-Tomato Salad, Marinated Eggplant, Breadsticks, Ricotta Cheesecake and Assorted Grapes

Veal with Tuna Sauce

3- pound boned, rolled and tied leg of veal
2 tablespoons olive or vegetable oil
½ cup chicken broth
½ cup dry white wine
½ teaspoon salt
½ teaspoon dried basil leaves
¼ teaspoon pepper
3 cloves garlic, crushed
1 medium onion, chopped (about ½ cup)
  Tuna Sauce (right)
2 tablespoons capers
2 tablespoons snipped parsley

Cook veal in 2 tablespoons oil in 4-quart Dutch oven over medium heat until brown. Add chicken broth, wine, salt, basil, pepper, garlic and onion. Heat to boiling; reduce heat. Cover and simmer until veal is tender, about 2¼ hours. Remove veal from broth. Cover and refrigerate until cold, at least 4 hours. Reserve ¼ cup broth. Cover and refrigerate.

Prepare Tuna Sauce. Cut veal into thin slices; arrange on serving platter. Spoon Tuna Sauce over veal. Cover and refrigerate at least 3 hours but no longer than 24 hours.

Sprinkle with capers and parsley; garnish with lemon if desired.

Tuna Sauce

1 can (6½ ounces) tuna in oil, undrained
¼ cup reserved veal broth
¼ cup olive or vegetable oil
¼ cup mayonnaise or salad dressing
2 tablespoons lemon juice
1 clove garlic
¼ teaspoon salt

Place all ingredients in blender container. Cover and blend on medium speed, stopping blender occasionally to scrape down sides, until mixture is smooth and creamy, about 2 minutes.

FOOD PROCESSOR DIRECTIONS: Place all ingredients in workbowl fitted with steel blade. Cover and process until smooth, 5 to 10 seconds.

Pasta-Tomato Salad

4 *medium tomatoes, chopped (about 4 cups)*
4 *green onions (with tops), sliced*
3 *cloves garlic, crushed*
⅓ *cup snipped parsley*
1 *teaspoon salt*
1 *teaspoon dried basil leaves*
¼ *teaspoon coarsely cracked pepper*
¼ *cup olive or vegetable oil*
1 *package (16 ounces) rigatoni or ziti*

Mix tomatoes, onions, garlic, parsley, salt, basil, pepper and oil. Cook rigatoni as directed on package; drain. Toss with tomato mixture. Cover and refrigerate at least 2 hours but no longer than 24 hours.

Toss before serving. Serve with freshly ground pepper if desired.

Marinated Eggplant

2 *medium eggplants (about 1½ pounds each)*
   Olive or vegetable oil
¼ *teaspoon coarsely ground pepper*
¾ *cup olive or vegetable oil*
3 *cloves garlic, crushed*
2 *medium green peppers, cut into ¼-inch*
     strips
¼ *cup lemon juice*
1½ *teaspoons salt*
1 *teaspoon dried oregano leaves*

Rub eggplants with oil. Bake eggplants on oven rack in 350° oven until tender when pierced with a fork, about 30 minutes; cool. Cut eggplants into 1-inch cubes. Place in glass or plastic bowl; sprinkle with pepper.

Heat ¾ cup oil and the garlic in 10-inch skillet over medium-high heat until hot. Add peppers. Cook and stir until peppers begin to blister, about 4 minutes; remove from heat. Remove peppers with slotted spoon and arrange on eggplant. Stir lemon juice, salt and oregano into oil in skillet; pour over vegetables. Cover and refrigerate at least 6 hours but no longer than 24 hours.

Ricotta Cheesecake

⅓ *cup rum*
¼ *cup finely cut-up mixed candied fruit*
¼ *cup golden raisins*
   Cheesecake Pastry (below)
1½ *pounds ricotta cheese, well drained*
½ *cup granulated sugar*
3 *tablespoons flour*
3 *eggs*
1 *teaspoon shredded orange peel*
1 *teaspoon vanilla*
¼ *teaspoon salt*
2 *tablespoons finely chopped blanched almonds*
¾ *cup chilled whipping cream*
2 *tablespoons powdered sugar*
   Mixed candied fruit

Pour rum over ¼ cup fruit and the raisins; let stand at room temperature at least 1 hour.

Prepare Cheesecake Pastry. Beat ricotta cheese, granulated sugar, flour, eggs, orange peel, vanilla and salt in large bowl on high speed until smooth and creamy, about 4 minutes. Stir in rum mixture and almonds. Pour into pastry-lined pan.

Reduce oven temperature to 350°. Bake until center is set and top is golden brown, 1¼ to 1½ hours; cool. Refrigerate at least 12 hours but no longer than 48 hours.

Remove outer rim and bottom of pan. Beat whipping cream and powdered sugar in chilled 1-quart bowl until stiff. Spread over cheesecake; garnish with candied fruit. Refrigerate no longer than 4 hours.

Cheesecake Pastry

¾ *cup all-purpose flour*
⅓ *cup margarine or butter, softened*
2 *tablespoons sugar*
⅛ *teaspoon salt*

Heat oven to 475°. Mix all ingredients until blended. Press evenly in bottom of ungreased springform pan, 9 × 3 inches. Bake 5 minutes.

An Easter Buffet

Menu

12 servings

Glazed Buffet Ham*

Elegant Rice*

Asparagus Spears

Melon-Cucumber Salad*

Croissants

Strawberry Puff Revel*

Coffee   Tea

***Recipe included**

Several days before buffet:
- ☐ Bake Petits Choux for Strawberry Puff Revel; fill with ice cream and freeze.

1 day before:
- ☐ Cook rice for Elegant Rice; cover and refrigerate.

Several hours before serving:
- ☐ Prepare Melon-Cucumber Salad; refrigerate.
- ☐ Prepare vegetables for Elegant Rice; cover and refrigerate.

About 2 hours 15 minutes before:
- ☐ Bake Glazed Buffet Ham.

About 30 minutes before:
- ☐ Prepare strawberries for Strawberry Puff Revel.
- ☐ Cook Elegant Rice.
- ☐ Cook Asparagus Spears.
- ☐ Heat Croissants.
- ☐ Brush ham with apricot mixture.
- ☐ Complete Melon-Cucumber Salad.
- ☐ Prepare Coffee and Tea.

At dessert time:
- ☐ Complete Strawberry Puff Revel.

Glazed Buffet Ham

5- to 5½-pound fully cooked boneless smoked
    ham, cut into ¼-inch slices and tied*
1 jar (12 ounces) apricot preserves
1 tablespoon prepared mustard

Place ham, fat side up, on rack in open shallow roasting pan. Insert meat thermometer so tip is in center of thickest part of ham and does not rest in fat.

Bake in 325° oven 1 hour 45 minutes. Heat apricot preserves and mustard over low heat until preserves are melted; brush ham evenly with half of the apricot mixture. Bake until thermometer registers 140°, about 20 minutes. Brush ham with remaining apricot mixture.

*Ask your meat retailer to cut the ham, reassemble and tie with cord.

Elegant Rice

¼ cup slivered almonds
¼ cup margarine or butter
2 medium stalks celery, sliced (about 1½ cups)
4 ounces mushrooms, sliced (about 1½ cups)
3 cups cooked wild rice
3 cups cooked white rice
1 teaspoon salt
1 teaspoon dried basil leaves
¼ cup sliced green onions (with tops)

Cook and stir almonds in margarine in 3-quart saucepan over medium heat until brown; remove and reserve. Cook and stir celery and mushrooms in same saucepan until celery is tender, about 5 minutes. Stir in wild rice, white rice, salt and basil. Cook, stirring occasionally, until rice is hot, about 10 minutes. Stir in onions; sprinkle with reserved almonds.

Melon-Cucumber Salad

½ cup vegetable oil
¼ cup lemon juice
1 teaspoon sugar
½ teaspoon salt
    Dash of freshly ground pepper
6 cups ¾-inch pieces melon (honeydew,
    cantaloupe, watermelon)
3 medium cucumbers, thinly sliced
    Crisp salad greens

Mix oil, lemon juice, sugar, salt and pepper in tightly covered container; toss with melon and cucumbers. Cover and refrigerate no longer than 8 hours. Drain; serve on salad greens.

Strawberry Puff Revel

Petits Choux (right)
1 pint vanilla ice cream
1 pint strawberries, sliced
½ cup powdered sugar
1 cup chilled whipping cream
2 tablespoons powdered sugar

Bake Petits Choux; cool. Cut off tops of puffs; pull out any filaments of soft dough. Fill puffs generously with ice cream; replace tops. Freeze at least 1 hour but no longer than 1 week.

Mix strawberries and ½ cup powdered sugar; let stand at least 1 hour. Just before serving, beat whipping cream and 2 tablespoons powdered sugar in chilled bowl until stiff. Remove puffs from freezer. Alternate layers of puffs, whipped cream and strawberries (with juice) in 1½- to 2-quart glass serving bowl. Garnish with mint leaves if desired.

Petits Choux

½ cup water
¼ cup margarine or butter
½ cup all-purpose flour
2 eggs

Heat oven to 400°. Heat water and margarine to rolling boil in 1-quart saucepan. Stir in flour. Stir vigorously over low heat until mixture forms a ball, about 1 minute; remove from heat. Beat in eggs, all at once; continue beating until smooth. Drop dough by slightly rounded teaspoonfuls about 1 inch apart onto ungreased cookie sheet. Bake until puffed and golden, 25 to 30 minutes. About 30 puffs.

Preparing Strawberry Puff Revel

Remove tops and filaments of soft dough from puffs; fill generously with ice cream.

Clockwise from top: Glazed Buffet Ham, Elegant Rice and Melon-Cucumber Salad

Alternate layers of frozen puffs, whipped cream and strawberries in serving bowl.

An Off-the-Shelf Buffet

Menu

8 servings

Dilled Seafood Medley*

**Green Noodles or
Buttered Rice**

Corn Almondine*

Spiced Crabapples

Double Cherry Dessert*

Coffee   Tea

***Recipe included**

About 1 hour before serving:
☐ Bake Double Cherry Dessert.

About 20 minutes before:
☐ Cook Green Noodles or Buttered Rice.
☐ Prepare Coffee and Tea.
☐ Cook Corn Almondine.
☐ Cook Dilled Seafood Medley.

Dilled Seafood Medley

1 can (10¾ ounces) condensed cream of
   chicken soup
1 can (10¾ ounces) condensed cream of
   mushroom soup
1½ cups milk
1 teaspoon dry mustard
½ teaspoon dried dill weed
1 can (8 ounces) mushroom stems and pieces,
   drained
1 can (7 ounces) minced clams, drained
1 can (6½ ounces) tuna, drained
1 can (4¼ ounces) shrimp, rinsed and drained
1 jar (2 ounces) sliced pimientos, drained

Heat condensed chicken soup, condensed mushroom soup, milk, dry mustard and dill weed in 3-quart saucepan, stirring occasionally, until smooth. Stir in remaining ingredients. Heat to boiling, stirring occasionally; reduce heat. Simmer uncovered, stirring occasionally, until hot, about 5 minutes.

Corn Almondine

⅓ cup slivered almonds
¼ cup margarine or butter

2 cans (16 ounces each) whole kernel corn,
   drained
⅛ teaspoon pepper

Cook and stir almonds in margarine in 10-inch skillet over medium heat until almonds are golden brown, about 8 minutes. Stir in corn and pepper. Heat, stirring occasionally, until corn is hot, about 5 minutes.

Double Cherry Dessert

1 can (21 ounces) cherry pie filling
1 can (16 ounces) pitted dark sweet cherries,
   drained
⅔ cup quick-cooking oats
½ cup packed brown sugar
½ cup buttermilk baking mix
¼ cup firm margarine or butter
¼ cup chopped nuts, if desired
1 teaspoon ground cinnamon

Mix pie filling and cherries in ungreased square pan, 8 × 8 × 2 inches. Mix remaining ingredients until crumbly; sprinkle over fruit. Bake in 375° oven until fruit is hot and bubbly and topping is brown, about 45 minutes.

An Out-of-Town Guest Buffet

Menu

8 servings

Scallops and Shrimp au Vin*

Bulgur Wheat*

Marinated Cauliflower and Broccoli*

Popovers (page 49)

Crimson Pears*

Coffee   Tea

*****Recipe included**

---

2 days before buffet:
- ☐ Prepare pears for Crimson Pears; refrigerate.

1 day before:
- ☐ Prepare scallops and mushroom mixture for Scallops and Shrimp au Vin; refrigerate.
- ☐ Prepare Marinated cauliflower and Broccoli; refrigerate.

About 45 minutes before serving:
- ☐ Bake Popovers.

About 20 minutes before:
- ☐ Cook Bulgur Wheat.
- ☐ Prepare Coffee and Tea.
- ☐ Unmold Marinated Cauliflower and Broccoli.
- ☐ Complete Scallops and Shrimp au Vin.

At dessert time:
- ☐ Complete Crimson Pears.

Scallops and Shrimp au Vin

1 package (12 ounces) frozen scallops, thawed, or 12 ounces fresh scallops
4 ounces mushrooms, sliced (about 1½ cups)
1 small red or green pepper, chopped (about ½ cup)
¼ cup margarine or butter
2 tablespoons all-purpose flour
½ teaspoon salt
1 cup half-and-half
½ cup dry white wine
1 can (14 ounces) artichoke hearts, drained and cut into halves
1 package (6 ounces) frozen cooked shrimp, thawed
¼ cup grated Parmesan cheese
2 tablespoons snipped parsley

If scallops are large, cut into 1½-inch pieces. Cover scallops with water. Heat to boiling; reduce heat. Simmer uncovered until scallops are tender, about 5 minutes; drain. Cover and refrigerate no longer than 24 hours.

Cook and stir mushrooms and red pepper in margarine over medium heat until tender, about 4 minutes; remove vegetables with slotted spoon. Stir flour and salt into margarine. Cook, stirring constantly, until smooth and bubbly; remove from heat. Stir in half-and-half. Heat to boiling, stirring constantly. Boil and stir 1 minute; stir in vegetables. Cover and refrigerate no longer than 24 hours.

Heat mushroom mixture in 2-quart saucepan, stirring occasionally, until hot. Stir in wine, artichoke hearts, shrimp and scallops. Heat until scallops and shrimp are hot, about 10 minutes. Pour into serving dish or chafing dish; sprinkle with cheese and parsley.

Bulgur Wheat

1 *small onion, chopped (about ¼ cup)*
¼ *cup margarine or butter*
2 *cans (10¾ ounces each) condensed chicken broth*
2 *cups water*
2 *cups uncooked cracked wheat (bulgur)*
½ *teaspoon salt*
¼ *teaspoon pepper*

Cook and stir onion in margarine in 3-quart saucepan over medium heat until onion is tender, about 5 minutes. Stir in remaining ingredients. Cover and heat to boiling; reduce heat. Simmer until all liquid is absorbed, about 15 minutes.

Marinated Cauliflower and Broccoli

Pepper Marinade (right)
1 *medium head cauliflower (about 1½ pounds)*
1½ *pounds broccoli*

Prepare Pepper Marinade. Separate cauliflower into flowerets. Cut flowerets from broccoli spears, leaving a 1-inch stem on each floweret. (Use broccoli stems in other recipes.)

Heat 1 inch salted water (½ teaspoon salt to 1 cup water) to boiling. Add cauliflower. Heat to boiling; reduce heat. Cover and simmer just until cauliflower is tender, 8 to 10 minutes. Remove cauliflower with slotted spoon; drain. Add broccoli flowerets to water. Heat to boiling; reduce heat. Cover and simmer just until tender, 5 to 8 minutes; drain. Cool cauliflower and broccoli.

Arrange some of the cauliflower, floweret sides down, in a circle in 1½-quart bowl. Alternate rows of broccoli and cauliflower, pressing flowerets to side of bowl, until it is about 5 inches high. Place remaining cauliflower and broccoli in center. Press down firmly; drain.

Let stand at room temperature 30 minutes; drain. Pour Pepper Marinade evenly over vegetables. Cover and refrigerate at least 4 hours but no longer than 24 hours.

Carefully drain marinade from vegetables; reserve. Press vegetables down firmly; invert on plate. Serve with reserved marinade.

Pepper Marinade

⅓ *cup olive or vegetable oil*
½ *teaspoon dried crushed red pepper*
2 *tablespoons vinegar*
1 *teaspoon sugar*
½ *teaspoon salt*
2 *cloves garlic, crushed*

Shake oil and red pepper in tightly covered container; let stand at room temperature at least 2 hours. Add remaining ingredients; cover tightly and shake.

Assembling Marinated Cauliflower and Broccoli

Alternate rows of broccoli and cauliflower, pressing flowerets to side of bowl. Place any remaining broccoli and cauliflower in center. Press down firmly; drain.

Crimson Pears

⅓ cup sugar
⅓ cup water
2 tablespoons lemon juice
8 pears
1 package (10 ounces) frozen raspberries,
  thawed
1 carton (8 ounces) frozen whipped topping,
  thawed
  Mint leaves

Mix sugar, water and lemon juice in un-greased 3-quart casserole until sugar is dissolved. Pare pears (do not core or remove stems). Arrange pears in sugar mixture, turning pears to coat with sugar mixture. Cover and bake in 350° oven until pears are tender when pierced with a fork, 45 to 60 minutes (baking time may vary due to size of pears).

Carefully remove pears; pour off sugar mixture. Return pears to casserole. Sieve raspberries over pears; turn to coat with raspberry syrup. Cool 30 minutes. Refrigerate, turning pears occasionally to coat evenly with raspberry syrup, at least 12 hours but no longer than 48 hours.

Divide whipped topping among 8 individual dishes or serving dish. Place pears on topping. Serve raspberry syrup with pears. Garnish each with mint leaf.

Scallops and Shrimp Au Vin, Bulgur Wheat, Popovers, Marinated Cauliflower and Broccoli and Crimson Pears

Spinach-Stuffed Fish Rolls, Whole Green Beans, Asparagus-Artichoke Salad, Butter Curls and Croissants

A Country French Buffet

Menu
8 servings

Spinach-stuffed Fish Rolls*

Green Beans with Almonds

Asparagus-Artichoke Salad*

Croissants

Crème Brûlée*

Coffee   Tea

***Recipe included**

1 day before buffet:
- ☐ Prepare custard for Crème Brûlée; refrigerate.
- ☐ Prepare Asparagus-Artichoke Salad; refrigerate.

Several hours before serving:
- ☐ Prepare Spinach-stuffed Fish Rolls; refrigerate.
- ☐ Prepare fresh fruit for Crème Brûlée; cover and refrigerate.

About 45 minutes before:
- ☐ Bake Spinach-stuffed Fish Rolls.

About 30 minutes before:
- ☐ Prepare Coffee and Tea.
- ☐ Prepare Green Beans with Almonds.
- ☐ Complete Asparagus-Artichoke Salad.
- ☐ Arrange Croissants in serving container.
- ☐ Prepare hollandaise sauce; serve with Spinach-stuffed Fish Rolls.

At serving time:
- ☐ Complete Crème Brûlée. Spoon over fruit.

Spinach-stuffed Fish Rolls

1 package (12 ounces) frozen spinach soufflé
8 small fish fillets (about 2 pounds)
1 tablespoon lemon juice
¼ cup margarine or butter, melted
2 packages (1¼ ounces each) hollandaise sauce
   mix

Thaw spinach soufflé slightly at room temperature about 20 minutes. Cut soufflé lengthwise into halves. Cut each half crosswise into 4 pieces. Drizzle fish fillets with lemon juice. Place 1 piece spinach soufflé at end of each fish fillet; roll up. Place fish roll, seam side down, in lightly greased rectangular baking dish, 13 × 9 × 2 inches. Repeat with remaining fillets. Cover and refrigerate no longer than 8 hours.

Drain off any liquid in baking dish. Pour margarine over fish rolls. Bake uncovered in 350° oven until fish flakes easily with a fork, 30 to 35 minutes. Remove fish rolls with slotted spatula to serving platter. Prepare sauce mix as directed on package. Spoon half of the sauce over fish rolls. Sprinkle with paprika if desired. Serve remaining hollandaise sauce with fish rolls.

Asparagus-Artichoke Salad

Mustard Dressing (below)
1 cup sliced mushrooms
1 can (15 ounces) white asparagus spears,
   drained and cut crosswise into halves
1 can (14 ounces) artichoke hearts, drained and
   cut into halves
Lettuce leaves
8 small pitted ripe olives

Prepare Mustard Dressing. Place mushrooms, asparagus and artichoke hearts in glass or plastic dish. Pour dressing over vegetables. Cover and refrigerate no longer than 24 hours.

Remove vegetables with slotted spoon; reserve Mustard Dressing. Arrange vegetables on lettuce leaves. Spoon reserved dressing over vegetables. Garnish with olives.

Mustard Dressing

½ cup olive or vegetable oil
¼ cup lemon juice
2 tablespoons snipped chives
1 tablespoon Dijon-style mustard
½ teaspoon salt
½ teaspoon grated lemon peel

Shake all ingredients in tightly covered jar.

Crème Brûlée

4 egg yolks
3 tablespoons granulated sugar
2 cups whipping cream
⅓ cup packed brown sugar
4 cups cut-up fresh fruit

Beat egg yolks until thick and lemon colored, about 5 minutes. Gradually beat in granulated sugar. Heat whipping cream in 2-quart saucepan over medium heat just until hot. Stir at least half of the hot cream gradually into egg yolks. Blend into hot cream in saucepan. Cook, stirring constantly, until mixture thickens, about 5 minutes (do not boil). Pour custard into pie plate, 9 × 1½ inches. Cover and refrigerate at least 2 hours but no longer than 24 hours.

Set oven control to broil and/or 550°. Sprinkle brown sugar over custard. Broil with top about 5 inches from heat until sugar melts and forms a glaze, about 3 minutes. Spoon over fruit.

Late Suppers

A Cold Late Supper

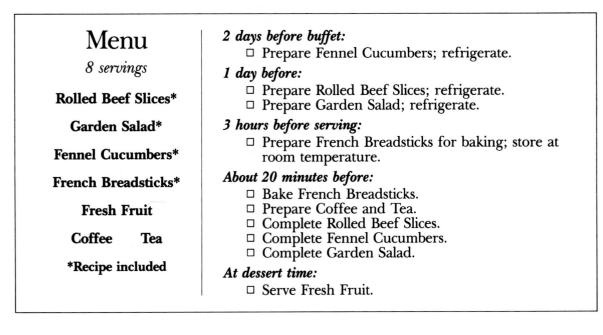

Menu

8 servings

Rolled Beef Slices*

Garden Salad*

Fennel Cucumbers*

French Breadsticks*

Fresh Fruit

Coffee   Tea

***Recipe included**

2 days before buffet:
- ☐ Prepare Fennel Cucumbers; refrigerate.

1 day before:
- ☐ Prepare Rolled Beef Slices; refrigerate.
- ☐ Prepare Garden Salad; refrigerate.

3 hours before serving:
- ☐ Prepare French Breadsticks for baking; store at room temperature.

About 20 minutes before:
- ☐ Bake French Breadsticks.
- ☐ Prepare Coffee and Tea.
- ☐ Complete Rolled Beef Slices.
- ☐ Complete Fennel Cucumbers.
- ☐ Complete Garden Salad.

At dessert time:
- ☐ Serve Fresh Fruit.

A Cold Late Supper

1. Rolled Beef Slices, 2. Fennel Cucumbers, 3. Garden Salad, 4. French Breadsticks

Rolled Beef Slices

1½- pound beef flank steak
¾ cup dry red wine
1 teaspoon salt
1 teaspoon dried basil leaves
1 teaspoon dried oregano leaves
2 cloves garlic, crushed
1 pound bulk pork sausage
1 small onion, chopped (about ¼ cup)
¼ cup dry bread crumbs
½ teaspoon salt
1 can (4 ounces) chopped green chilies, drained
1 medium carrot
3 hard-cooked eggs
2 tablespoons olive or vegetable oil
1 cup water
1 jar (12 ounces) salsa

Split beef steak lengthwise almost into halves; open and place in shallow glass or plastic dish. Mix wine, 1 teaspoon salt, the basil, oregano and garlic; pour over beef. Cover and refrigerate at least 1 hour. Drain; reserve marinade.

Cook and stir sausage and onion in 4-quart Dutch oven over medium heat until sausage is done; drain. Stir in bread crumbs, ½ teaspoon salt and the chilies. Spread sausage mixture on cut side of open beef to within 1 inch of edge. Cut carrot lengthwise into halves; cut each half lengthwise into 3 strips. Arrange carrot crosswise on sausage mixture. Place peeled eggs in a row along one narrow edge. Roll up, beginning at end with eggs; tie with string or secure with wooden picks.

Cook beef roll in oil in same Dutch oven over medium heat, turning carefully, until brown on all sides; drain. Add reserved marinade and water. Heat to boiling; reduce heat. Cover and simmer until beef is tender, about 1 hour. Remove beef from liquid. Cover and refrigerate until cold, at least 6 hours but no longer than 24 hours.

Spread salsa on serving platter or plate. Cut beef roll into slices; arrange on salsa. Serve with additional salsa if desired.

Garden Salad

1 bunch leaf lettuce, torn into bite-size pieces
1 bunch romaine, torn into bite-size pieces
1 cup sliced radishes
6 green onions (with tops), cut into julienne
  Chive Dressing (below)

Place greens, radishes and onions in large plastic bag. Fasten bag and refrigerate no longer than 24 hours. Prepare Chive Dressing; refrigerate. Just before serving, add dressing to bag. Fasten bag securely and shake until greens are evenly coated.

Chive Dressing

½ cup vegetable oil
¼ cup vinegar
2 tablespoons finely snipped chives
1 teaspoon sugar
1 teaspoon dry mustard
¾ teaspoon salt
⅛ teaspoon red pepper sauce

Shake all ingredients in tightly covered container. Refrigerate no longer than 24 hours.

Fennel Cucumbers

4 medium cucumbers
⅓ cup vegetable oil
2 tablespoons lemon juice
1 teaspoon fennel seed
1 teaspoon salt
1 small onion, finely chopped (about ¼ cup)
  Green Mayonnaise (below)

Cut cucumbers lengthwise into halves; remove seeds. Cut each half lengthwise into 4 strips. Cut each strip into pieces, about 2 inches long. Place cucumbers in glass or plastic bowl. Shake oil, lemon juice, fennel seed, salt and onion in tightly covered jar; pour over cucumbers. Cover and refrigerate, stirring occasionally, at least 12 hours but no longer than 48 hours. Prepare Green Mayonnaise. Drain cucumbers. Serve with Green Mayonnaise.

Green Mayonnaise

1 cup mayonnaise or salad dressing
¼ cup finely chopped spinach
¼ cup snipped parsley
1½ teaspoons dried dill weed
2 teaspoons tarragon vinegar

Place all ingredients in blender container. Cover and blend on high speed until smooth. Refrigerate at least 2 hours but no longer than 48 hours.

French Breadsticks

½ loaf (1-pound size) French bread
⅓ cup margarine or butter, melted
1 clove garlic, crushed
2 tablespoons grated Parmesan cheese

Split bread lengthwise into halves. Cut each half crosswise into 3 equal pieces. Cut each piece lengthwise into 3 sticks. Place sticks in ungreased jelly roll pan, 15½ × 10½ × 1 inch. Mix margarine and garlic; brush on cut sides of sticks. Sprinkle sticks with Parmesan cheese. Cover and store at room temperature no longer than 3 hours.

Bake uncovered in 425° oven until golden and crisp, 12 to 15 minutes. 18 sticks.

An Italian-Style Late Supper

This Italian-style menu suggests an informal, relaxing way to entertain late in the evening. The colorful antipasto can be served as the appetizer in the living room. Guests help themselves to soup, bread and crackers and sit wherever it is comfortable. They can return to the buffet table for fresh fruit, which also can be the centerpiece, and Espresso.

Menu

12 servings

Antipasto Salad Platter*

Meatball Minestrone*

Sesame Sticks*

Assorted Crackers

Fresh Fruit

Espresso

***Recipe included**

Several weeks before buffet:
- [ ] Prepare Mini Meatballs for Meatball Minestrone; freeze.

1 day before:
- [ ] Prepare Meatball Minestrone; refrigerate.
- [ ] Prepare greens and vegetables for Antipasto Salad Platter; refrigerate.

Several hours before serving:
- [ ] Prepare Sesame Sticks for baking; refrigerate.

About 20 minutes before:
- [ ] Bake Sesame Sticks.
- [ ] Complete Meatball Minestrone.
- [ ] Prepare Espresso.
- [ ] Complete Antipasto Salad Platter.
- [ ] Arrange Assorted Crackers in serving container.

At dessert time:
- [ ] Serve Fresh Fruit.

Antipasto Salad Platter

2 bunches romaine, torn into bite-size pieces
1 small head lettuce, torn into bite-size pieces
1 small green pepper, chopped (about 1/2 cup)
1 small red onion, thinly sliced
1 can (14 ounces) artichoke hearts, drained
1 jar (2 1/2 ounces) whole mushrooms, drained
1 cup bottled creamy Italian salad dressing
1/4 cup grated Parmesan cheese
12 thin slices provolone or mozzarella cheese
12 thin slices salami
12 cherry tomatoes
12 large pitted ripe olives

Divide romaine, lettuce, green pepper, onion, artichoke hearts and mushrooms between 2 large plastic bags. Fasten bags and refrigerate no longer than 24 hours.

Shake salad dressing and Parmesan cheese in tightly covered container. Add about 1/2 cup to each bag. Fasten bags securely and shake until ingredients are coated. Place salad on platter. Garnish with tomatoes and olives. Roll cheese and salami; arrange around salad.

Antipasto Salad Platter and Meatball Minestrone

Meatball Minestrone

Mini Meatballs (below)
1 *can (28 ounces) whole tomatoes, undrained*
1 *can (15 ounces) kidney beans, undrained*
1 *can (12 ounces) vacuum-packed whole kernel*
   corn, undrained
2 *cups water*
1/2 *cup dry red wine or water*
1 *tablespoon Italian seasoning*
1 *teaspoon salt*
1/2 *teaspoon pepper*
2 *stalks celery, sliced (about 1 cup)*
1 *medium onion, chopped (about 1/2 cup)*
1 *cup elbow spaghetti or broken spaghetti*
2 *zucchini, sliced (about 2 cups)*

Prepare Mini Meatballs. Mix tomatoes, beans, corn, water, wine, Italian seasoning, salt, pepper, celery and onion in 4-quart Dutch oven; break up tomatoes with fork. Heat to boiling; add frozen Mini Meatballs. Cover and refrigerate no longer than 24 hours.

Heat meatball mixture to boiling. Add spaghetti and zucchini. Heat to boiling; reduce heat. Cover and simmer, stirring occasionally, until meatballs are hot and spaghetti and zucchini are tender, about 12 minutes. Serve with grated Parmesan cheese if desired.

Mini Meatballs

1 *pound ground beef*
1 *egg*
1 *small onion, chopped (about 1/4 cup)*
1/4 *cup dry bread crumbs*
1/4 *cup milk*
1 *clove garlic, crushed*
2 *tablespoons snipped parsley*
1 *teaspoon fennel seed*
1/2 *teaspoon dried basil leaves*
1/2 *teaspoon salt*
1/8 *teaspoon pepper*

Mix all ingredients. Shape mixture into about thirty-six 1-inch balls. (For ease in shaping meatballs, occasionally wet hands with cold water.) Place meatballs in lightly greased jelly roll pan, 15 1/2 × 10 1/2 × 1 inch, or 2 rectangular pans, 13 × 9 × 2 inches. Bake uncovered in 400° oven until brown, 15 to 20 minutes; cool slightly. Place meatballs on ungreased cookie sheet. Freeze uncovered until firm, about 3 hours. Place in freezer containers; label and freeze no longer than 3 months.

Sesame Sticks

2 *cups buttermilk baking mix*
2/3 *cup milk*
1/3 *cup margarine or butter, melted*
1 *tablespoon sesame seed*

Mix baking mix and milk until soft dough forms; beat vigorously 30 seconds. Turn onto cloth-covered board well dusted with baking mix. Gently roll in baking mix to coat; shape into ball. Knead 10 times. Roll dough into rectangle, 10 × 6 inches. Cut lengthwise into halves. Cut each half into 12 strips, each about 3/4 inch wide.

Pour margarine into ungreased rectangular pan, 13 × 9 × 2 inches. Dip sticks into margarine, turning to coat all sides; arrange in pan. Sprinkle with sesame seed. Cover and refrigerate no longer than 6 hours.

Bake uncovered in 450° oven until golden brown, 15 to 20 minutes. Serve hot. 24 sticks.

THE GUEST LIST

Begin by listing the guests you wish to invite; then count the names and consider whether you can accommodate them comfortably. Consider your kitchen area, refrigerator and freezer space, and the cooking and serving equipment you have. If arrangements will be crowded or inconvenient, you may wish to give more than one party or a cocktail party.

Ten days to two weeks in advance of your party date, depending on the patterns of your community, telephone or send handwritten invitations — the choice is yours. Written invitations are festive and fun, especially if the party has a theme.

Braised Meatballs, Cheesy Rice, Crusty Bread, Roasted Pepper Salad, Gorgonzola Cheese and Fresh Fruit

A Late Summer Supper

The three courses — salad, cheese and fruit — in that order, are thought to "cleanse the palate." This menu lends itself nicely to the European style of eating. After the main course, your guests may want to return to the buffet table for a salad and then end the meal with a piece of crusty bread, a slice of Gorgonzola cheese and a selection from the beautifully arranged fruit bowl.

Menu

8 servings

Braised Meatballs*

Cheesy Rice*

Roasted Pepper Salad*

Crusty Bread

Gorgonzola Cheese

Fresh Fruit

Coffee   Tea

*Recipe included

1 day before buffet:
☐ Prepare Roasted Pepper Salad; refrigerate.
☐ Prepare Braised Meatballs; refrigerate.

About 30 minutes before serving:
☐ Remove Gorgonzola Cheese from refrigerator; let stand at room temperature.
☐ Prepare Cheesy Rice.
☐ Prepare Coffee and Tea.
☐ Heat Braised Meatballs.
☐ Arrange Fresh Fruit in serving container.
☐ Arrange Crusty Bread in serving container.

Braised Meatballs

2 pounds ground beef
⅓ cup grated Parmesan cheese
1 teaspoon fennel seed
½ teaspoon salt
½ teaspoon pepper
½ cup all-purpose flour
¼ cup olive or vegetable oil
1 teaspoon salt
3 cloves garlic, crushed
1 can (28 ounces) whole tomatoes, undrained

Mix ground beef, cheese, fennel seed, ½ teaspoon salt and the pepper. Shape mixture into 16 balls, each about 1¾ inches in diameter. Roll meatballs in flour. Heat oil in 12-inch skillet over medium heat. Cook meatballs until brown, about 8 minutes. Remove meatballs with slotted spoon and reserve; drain skillet. Mix 1 teaspoon salt, the garlic and tomatoes in same skillet; break up tomatoes with fork. Heat to boiling; reduce heat. Add meatballs. Cover and simmer until meatballs are done, about 15 minutes. Cover and refrigerate no longer than 24 hours.

Remove excess fat if necessary. Heat meatball mixture to boiling; reduce heat. Simmer uncovered until hot, about 20 minutes.

Cheesy Rice

1½ cups uncooked regular rice
3 cups water
1 teaspoon salt
1½ cups shredded Monterey Jack cheese (6 ounces)
½ cup grated Parmesan cheese
¼ cup margarine or butter, softened

Heat rice, water and salt to boiling, stirring once or twice; reduce heat. Cover and simmer 14 minutes (do not lift cover or stir); remove from heat. Fluff rice lightly with fork. Cover and let steam 5 to 10 minutes. Stir in cheeses and margarine. Sprinkle with snipped parsley if desired.

Roasted Pepper Salad

3 large green peppers
3 large red peppers
¼ cup olive or vegetable oil
2 tablespoons snipped parsley
2 tablespoons lemon juice
2 tablespoons lime juice
½ teaspoon salt
¼ teaspoon dried oregano leaves
¼ teaspoon dried basil leaves
⅛ teaspoon pepper
⅛ teaspoon dried sage leaves
2 large cloves garlic, finely chopped

Set oven control to broil and/or 550°. Place peppers on rack in broiler pan. Broil peppers with tops 4 to 5 inches from heat until skin blisters and browns, about 5 minutes on each side. Wrap in towels; let stand 5 minutes. Remove skin, stems, seeds and membrane from peppers; cut peppers into ¼-inch slices. Shake remaining ingredients in tightly covered container; pour over peppers. Cover and refrigerate at least 4 hours but no longer than 24 hours.

A Late Evening Supper

Menu

8 servings

Pink Colada*

Chicken Salad Shortcake*

Steamed Broccoli

Mushroom-Tomato Salad*

Chocolate Apricots*

Pirouettes

Coffee   Tea

***Recipe included**

1 day before buffet:
- ☐ Prepare Chicken Salad Shortcake; refrigerate.
- ☐ Prepare mushrooms for Mushroom-Tomato Salad; refrigerate.
- ☐ Prepare Chocolate Apricots; refrigerate.
- ☐ Refrigerate sparkling water for Pink Colada.

When guests arrive:
- ☐ Prepare Pink Colada and serve.

About 20 minutes before serving:
- ☐ Prepare Steamed Broccoli.
- ☐ Complete Mushroom-Tomato Salad.
- ☐ Complete Chicken Salad Shortcake.
- ☐ Prepare Coffee and Tea.

At dessert time:
- ☐ Serve Chocolate Apricots and Pirouettes.

Chicken Salad Shortcake

Pink Colada

*2 cans (12 ounces each) frozen limeade
   concentrate, thawed*
1 can (15½ ounces) coconut cream
½ cup grenadine syrup
*2 bottles (28 ounces each) sparkling water,
   chilled*

Mix limeade concentrate, coconut cream and
grenadine syrup; add sparkling water. Serve
over ice and garnish with lime slice if desired.
24 servings (about ½ cup each).

Chicken Salad Shortcake

Cheese Bread (below)
2½ cups cut-up cookèd chicken or turkey
1 cup toasted slivered almonds
½ cup sliced ripe olives
2 stalks celery, sliced (about 1 cup)
*1 can (20 ounces) crushed pineapple, well
   drained*
1 teaspoon salt
1½ cups dairy sour cream
1 cup mayonnaise or salad dressing

Bake Cheese Bread. Mix chicken, almonds,
olives, celery, pineapple and salt. Mix sour
cream and mayonnaise. Mix 1½ cups sour
cream mixture into chicken mixture.

Place 1 Cheese Bread, sesame seed side down,
on serving plate. Spoon chicken mixture over
bread; top with remaining Cheese Bread,
sesame seed side up. Spread remaining sour
cream mixture over bread. Cover loosely with
aluminum foil. Refrigerate at least 4 hours but
no longer than 24 hours.

Cheese Bread

3 cups buttermilk baking mix
2 eggs
½ cup milk
1 cup shredded Cheddar cheese (4 ounces)
2 tablespoons sesame seed
¼ cup margarine or butter, melted

Heat oven to 400°. Mix baking mix, eggs, milk
and cheese. Divide dough into halves; pat each

half in greased round pan, 9 × 1½ inches.
Sprinkle each with 1 tablespoon sesame seed.
Pour 2 tablespoons margarine evenly over
each. Bake until golden brown, 20 to 25 minutes. Remove from pans; cool.

Mushroom-Tomato Salad

¼ cup vinegar
¼ cup olive oil
¼ cup vegetable oil
1 tablespoon sugar
1 teaspoon dried basil leaves
½ teaspoon salt
2 cloves garlic, crushed
8 ounces mushrooms, sliced (about 3 cups)
4 medium tomatoes, each cut into 4 slices
Lettuce leaves

Mix vinegar, olive oil, vegetable oil, sugar,
basil, salt and garlic in tightly covered container. Pour over mushrooms in glass or plastic
bowl. Cover and refrigerate at least 4 hours
but no longer than 24 hours.

Arrange tomato slices on lettuce leaves. Spoon
mushroom mixture on tomatoes.

Chocolate Apricots

Heat ½ cup semisweet chocolate chips and 2
teaspoons shortening over low heat, stirring
occasionally, until melted. Coat 24 dried apricots about ¾ of the way with chocolate mixture; place on waxed paper on cookie sheet.
Refrigerate uncovered until chocolate is firm,
at least 30 minutes but no longer than 24
hours. 24 apricots.

An After-Caroling Late Supper

Menu

12 servings

Hot Buttered Rum*

Spiced Cran-Apple Cider*

Chicken-Vegetable Soup*

Creamy Split Pea Soup*

Crisp Vegetable Relishes

Assorted Crackers

Parmesan Ring*

Cookies and Bars

Coffee   Tea

***Recipe included**

1 month before buffet:
☐ Prepare Hot Buttered Rum mixture; freeze.

1 day before:
☐ Bake Parmesan Ring; store at room temperature.
☐ Prepare Chicken-Vegetable Soup; refrigerate.
☐ Prepare Crisp Vegetable Relishes; cover and refrigerate.
☐ Slice sausage for Creamy Split Pea Soup; cover and refrigerate.

When guests arrive:
☐ Prepare Spiced Cran-Apple Cider.
☐ Complete Hot Buttered Rum and serve beverages.

About 30 minutes before serving:
☐ Heat Parmesan Ring.
☐ Heat Chicken-Vegetable Soup.
☐ Prepare Creamy Split Pea Soup.
☐ Place Assorted Crackers and Crisp Vegetable Relishes in serving containers.
☐ Prepare Coffee and Tea.

At dessert time:
☐ Arrange Cookies and Bars on serving plate.

Hot Buttered Rum

¾ cup packed brown sugar
½ cup butter, softened
½ cup whipping cream
1 cup powdered sugar
¼ teaspoon ground nutmeg
⅛ teaspoon ground cloves
⅛ teaspoon ground cinnamon
    Rum
    Boiling water
    Ground nutmeg

Beat brown sugar and butter on medium speed until fluffy, about 5 minutes. Beat in whipping cream and powdered sugar alternately on low speed until smooth. Stir in ¼ teaspoon nutmeg, the cloves and cinnamon. Spoon into 2½-cup freezer container. Cover, label and freeze no longer than 1 month.

For each serving, place 2 tablespoons butter mixture and 2 tablespoons rum in mug. Stir in ½ cup boiling water; sprinkle with nutmeg.

Spiced Cran-Apple Cider

1 quart apple cider
1 quart cranberry juice cocktail
¼ cup packed brown sugar
1½ teaspoons whole allspice
4 3-inch sticks cinnamon
    Orange slices

Heat all ingredients except orange slices to boiling; reduce heat. Simmer uncovered 15 minutes; remove spices. Garnish with orange slices. 12 servings (about ¾ cup each).

Chicken-Vegetable Soup

2½- to 3-pound broiler-fryer chicken, cut up
  6 cups water
  2 medium carrots, cut into ½-inch slices (about
     1 cup)
  2 medium stalks celery, cut into ½-inch slices
     (about 1 cup)
  1 tablespoon salt
  1 tablespoon instant chicken bouillon
  ¼ teaspoon pepper
  1 package (10 ounces) frozen whole kernel
     corn
  2 medium zucchini, chopped (about 1 cup)
  1 can (4 ounces) chopped green chilies,
     drained
  1 can (2.2 ounces) sliced ripe olives, drained

Heat chicken, water, carrots, celery, salt, chicken bouillon (dry) and pepper to boiling in 4-quart Dutch oven; reduce heat. Cover and simmer until chicken is done, about 45 minutes. Skim fat if necessary.

Remove chicken from broth; cool slightly. Remove skin from chicken; remove chicken from bones. Cut chicken into bite-size pieces. Rinse corn under running cold water to separate; drain. Stir chicken, corn and remaining ingredients into broth. Cover and refrigerate no longer than 24 hours.

Heat to boiling, stirring occasionally; reduce heat. Cover and simmer until vegetables are hot, about 10 minutes.

Creamy Split Pea Soup

  1 pound fully cooked smoked kielbasa or Polish
     sausage, thinly sliced
  3 cans (11½ ounces each) condensed pea soup
     with ham and bacon
  2 cups water
  2 tablespoons prepared mustard
1½ cups half-and-half
1½ teaspoons curry powder
  1 jar (2 ounces) diced pimientos, drained

Cook and stir kielbasa in 3-quart saucepan over medium heat about 5 minutes; drain. Stir in soup, water and mustard. Heat to boiling, stirring occasionally. Stir in half-and-half, curry powder and pimientos; heat just until hot, about 5 minutes. Sprinkle with Cheddar cheese if desired.

Parmesan Ring

  1 package active dry yeast
  ¼ cup warm water (105 to 115°)
  ¾ cup lukewarm milk (scalded then cooled)
  ¼ cup sugar
  1 teaspoon salt
  1 egg
  ¼ cup margarine or butter, softened
3½ to 3¾ cups all-purpose flour
  ½ cup margarine or butter, melted
  1 cup grated Parmesan cheese (4 ounces)

Dissolve yeast in warm water in large bowl. Stir in milk, sugar, salt, egg, ¼ cup margarine and 2 cups of the flour. Beat until smooth. Mix in enough remaining flour to make dough easy to handle.

Turn dough onto lightly floured surface; knead until smooth and elastic, about 5 minutes. Place in greased bowl; turn greased side up. Cover; let rise in warm place until double, about 2 hours. (Dough is ready if indentation remains when touched.)

Line tube pan, 10 × 4 inches, with aluminum foil; grease. Punch down dough. Turn onto lightly floured surface; divide into 24 equal pieces. Dip each piece into melted margarine; roll in cheese. Place 12 pieces in pan in one layer; make second layer with remaining pieces. Cover; let rise until double.

Heat oven to 375°. Bake until golden brown, about 35 minutes. Remove from pan. Carefully remove foil; cool. Wrap in aluminum foil and store at room temperature no longer than 24 hours.

Heat wrapped Parmesan Ring in 350° oven until warm, about 30 minutes.

Clockwise from top; Cookies and Bars, Parmesan Ring, Crisp Vegetable Relishes, Creamy Split Pea Soup, Chicken-Vegetable Soup and Creamy Split Pea Soup

Clockwise from top: Asparagus-Artichoke Salad, Green Tortellini, Salmon Glacés and Brioche

An Elegant Late Supper

After a very special evening event, serve your guests an elegant late supper meal using your best china and linens. Let them enjoy fresh raspberries in champagne in the living room while you put the final touches on the food for the buffet table. Your guests will be impressed that you can spend an evening out and still entertain with an elegant meal.

Menu

8 servings

Raspberries in Champagne

Salmon Glacés*

Green Tortellini*

Asparagus-Artichoke Salad (page 73)

Brioche

Rich Chocolate Custard*

Coffee   Tea

***Recipe included**

1 day before buffet:
- ☐ Prepare Salmon Glacés; refrigerate.
- ☐ Prepare green sauce for Green Tortellini; refrigerate.
- ☐ Prepare vegetables for Asparagus-Artichoke Salad; refrigerate.
- ☐ Prepare Rich Chocolate Custard; refrigerate.

About 20 minutes before serving:
- ☐ Complete Green Tortellini.
- ☐ Prepare Coffee and Tea.
- ☐ Heat Brioche.

At serving time:
- ☐ Complete Asparagus-Artichoke Salad.
- ☐ Place Salmon Glacés on serving plate.
- ☐ Prepare Raspberries in Champagne.

At dessert time:
- ☐ Complete Rich Chocolate Custard.

Salmon Glacés

8   cups water
2   teaspoons salt
6   peppercorns
4   lemon slices
3   parsley sprigs
1   medium onion, sliced
1   bay leaf
8   small salmon steaks, 1 inch thick (about 3
      pounds)
1   envelope unflavored gelatin
2   cups dry white wine
    Pitted ripe olives
    Pimiento
    Green onion tops
    Chives
    Parsley sprigs

Heat water, salt, peppercorns, lemon, parsley, onion and bay leaf to boiling in 12-inch skillet. Arrange 4 of the salmon steaks in skillet; reduce heat. Simmer uncovered until salmon flakes easily with fork, about 12 minutes. Remove salmon with slotted spatula; place in rectangular baking dish, 13 × 9 × 2 inches. Remove skin and discard. Repeat with remaining salmon steaks. Pour enough of the poaching liquid into dish to cover salmon. Cover and refrigerate until cool, about 4 hours.

Sprinkle gelatin on ½ cup of the wine in small bowl. Place bowl in pan of hot water over low heat until gelatin is dissolved, about 5 minutes. Stir in remaining wine. Place bowl in pan of ice and water, stirring occasionally, until mixture begins to thicken, 20 to 25 minutes (mixture should be consistency of unbeaten egg white).

Remove salmon from liquid; drain and pat dry. Place salmon on wire rack in shallow pan. Spoon ⅔ of the glaze over salmon steaks until completely coated. Decorate with olives, pimiento, green onion tops and chives; spoon remaining glaze over decorations. (If glaze begins to thicken, place bowl in pan of hot water.) Refrigerate until glaze is firm, at least 6 hours but no longer than 24 hours.

Remove salmon steaks from rack; place on serving plate. Garnish with parsley if desired.

Green Tortellini

1   cup parsley sprigs
⅓   cup grated Parmesan cheese
1½ cups creamed cottage cheese (large curd)
1   tablespoon lemon juice
1   tablespoon milk
½   teaspoon dried basil leaves
½   teaspoon salt
⅛   teaspoon pepper
4   to 6 drops red pepper sauce
2   cloves garlic, crushed
1   package (7 ounces) tortellini

Place all ingredients except tortellini in blender container. Cover and blend on high speed, stopping blender occasionally to scrape down sides, until smooth, about 3 minutes. Cover and refrigerate at least 2 hours but no longer than 24 hours. Cook tortellini as directed on package; drain. Toss with green sauce.

Rich Chocolate Custard

2¼ cups half-and-half
1   package (6 ounces) semisweet chocolate chips
4   eggs
½   cup sugar
¼   teaspoon salt
¾   cup chilled whipping cream
2   tablespoons sugar

Heat half-and-half and chocolate chips, stirring constantly, until chocolate is melted and mixture is smooth; cool slightly. Beat eggs, ½ cup sugar and the salt; gradually stir into chocolate mixture. Pour into 8 ungreased 6-ounce custard cups or ovenproof pot de crème cups. Place cups in 2 square pans, 8 × 8 × 2 inches, on oven rack. Pour boiling water into pans within ½ inch of tops of cups.

Bake in 350° oven until set, 20 to 25 minutes. Remove cups from water; cool slightly. Cover and refrigerate at least 4 hours but no longer than 24 hours. Beat whipping cream and 2 tablespoons sugar in chilled bowl until stiff. Top each serving with whipped cream.

Fish-Stuffed Tomato, Hard Roll and Mandarin Salad

An After-the-Concert Late Supper

Menu

8 servings

Fish-stuffed Tomatoes*

Mandarin Salad*

Hard Rolls

Chocolate Frango*

Coffee   Tea

***Recipe included**

2 days before buffet:
- ☐ Prepare Chocolate Frango; freeze.

1 day before:
- ☐ Prepare Fish-stuffed Tomatoes for baking; refrigerate.
- ☐ Prepare almonds for Mandarin Salad; store at room temperature.
- ☐ Prepare vegetables for Mandarin Salad; refrigerate.

About 30 minutes before serving:
- ☐ Bake Fish-stuffed Tomatoes.

About 15 minutes before:
- ☐ Prepare Coffee and Tea.
- ☐ Arrange Hard Rolls in serving container.
- ☐ Prepare cheese sauce for Fish-stuffed Tomatoes.
- ☐ Complete Mandarin Salad.

Fish-stuffed Tomatoes

8 large tomatoes
1/8 teaspoon salt
1/8 teaspoon pepper
1/3 cup soft bread crumbs
8 fish fillets (about 1 1/2 pounds)
1 tablespoon margarine or butter, melted
1/4 teaspoon salt
1/8 teaspoon pepper
2 cups soft bread crumbs
1/3 cup snipped parsley
1/3 cup margarine or butter, melted
3 tablespoons finely chopped onion
3 tablespoons lemon juice
1 teaspoon salt
1/2 teaspoon dried thyme leaves
1/2 teaspoon ground savory
1/4 teaspoon pepper
2 packages (about 1 1/4 ounces each) cheese sauce mix

Cut slice from top of each tomato. Remove pulp from each, leaving a 1/4-inch wall. Place tomatoes, cut sides down, on wire rack to drain. Sprinkle insides of tomatoes with 1/8 teaspoon salt and 1/8 teaspoon pepper; divide 1/3 cup bread crumbs among tomatoes. Brush fish fillets with 1 tablespoon margarine; sprinkle with 1/4 teaspoon salt and 1/8 teaspoon pepper. Mix remaining ingredients except cheese sauce mix. Spread about 2 tablespoons bread mixture on each fish fillet. Roll up and place in tomato cups. Place in ungreased rectangular baking dish, 13 × 9 × 2 inches. Cover and refrigerate no longer than 24 hours.

Bake uncovered in 350° oven until fish flakes easily with a fork, about 30 minutes. Prepare cheese sauce as directed on package; serve with tomato cups.

Mandarin Salad

1/2 cup sliced almonds
3 tablespoons sugar
4 heads Bibb lettuce, torn into bite-size pieces (about 6 cups)
1 cup chopped celery
2 green onions (with tops), thinly sliced
1 can (11 ounces) mandarin orange segments, drained
1/3 cup bottled oil and vinegar dressing

Cook almonds and sugar over low heat, stirring constantly, until sugar is melted and almonds are coated. Cool and break apart. Cover and store at room temperature no longer than 24 hours. Place lettuce, celery and onions in plastic bag; fasten and refrigerate no longer than 24 hours.

Add mandarin oranges and dressing to bag. Fasten bag securely and shake until greens and oranges are well coated. Add almonds and shake.

Chocolate Frango

2 cups chilled whipping cream
1 can (5.5 ounces) chocolate-flavored syrup
1/4 cup almond-flavored liqueur

Beat whipping cream in chilled bowl until stiff. Fold syrup and liqueur into whipped cream. Pour into ungreased square pan, 9 × 9 × 2 inches. Cover and freeze at least 4 hours but no longer than 48 hours.

A Mexican Late Supper

Menu

12 servings

Sangria*

Cheese Enchiladas*

Fiesta Rice*

Cauliflower-Avocado Salad*

Caramel Flans*

Coffee   Tea

***Recipe included**

1 day before buffet:
- ☐ Prepare Cheese Enchiladas for baking; refrigerate.
- ☐ Bake Caramel Flans; refrigerate.
- ☐ Cook cauliflowers and prepare avocado mixture for Cauliflower-Avocado Salad; refrigerate.

Several hours before serving:
- ☐ Prepare Sangria except for ginger ale; refrigerate.
- ☐ Slice orange and lemon; cover and refrigerate. Refrigerate ginger ale.
- ☐ Cook rice for Fiesta Rice; cover and refrigerate.

When guests arrive:
- ☐ Complete Sangria; serve.

About 30 minutes before serving:
- ☐ Bake Cheese Enchiladas.
- ☐ Prepare Fiesta Rice.
- ☐ Prepare Cauliflower-Avocado Salad.
- ☐ Prepare Coffee and Tea.

At dessert time:
- ☐ Unmold Caramel Flans.

Cheese Enchiladas, Cauliflower-Avocado Salad, Fiesta Rice and Sangria

Cheese Enchiladas

2 *large onions, chopped (about 2 cups)*
4 *large cloves garlic, crushed*
2 *tablespoons chili powder*
¼ *cup vegetable oil*
2 *cans (28 ounces each) whole tomatoes, undrained*
2 *teaspoons ground cumin*
2 *teaspoons dried oregano leaves*
1 *teaspoon salt*
¼ *teaspoon pepper*
3 *cups shredded Cheddar cheese (12 ounces)*
3 *cups shredded Monterey Jack cheese (12 ounces)*
½ *cup vegetable oil*
2 *packages (8 or 9 ounces each) 6- or 7-inch corn tortillas (24 tortillas)*
3 *cups shredded lettuce*
1 *cup sliced radishes*
½ *cup sliced ripe olives*
Dairy sour cream

Cook and stir onions, garlic and chili powder in ¼ cup oil in 4-quart Dutch oven until onions are tender, about 5 minutes. Stir in tomatoes, cumin, oregano, salt and pepper; break up tomatoes with fork. Heat to boiling; reduce heat. Simmer uncovered until sauce thickens, about 30 minutes.

Mix Cheddar and Monterey Jack cheese. Heat ½ cup oil in 8-inch skillet until hot. Dip each tortilla lightly into hot oil to soften; drain. Dip each tortilla into tomato sauce to coat both sides. Spoon about 2 tablespoons cheese on each tortilla; roll tortilla around cheese. Place seam side down in 2 ungreased rectangular baking dishes, 13 × 9 × 2 inches. Pour half of the remaining tomato sauce over enchiladas in each dish; sprinkle each with half of the remaining cheese. Cover and refrigerate no longer than 24 hours.

Bake uncovered in 350° oven until cheese is melted and enchiladas are hot, about 25 minutes. Top with lettuce, radishes and olives. Serve with sour cream.

NOTE: For spicier enchiladas, serve with a hot bottled salsa or taco sauce.

Fiesta Rice

1 medium onion, finely chopped
1 small green pepper, chopped
¼ cup margarine or butter
1 can (16 ounces) stewed tomatoes
1 teaspoon salt
¼ teaspoon pepper
6 cups cooked rice

Cook and stir onion and green pepper in margarine in 3-quart saucepan until onion is tender. Stir in remaining ingredients. Simmer uncovered over low heat, stirring constantly until hot, about 15 minutes.

Cauliflower-Avocado Salad

2 medium heads cauliflower (about 2 pounds each)
4 very ripe large avocados, mashed
1 medium onion, chopped (about ½ cup)
1 jalapeño pepper, seeded and finely chopped
2 tablespoons lemon or lime juice
2 teaspoons finely snipped cilantro or ½ teaspoon ground coriander
½ teaspoon salt
Lettuce leaves
¼ cup toasted slivered almonds

Trim outer leaves from each cauliflower; slice off stem end so cauliflower stands evenly. Heat 1 inch salted water (1 teaspoon salt to 1 cup water) to boiling in 4-quart Dutch oven. Add cauliflowers. Heat to boiling; reduce heat. Cover and simmer until tender, 20 to 25 minutes; drain. Cover and refrigerate no longer than 24 hours. Mix avocados, onion, jalapeño pepper, lemon juice, cilantro and salt. Cover and refrigerate at least 1 hour but no longer than 24 hours.

Place cauliflowers on lettuce-lined plate. Spread half of the avocado mixture over each cauliflower; sprinkle each with 2 tablespoons almonds. Cut each cauliflower into 6 wedges.

Sangria

1 bottle (750 ml) dry red wine, chilled
½ cup brandy
½ cup fresh orange juice
1 can (6 ounces) frozen lemonade concentrate, thawed
2 cups ginger ale, chilled
1 orange, thinly sliced
1 lemon, thinly sliced

Mix wine, brandy, orange juice and lemonade concentrate. Cover and refrigerate no longer than 24 hours.

Stir in ginger ale. Pour over ice; garnish with orange and lemon slices.

Caramel Flans

6 eggs, slightly beaten
⅔ cup sugar
2 teaspoons vanilla
Dash of salt
5 cups milk, scalded
½ cup caramel ice-cream topping

Mix eggs, sugar, vanilla and salt. Stir in milk gradually. Place 2 teaspoons ice-cream topping in each of twelve 6-ounce custard cups. Pour milk mixture into cups. Place cups on oven racks in 2 rectangular pans, 13 × 9 × 2 inches. Pour very hot water into pans to within ½ inch of tops of cups.

Bake in 350° oven until knife inserted halfway between center and edge comes out clean, about 45 minutes. Remove cups from water. Refrigerate at least 4 hours but no longer than 24 hours.

To unmold, carefully loosen side of custard with knife or small spatula. Place dessert dish or plate on top of cup and, holding tightly, invert dish and cup. Shake cup gently to loosen and remove.

A Soup and Sandwich Late Supper

End an evening out with friends — whether at a sports event, movie, or concert — with soup and sandwiches. Everything, except the Dilled Tomato Bisque, can be prepared before leaving home. Guests help themselves to mugs of soup, and make their own sandwiches. The Strawberry Cream is refreshing but not too rich or heavy to end a late evening.

Menu

12 servings

Cold Potato Soup*

Dilled Tomato Bisque*

Meat and Cheese Tray*

Assorted Vegetables*

Breads and Rolls

Strawberry Cream*

Scotch Shortbread*

Coffee   Tea

***Recipe included**

About 4 days before buffet:
- ☐ Bake Scotch Shortbread; store at room temperature.

1 day before:
- ☐ Prepare Cold Potato Soup; refrigerate.
- ☐ Prepare Strawberry Cream; refrigerate.

About 6 hours before serving:
- ☐ Prepare Meat and Cheese Tray; refrigerate.
- ☐ Prepare Assorted Vegetables; refrigerate.

About 20 minutes before:
- ☐ Unmold Strawberry Cream; garnish and refrigerate.
- ☐ Prepare Coffee and Tea.
- ☐ Prepare Dilled Tomato Bisque.
- ☐ Complete Cold Potato Soup.
- ☐ Arrange Breads and Rolls in serving containers.

At dessert time:
- ☐ Serve Strawberry Cream and Scotch Shortbread.

Cold Potato Soup

- 1 large onion, chopped (about 1 cup)
- 1 medium stalk celery, chopped (about ½ cup)
- 1 tablespoon margarine or butter
- 4 medium potatoes, chopped
- 2 cans (10¾ ounces each) condensed chicken broth
- 2 cups half-and-half
- 1 teaspoon salt
- ¼ teaspoon pepper
- 1¾ to 2 cups half-and-half

Cook and stir onion and celery in margarine in 3-quart saucepan until onion is tender, about 5 minutes. Add potatoes and broth. Heat to boiling; reduce heat. Cover and simmer until potatoes are tender, 15 to 20 minutes.

Pour half of the potato mixture into blender container. Cover and blend on medium speed until mixture is smooth, about 45 seconds.

Repeat with remaining potato mixture. Stir in 2 cups half-and-half, the salt and pepper. Cover and refrigerate at least 6 hours but no longer than 24 hours.

At serving time, stir in enough half-and-half until desired consistency.

Dilled Tomato Bisque

- 3 cans (11 ounces each) condensed tomato bisque
- 2½ cups water
- 1 teaspoon dried dill weed
- 12 lemon slices

Heat soup and water to boiling in 3-quart saucepan over medium heat, stirring occasionally. Stir in dried dill weed; garnish with lemon slices.

Meat and Cheese Tray

1 pound thinly sliced cooked roast beef
1 pound thinly sliced cooked turkey breast
1 pound thinly sliced Thuringer sausage
½ pound sliced Swiss cheese
½ pound sliced provolone cheese
Mayonnaise or salad dressing
Mustard
Sandwich spread

Roll some of the slices of meat for variety. Arrange meat and cheese on tray, two platters or assorted plates. (If using more than one platter or plate, either serve both platters, or serve one platter and replace with second platter when it is almost empty.) Garnish tray with lettuce leaves and relishes (radish roses, chili peppers, olives, carrot curls) if desired. Place a dampened towel over top of tray. Cover tightly with plastic wrap and refrigerate no longer than 6 hours.

To serve, place tray on buffet table or serve two trays, one at each end of table, or serve one tray and replace with fresh tray. Serve with mayonnaise, mustard and sandwich spread for guests to build their own sandwiches.

Assorted Vegetables

4 medium tomatoes, sliced
2 medium onions, thinly sliced
1 medium green or red pepper, thinly sliced
1 medium cucumber, thinly sliced
1 small head lettuce, shredded
1 pint alfalfa sprouts
1 pint creamy-style coleslaw

Select 4 or more of the vegetables. Arrange on tray, assorted plates and bowls or lazy Susan. Cover tightly with plastic wrap and refrigerate no longer than 6 hours.

Strawberry Cream

2 packages (10 ounces each) frozen sliced
* strawberries, thawed*
1 package (6 ounces) strawberry-flavored gelatin
2 cups chilled whipping cream
1 teaspoon almond extract

Drain strawberries, reserving juice; add enough cold water to juice to measure 2 cups. Prepare gelatin as directed on package except use strawberry juice for the cold water. Refrigerate until mixture mounds slightly when dropped from a spoon.

Beat whipping cream and almond extract in chilled 3½-quart bowl until stiff. Beat gelatin until light and fluffy. Fold gelatin and strawberries into whipped cream. Pour into 8-cup mold, two 4-cup molds or 12 individual molds. Refrigerate until firm, at least 6 hours but no longer than 24 hours.

Unmold on serving plate; garnish with whipped cream and sliced almonds if desired.

Scotch Shortbread

¾ cup margarine or butter, softened
¼ cup sugar
2 cups all-purpose flour

Heat oven to 350°. Mix margarine and sugar. Mix in flour (using hands if necessary). If dough is crumbly, mix in 1 to 2 tablespoons margarine or butter, softened. Roll dough about ½ inch thick on lightly floured board. Cut into small squares, rectangles, diamonds or triangle shapes. Place about ½ inch apart on ungreased cookie sheet.

Bake until set but not brown, about 20 minutes. Immediately remove from cookie sheet; cool completely. Store in tightly covered container no longer than 4 days. About 2 dozen 1½ × 1-inch cookies.

Dilled Tomato Bisque, Cold Potato Soup, Breads and Rolls, Meats and Cheese Tray and Assorted Vegetables

Special Occasions

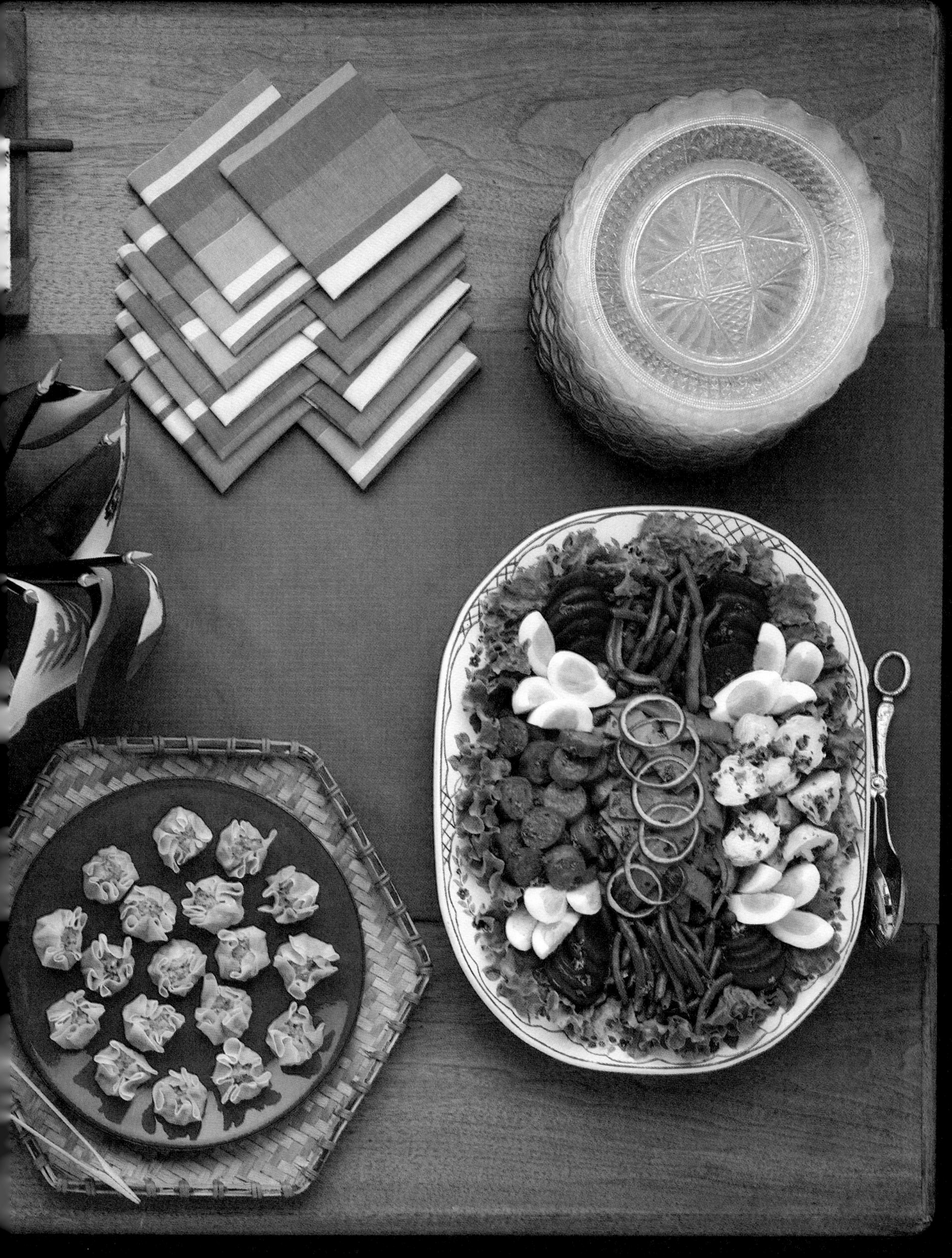

An International Cocktail Buffet

Menu

24 servings

Mexican Platter*

Scandinavian Canapés*

Greek Cheese Puffs*

Hummus (page 52)

Chinese Pork Dumplings*

Melon and Berries

Assorted Cheeses

***Recipe included**

2 days before buffet:
☐ Prepare Hummus; refrigerate.

1 day before:
☐ Prepare Mexican Platter; refrigerate.
☐ Prepare Greek Cheese Puffs for baking; refrigerate.
☐ Prepare Chinese Pork Dumplings for steaming; refrigerate.

About 6 hours before serving:
☐ Prepare Scandinavian Canapés; refrigerate.

About 1½ hours before:
☐ Steam Chinese Pork Dumplings.
☐ Remove Hummus from refrigerator; let stand at room temperature.
☐ Arrange Assorted Cheeses; let stand at room temperature.
☐ Prepare pita bread wedges for Hummus.
☐ Arrange Melon and Berries.

About 30 minutes before:
☐ Bake Greek Cheese Puffs.

An International Cocktail Buffet

1. Mexican Platter, 2. Chinese Pork Dumplings, 3. Scandinavian Canapés, 4. Hummus, 5. Greek Cheese Puffs, 6. Melon and Berries, 7. Assorted Cheeses

Mexican Platter

Herbed Vinaigrette (page 101)
1½ pounds cooked roast beef, cut into julienne strips
4 chorizo sausages, cooked and cut into ¼-inch slices
6 hard-cooked eggs, cut into fourths
1 can (16 ounces) sliced beets, drained
1 can (16 ounces) whole green beans, drained
1 can (14 ounces) artichoke hearts, drained and cut into halves
Lettuce leaves
1 small red onion, thinly sliced
2 tablespoons capers

Prepare Herbed Vinaigrette. Arrange meats, eggs and vegetables in sections on lettuce on 2 or more platters or trays. Pour on Herbed Vinaigrette; garnish with onion and capers. Cover and refrigerate at least 1 hour but no longer than 24 hours. Serve with cocktail forks or wooden or plastic picks or thin slices of crusty bread.

Herbed Vinaigrette

½ cup olive or vegetable oil
1 tablespoon snipped parsley
2 tablespoons red wine vinegar
2 tablespoons lemon juice
½ teaspoon salt
½ teaspoon dry mustard
¼ teaspoon dried oregano leaves
¼ teaspoon dried basil leaves
⅛ teaspoon pepper
1 clove garlic, crushed

Shake all ingredients in tightly covered jar.

Chinese Pork Dumplings

1 pound ground pork
½ cup finely chopped canned bamboo shoots
¼ cup finely chopped green onions (with tops)
10 medium mushrooms, finely chopped
1 egg white
2 tablespoons cornstarch
2 teaspoons salt
2 teaspoons soy sauce
½ teaspoon sesame oil, if desired
¼ teaspoon white pepper
40 wonton skins

Mix ground pork, bamboo shoots, onions, mushrooms, egg white, cornstarch, salt, 2 teaspoons soy sauce, the sesame oil and white pepper. Cut corners from wonton skins to make circles. Place 1 tablespoon pork mixture in center of circle. Bring edge up around filling, leaving top open. Repeat with remaining circles. Cover dumplings with dampened towel; wrap with plastic wrap. Refrigerate no longer than 24 hours.

Place rack in water in Dutch oven or skillet (water should not touch bottom of rack). Place about half of the dumplings in single layer on rack. Cover tightly and heat to boiling; reduce heat. Steam until pork mixture is done, about 25 minutes (add boiling water if necessary). Repeat with remaining dumplings. Serve with soy sauce if desired. 40 dumplings.

Scandinavian Canapés

12 slices day-old white sandwich bread
¼ cup margarine or butter, softened
⅛ teaspoon dried dill weed
6 thin slices fully cooked smoked ham
6 thin slices cooked turkey
1 can (11 ounces) mandarin orange segments, drained
1 cup seedless grape halves
1 kiwi fruit, thinly sliced and cut into fourths

Trim crusts from bread slices. Mix margarine and dill weed; spread over bread slices. Arrange ham or turkey slice on each bread slice; cut into desired shapes. Top each with pieces of fruit. Garnish with watercress, mint or lettuce if desired. Arrange canapés on trays. Cover with dampened towel; wrap with plastic wrap. Refrigerate no longer than 24 hours. About 48 canapés.

Greek Cheese Puffs

1 pound feta or finely shredded Monterey Jack cheese
2 eggs, slightly beaten
¼ cup finely snipped chives
¼ teaspoon white pepper
1 pound frozen phyllo leaves, thawed
¼ cup margarine or butter, melted

Crumble cheese in small bowl; mash with fork. Stir in eggs, chives and white pepper until well mixed. Cut phyllo leaves lengthwise into 3 strips. (Use 2 layers phyllo leaves for each strip.) Cover with damp towel to prevent them from drying out. Place 1 heaping teaspoon filling on one end of strip; fold end over end, in triangular shape, to opposite end. Place on greased cookie sheet. Repeat with remaining filling and strips. Brush triangles with margarine. Cover and refrigerate no longer than 24 hours.

Heat oven to 350°. Bake triangles until puffed and golden brown, about 20 minutes. About 30 appetizers.

A Patio Cocktail Party

Menu

12 servings

Chili-Cheese Squares*

Pickled Mushrooms*

**Cherry Tomato
Appetizers***

Melon with Salmon*

Spiced Pecans*

**Assorted Cocktail
Crackers**

***Recipe included**

5 days before buffet:
- ☐ Prepare Pickled Mushrooms; refrigerate.
- ☐ Prepare Spiced Pecans; store at room temperature.

About 6 hours before serving:
- ☐ Prepare Melon with Salmon; refrigerate.
- ☐ Prepare Cherry Tomato Appetizers; refrigerate.

About 45 minutes before:
- ☐ Bake Chili-Cheese Squares. Set up bar.

At serving time:
- ☐ Arrange Cherry Tomato Appetizers and Melon with Salmon on serving plate.
- ☐ Place Pickled Mushrooms and Spiced Pecans in serving containers.
- ☐ Arrange Assorted Cocktail Crackers in serving container.
- ☐ Cut Chili-Cheese Squares; arrange on serving plate.

Chili-Cheese Squares

1 can (4 ounces) chopped green chilies, drained
*2 cups shredded Monterey Jack or Cheddar
   cheese (8 ounces)*
1 cup buttermilk baking mix
1 cup half-and-half
4 eggs
1/8 teaspoon red pepper sauce, if desired

Heat oven to 375°. Grease square pan, 9 × 9 × 2 inches. Sprinkle chilies and cheese in pan. Beat remaining ingredients until smooth, 15 seconds in blender on high speed or 1 minute with hand beater. Pour into pan. Bake until golden brown and knife inserted in center comes out clean, 30 to 35 minutes. Let stand 10 minutes before cutting. Cut into about 1¼-inch squares. 36 appetizers.

Melon with Salmon

1 lime or lemon, cut into halves
*24 pieces honeydew melon or cantaloupe, 2 × 1/2
   inch*
24 thin strips smoked salmon, 3 × 1 inch
1/2 pound seedless green grapes

Squeeze juice from lime over melon pieces; toss until evenly coated. Wrap 1 salmon strip crosswise around center of each melon piece. Separate grapes into small clusters. Arrange melon pieces on serving plate; garnish with grapes. Cover and refrigerate no longer than 6 hours. 24 appetizers.

Cherry Tomato Appetizers

12 cherry tomatoes
1 package (3 ounces) cream cheese, softened
2 ounces blue cheese, finely crumbled
1 tablespoon prepared horseradish
1 tablespoon milk

Cut each tomato into halves; cut very thin slice from bottom of each half, if necessary, to prevent tipping. Place halves, cut sides up, in ungreased square baking dish, 8 × 8 × 2 inches. Beat remaining ingredients on medium speed until smooth and fluffy, about 1 minute. Place in pastry bag or decorator tube fitted with star tip. Top each tomato half with cheese mixture. Garnish with a caper, piece of olive, pimiento or parsley if desired. Cover and refrigerate no longer than 6 hours.

Arrange tomatoes on serving plate. Garnish plate with olives and parsley if desired. 24 appetizers.

NOTE: To crumble blue cheese, freeze first (it is easier to handle). After crumbling, wrap and freeze. Separate into pieces before adding to cream cheese.

Spiced Pecans

2 cups pecan halves
2 tablespoons margarine or butter
1 egg white
1/2 teaspoon salt
1/2 teaspoon ground ginger
1/4 teaspoon garlic powder
1 teaspoon grated orange peel

Spread pecans in ungreased rectangular pan, 13 × 9 × 2 inches. Bake in 325° oven, stirring occasionally, until toasted, about 10 minutes. Remove pecans from pan; reserve.

Heat margarine in same pan in oven until melted; tilt pan to spread margarine evenly. Beat egg white, salt, ginger and garlic powder on medium speed until foamy, about 20 seconds; stir in orange peel and reserved pecans until evenly coated. Spread pecans evenly in margarine.

Bake uncovered, stirring occasionally, until shiny and dark golden brown, about 20 minutes; cool completely. Store in tightly covered container at room temperature no longer than 5 days. 2 cups.

Pickled Mushrooms

24 small mushrooms
2 tablespoons finely chopped onion
1 jar (2 ounces) diced pimientos, drained
1/4 cup vinegar
1/4 cup olive oil
1/4 cup vegetable oil
1 tablespoon sugar
1/2 teaspoon salt
1/4 teaspoon dried dill weed
2 cloves garlic, crushed

Place mushrooms, onion and pimientos in 1-quart jar. Shake remaining ingredients in tightly covered container; pour over vegetables. Cover tightly and refrigerate, shaking jar occasionally, at least 24 hours but no longer than 5 days.

Drain; serve with plastic picks. 24 appetizers.

COCKTAIL PARTY SUPPLIES

Be sure to have plenty of glasses — whether purchased, rented or borrowed — a jigger, bottle opener, strainer, and if possible, an ice crusher. Add a knife, spoon, wooden picks and stirrers. A bartender's guide is a must for mixing various drinks.

A supply of ice cubes, stored behind the bar in an insulated cooler, is essential. A variety of garnishes such as lemon and lime slices, olives, celery sticks, cocktail onions, maraschino cherries, fresh berries and mint leaves add that final touch. Plenty of towels and cocktail napkins complete the bar.

A Holiday Open House

Menu

24 servings

Hot Apple Cider   Glogg*

Ham Cheesecake Appetizer*

Caraway Cheese Spread*

Salmon Ball*

Apple Wedges

Assorted Crackers

Herring in Cream Sauce

Deviled Eggs*

Fruitcake

Holiday Cookies

Coffee   Tea

***Recipe included**

About 1 week before buffet:
- Prepare Caraway Cheese Spread; refrigerate.

2 days before:
- Prepare Ham Cheesecake Appetizer; refrigerate.
- Prepare Salmon Ball; refrigerate.

1 day before:
- Prepare Deviled Eggs; refrigerate.
- Prepare Glogg; refrigerate.

About 3 hours before serving:
- Arrange Assorted Crackers in serving container.
- Spoon Herring in Cream Sauce into serving container; cover and refrigerate.
- Arrange Fruitcake and Holiday Cookies on serving trays; cover Fruitcake until serving time.

About 2 hours before:
- Remove Ham Cheesecake Appetizer from refrigerator; let stand at room temperature.
- Remove Caraway Cheese Spread from refrigerator; let stand at room temperature.

About 20 minutes before:
- Prepare Coffee and Tea.
- Heat Hot Apple Cider.
- Heat Glogg.
- Arrange Apple Wedges in serving container.

Glogg

```
10  whole cloves
 7  cardamom pods, crushed
 2  sticks cinnamon
 2  cups water
10  blanched almonds
 1  orange, cut into fourths
 1  package (9 ounces) raisins
 2  bottles (750 ml each) dry red wine
1¾  cups vodka
1¾  cups brandy
 ⅓  cup sugar
```

Tie cloves, cardamom and cinnamon in cheesecloth bag. Heat spice bag, water, almonds, orange and raisins to boiling in 4-quart Dutch oven; reduce heat. Cover and simmer 45 minutes. Remove spice bag and orange. Stir in remaining ingredients. Cover and refrigerate no longer than 24 hours.

Heat just to boiling. Ladle several raisins into each cup; fill with hot Glogg. 24 servings (about ½ cup each).

Clockwise from top left: Glogg, Ham Cheesecake Appetizer, Salmon Ball and Apple Wedges

Ham Cheesecake Appetizer

½ cup bread crumbs
½ cup half-and-half
1 teaspoon dry mustard
1 teaspoon salt
⅛ teaspoon ground red pepper
4 eggs
3 packages (8 ounces each) cream cheese, softened
½ pound finely chopped fully cooked smoked ham
2 cups shredded Swiss cheese (8 ounces)

Grease springform pan, 9 × 3 inches; coat side and bottom with bread crumbs. Spread any remaining crumbs evenly on bottom of pan. Beat half-and-half, mustard, salt, red pepper, eggs and cream cheese in large bowl on medium speed until smooth, about 5 minutes. Stir in ham and Swiss cheese. Spread in pan. Bake in 325° oven until set, about 1 hour; cool. Cover and refrigerate no longer than 48 hours.

About 2 hours before serving, remove from refrigerator. Remove side and bottom of pan. Let stand at room temperature. Garnish with pimiento and parsley if desired.

Caraway Cheese Spread

½ cup margarine or butter, softened
½ cup dairy sour cream
2 tablespoons snipped chives
1 tablespoon caraway seed
1 tablespoon paprika
2 tablespoons anchovy paste
2 teaspoons capers
½ teaspoon dry mustard
1 package (8 ounces) cream cheese, softened

Place all ingredients in blender container. Cover and blend on high speed, stopping occasionally to scrape sides, until smooth, about 2 minutes. Spoon mixture into crock or serving container. Cover tightly and refrigerate until well chilled, at least 4 hours but no longer than 1 week.

About 2 hours before serving, remove from refrigerator. Let stand uncovered at room temperature. 2 cups.

Salmon Ball

1 tablespoon finely chopped onion
1 tablespoon lemon juice
¼ teaspoon salt
¼ teaspoon liquid smoke
1 can (16 ounces) salmon, drained and flaked
1 package (8 ounces) cream cheese, softened
⅓ cup snipped parsley

Mix all ingredients except parsley. Refrigerate until mixture begins to firm, about 3 hours. Shape salmon mixture into ball; roll in parsley. Cover and refrigerate no longer than 24 hours.

Deviled Eggs

12 hard-cooked eggs
⅓ cup mayonnaise or salad dressing
1 teaspoon dry mustard
½ teaspoon salt
½ teaspoon pepper
24 capers

Cut peeled eggs lengthwise into halves. Slip out yolks; mash with fork. Mix in mayonnaise, mustard, salt and pepper. Fill whites with egg yolk mixture, heaping it up lightly; top each with caper. Cover and refrigerate no longer than 24 hours. 24 eggs.

A Graduation Open House

Menu

24 servings

Ginger Punch*

Mixed Nuts

Mini Ham and Turkey Sandwiches*

Pickles   Olives

Pastel Cookie Slices*

Chocolate Squares*

Fruit in Honeydew Shells*

Coffee   Tea

*Recipe included

About 1 week before buffet:
- ☐ Bake Chocolate Squares; freeze.
- ☐ Prepare dough for Pastel Cookie Slices; refrigerate.

2 days before:
- ☐ Roast turkey for Mini Ham and Turkey Sandwiches; refrigerate.
- ☐ Prepare Grape Ice Ring for Ginger Punch; freeze.

1 day before:
- ☐ Complete Pastel Cookie Slices and Chocolate Squares; store at room temperature.
- ☐ Complete Mini Ham and Turkey Sandwiches; refrigerate.
- ☐ Prepare honeydew melons and fruit mixture for Fruit in Honeydew Shells; refrigerate.

About 30 minutes before serving:
- ☐ Arrange Mixed Nuts, Pickles and Olives in serving containers.
- ☐ Complete Fruit in Honeydew Shells.
- ☐ Arrange Pastel Cookie Slices and Chocolate Squares on serving plates.
- ☐ Prepare Coffee and Tea.

When guests arrive:
- ☐ Complete Ginger Punch.

Ginger Punch

Grape Ice Ring (right)
3 cans (12 ounces each) frozen lemonade
   concentrate, thawed
1 can (12 ounces) frozen grape juice
   concentrate, thawed
2½ quarts cold water
1 teaspoon ground ginger
2 bottles (28 ounces each) ginger ale, chilled

Prepare Grape Ice Ring. Mix concentrates, water and ginger in large punch bowl; stir in ginger ale. Place Grape Ice Ring, fruit side up, in punch bowl. 48 servings (about ½ cup each).

Grape Ice Ring

Seedless green grapes, if desired
Lemon slices, if desired
1 can (12 ounces) frozen grape juice concentrate,
   thawed
1 bottle (28 ounces) ginger ale, chilled, or 1
   bottle (32 ounces) sparkling water, chilled

Arrange grapes and lemon slices in 8-cup ring mold. Mix concentrate and ginger ale; pour into mold. Freeze until solid but no longer than 48 hours. To unmold, run cold water over inverted mold until ice ring releases.

Mini Ham and Turkey Sandwiches

5- pound frozen turkey breast, thawed*
2- pound fully cooked smoked boneless ham*
1 jar (10 ounces) mustard-mayonnaise
    sandwich and salad sauce or 1 jar (8
    ounces) Dijon-style mustard
2½ dozen cocktail buns (about 2 inches in
    diameter), sliced
2½ dozen rye cocktail buns (about 2 inches in
    diameter), sliced, or 5 dozen slices party
    cocktail rye bread
1 cup mayonnaise or salad dressing
¼ teaspoon ground cumin

Place turkey breast, skin side up, on rack in shallow roasting pan. Place meat thermometer in thickest part. Be sure it does not touch bone. Brush with vegetable oil. Roast uncovered in 325° oven until thermometer registers 180 to 185°, 1½ to 2 hours; cool. Cut into thin slices. Cover and refrigerate no longer than 24 hours.

Cut ham into thin slices. Spread sauce over ½ of the buns; fill with ham. Cover with dampened towel; wrap with plastic wrap. Refrigerate no longer than 24 hours.

Mix mayonnaise and cumin. Spread mayonnaise mixture over remaining buns; fill with turkey. Cover with dampened towel; wrap with plastic wrap. Refrigerate no longer than 24 hours.

At serving time, arrange sandwiches on trays. 5 dozen sandwiches.

*2 pounds each thinly sliced cooked turkey and fully cooked smoked ham can be substituted for the turkey breast and ham.

Pastel Cookie Slices

1 cup sugar
1 cup margarine or butter, softened
1½ teaspoons vanilla
2 eggs
3 cups all-purpose flour
1 teaspoon salt
½ teaspoon baking soda
2 egg whites
⅔ cup finely chopped nuts
    Pastel Frostings (below)

Mix sugar, margarine, vanilla and eggs. Mix in flour, salt and baking soda. Divide dough into 3 equal parts. Shape each part into roll, 1½ inches in diameter and about 7 inches long. Wrap and refrigerate at least 4 hours but no longer than 1 week.

Heat oven to 400°. Cut rolls into ⅛-inch slices. Place about 1 inch apart on ungreased cookie sheet. Beat egg whites slightly; stir in nuts. Spread ½ teaspoon nut mixture over ⅓ of the slices. Bake until set, 8 to 10 minutes. Immediately remove from cookie sheet; cool.

Prepare Pastel Frostings; frost remaining cookies. Wrap loosely and store at room temperature no longer than 24 hours.

Pastel Frostings

1 cup powdered sugar
2 teaspoons margarine or butter, softened
1 teaspoon grated lemon peel
1 tablespoon plus 1½ teaspoons lemon juice
1 drop green food color
1 drop yellow food color

Mix powdered sugar, margarine, lemon peel and lemon juice until smooth; divide into halves. Tint ½ with green food color; tint other half with yellow food color.

Chocolate Squares

1 cup margarine or butter
1 cup water
1/3 cup cocoa
2 cups all-purpose flour
2 cups sugar
1 teaspoon baking soda
1 teaspoon vanilla
1/2 teaspoon salt
2 eggs
1/2 cup dairy sour cream
    Chocolate-Nut Frosting (below)
3/4 cup finely chopped nuts

Heat oven to 375°. Grease jelly roll pan, 15½ × 10½ × 1 inch. Heat margarine, water and cocoa to boiling in 2-quart saucepan, stirring occasionally; remove from heat. Add flour, sugar, baking soda, vanilla, salt, eggs and sour cream; beat until smooth (batter will be very thin). Pour into pan.

Bake until wooden pick inserted in center comes out clean, 20 to 25 minutes; cool. Wrap, label and freeze no longer than 1 week.

Twenty-four hours before serving, remove from freezer. Unwrap and let stand 30 minutes at room temperature. Prepare Chocolate-Nut Frosting; frost cake and sprinkle with nuts. Cover and store at room temperature no longer than 24 hours. At serving time, cut into about 1½-inch squares. 70 squares.

Chocolate-Nut Frosting

1/2 cup margarine or butter
1/3 cup cocoa
1/3 cup milk
1 package (16 ounces) powdered sugar (about 4½ cups)
1 teaspoon almond extract

Heat margarine, cocoa and milk to boiling in 1½-quart saucepan, stirring occasionally; remove from heat. Add powdered sugar; beat until smooth. Stir in almond extract.

Fruit in Honeydew Shells

2 large honeydew melons (each about 7 inches in diameter)
1 small pineapple, cut into bite-size pieces
1 pound red seedless grapes
2 pounds green seedless grapes, separated into small clusters
2 small cantaloupe, cut into bite-size pieces

Cut top third from 1 honeydew melon, using a deep zigzag cut. Cover and refrigerate top portion to use as desired. Remove seeds and scoop balls from larger section of melon; reserve melon balls. Scoop remaining pulp from melon with large spoon to form shell; drain shell. Repeat with second melon. Cut thin slice from bottom of each shell to keep it from tipping. Cover and refrigerate no longer than 24 hours. Mix melon balls with remaining ingredients. Cover and refrigerate no longer than 24 hours.

Just before serving, divide fruit mixture between shells. Garnish with mint leaves if desired, and serve with wooden picks.

Fruit in Honeydew Shells

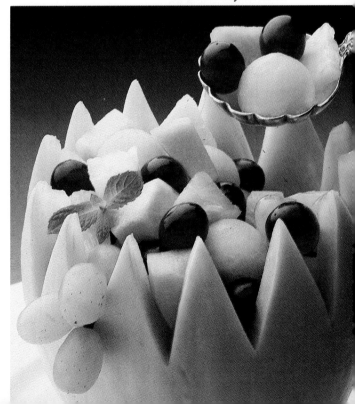

Grapes, Assorted Cheeses and Crackers, Liver Pâté, and Crusty Bread

An Anniversary Open House

Menu

24 servings

Sparkling Punch*

Liver Pâté*   Crusty Bread

**Salmon Mousse with
Green Sauce***

**Assorted Cheeses and
Crackers**

Fresh Vegetable Tray

Grapes

Celebration Cupcakes*

Coffee   Tea

***Recipe included**

2 days before buffet:
- ☐ Prepare Liver Pâté; refrigerate.

1 day before:
- ☐ Prepare Salmon Mousse with Green Sauce; refrigerate.
- ☐ Prepare Celebration Cupcakes; store at room temperature.
- ☐ Prepare vegetables for Fresh Vegetable Tray; cover and refrigerate.

About 2 hours before serving:
- ☐ Prepare fruit mixture for Sparkling Punch; refrigerate.
- ☐ Arrange Assorted Cheeses and Crackers on serving trays; store at room temperature.

About 45 minutes before:
- ☐ Remove Liver Pâté from refrigerator; let stand at room temperature.
- ☐ Cut Crusty Bread into thin slices; arrange in serving container.
- ☐ Arrange Fresh Vegetable Tray.
- ☐ Arrange Grapes in serving container.

About 20 minutes before:
- ☐ Prepare Coffee and Tea.
- ☐ Arrange Celebration Cupcakes on serving tray.
- ☐ Complete Sparkling Punch.

Celebration Cupcakes, Salmon Mousse with Green Sauce, and Fresh Vegetable Tray

Sparkling Punch

2 *packages (10 ounces each) frozen strawberries, thawed*
2 *cups vodka, if desired*
1 *cup lemon juice*
½ *cup water*
1 *can (6 ounces) frozen orange juice concentrate, thawed*
   Ice cubes
2 *bottles (28 ounces each) ginger ale, chilled*

Mix strawberries, vodka, lemon juice, water and orange juice concentrate. Refrigerate until cold, at least 2 hours.

Pour fruit mixture over ice cubes in punch bowl. Stir in ginger ale. Garnish punch with mint sprigs if desired. 24 servings (about ½ cup each).

PUNCH POINTERS

- Ingredients for punch should always be chilled before mixing.
- Carbonated beverages should always be added just before serving to prevent them from going flat.
- Use frozen ice cubes of tea, lemon, lime or orange juice for fruit punches.

Liver Pâté

2 *pounds chicken livers*
2 *cups margarine or butter, softened*
2 *teaspoons salt*
4 *teaspoons dry mustard*
1 *teaspoon ground nutmeg*
½ *teaspoon ground cloves*
⅛ *teaspoon ground red pepper*
1 *medium onion, chopped (about ½ cup)*
⅔ *cup coarsely chopped pistachio nuts*

Heat chicken livers and enough water to cover to boiling in 3-quart saucepan; reduce heat. Cover and simmer 15 minutes; drain and cool. Place a quarter of the livers and a quarter of the remaining ingredients except pistachio nuts in blender container. Cover and blend on high speed, scraping sides occasionally, until smooth, about 5 minutes. Repeat 3 times with remaining ingredients. Stir in pistachio nuts. Cover and refrigerate until firm, at least 3 hours but no longer than 48 hours. Divide liver mixture into halves. Spoon into 2 bowls or shape each half into a ball. Garnish with chopped pistachio nuts if desired.

Salmon Mousse with Green Sauce

2 cans (15½ ounces each) salmon, drained and flaked
2 medium stalks celery, chopped (about 1 cup)
3 cups whipping cream
1 small onion, chopped (about ¼ cup)
¼ cup lemon juice
1 teaspoon dried tarragon leaves
¾ teaspoon salt
⅛ teaspoon ground red pepper
4 envelopes unflavored gelatin
1 cup cold water
Green Sauce (below)

Place 1 can salmon, ½ cup celery, 1 cup whipping cream, 2 tablespoons onion, 2 tablespoons lemon juice and half of the tarragon, salt and red pepper in blender container. Cover and blend on high speed until smooth, about 2 minutes; repeat. Sprinkle gelatin on cold water in 1½-quart saucepan to soften; stir in remaining whipping cream. Heat over low heat, stirring constantly, until gelatin is dissolved; cool. Mix gelatin mixture and salmon mixture. Pour into lightly oiled 8-cup mold. Cover and refrigerate until firm, at least 3 hours but no longer than 24 hours. Prepare Green Sauce; serve with Mousse.

Green Sauce

1 cup parsley sprigs
1½ cups creamed cottage cheese (large curd)
3 tablespoons milk
1 tablespoon lemon juice
½ teaspoon salt
½ teaspoon dried basil leaves
⅛ teaspoon pepper
4 to 6 drops red pepper sauce

Place all ingredients in blender container. Cover and blend on high speed, stopping blender occasionally to scrape down sides, until smooth, about 3 minutes. Cover and refrigerate no longer than 24 hours.

Celebration Cupcakes

1 package white cake mix with pudding
  Buttercream Decorator Frosting (below)
  Cake Decorator Flowers*

Heat oven to 350°. Line 24 medium muffin cups, 2½ × 1¼ inches, with paper baking cups. Prepare cake mix as directed on package. Fill cups ⅔ full. Bake cupcakes as directed on package; cool. Prepare Buttercream Decorator Frosting. Frost cupcakes; reserve remaining frosting. Place reserved frosting in decorating bag with star tip #18 or 30. Pipe frosting around edge of each cupcake. Top with Cake Decorator Flowers. Cover and store at room temperature no longer than 24 hours. 24 cupcakes.

Buttercream Decorator Frosting

6 cups powdered sugar
¾ cup margarine or butter, softened
¾ cup shortening
3 tablespoons water
1½ teaspoons almond extract

Beat all ingredients on medium speed until smooth and of desired consistency. Stir in additional powdered sugar if necessary.

*Omit Cake Decorator Flowers. Remove 1 cup of the frosting; stir in 2 or 3 drops of food color and reserve. Frost cupcakes as directed. Place tinted frosting in decorating bag with writing tip #2. Write wedding date, initials of the anniversary couple or special wishes on each cupcake.

A Wedding Reception

Menu

36 servings

Champagne Punch*

Salmon Pinwheels*

Watercress Triangles*

Caviar Canapés*

Chicken-filled Puffs*

Assorted Relish Tray

Fresh Fruit

Mints   Mixed Nuts

Toasted Almond Wedding Cake*

Coffee   Tea

***Recipe included**

3 weeks before buffet:
- ☐ Prepare White Leaves for Toasted Almond Wedding Cake; freeze.

1 week before:
- ☐ Bake Mini Puffs for Chicken-filled Puffs; freeze.

3 days before:
- ☐ Prepare Sugared Flowers for Toasted Almond Wedding Cake; store at room temperature.

2 days before:
- ☐ Bake Toasted Almond Cake and Chocolate Fruitcake for Toasted Almond Wedding Cake.

1 day before:
- ☐ Prepare Salmon Pinwheels; refrigerate.
- ☐ Prepare Watercress Triangles; refrigerate.
- ☐ Prepare chicken mixture for Chicken-filled Puffs; refrigerate.
- ☐ Prepare toasted rounds for Caviar Canapés; store at room temperature.
- ☐ Complete Toasted Almond Wedding Cake; store at room temperature.

About 6 hours before serving:
- ☐ Arrange Assorted Relish Tray; cover and refrigerate.
- ☐ Place Mints and Mixed Nuts in serving containers.
- ☐ Complete Chicken-filled Puffs; refrigerate.
- ☐ Complete Caviar Canapés; refrigerate.

At serving time:
- ☐ Prepare Coffee and Tea.
- ☐ Prepare Champagne Punch.

Champagne Punch

6 bottles (750 ml each) champagne or 6 bottles (28 ounces each) ginger ale, chilled
3 quarts apple juice, chilled
1 lemon, thinly sliced

Mix 3 bottles champagne and 1½ quarts apple juice in punch bowl just before serving. Float lemon slices in punch and fresh strawberries if desired. Repeat as needed. 36 servings (about 1 cup each).

Clockwise from top: Fresh Fruit, Toasted Almond Wedding Cake, Champagne Punch, Chicken-Filled Puffs,

Salmon Pinwheels

- 2 *tablespoons lemon juice*
- 1/2 *teaspoon dried dill weed*
- 4 *packages (3 ounces each) cream cheese, softened*
- 6 *packages (3 ounces each) sliced smoked salmon or 30 pieces sliced smoked salmon, each 3 × 2½ inches*

Mix lemon juice, dill weed and cream cheese. Spread about 2½ teaspoons cream cheese mixture on each salmon slice. Roll up, beginning at narrow end. Cut rolls crosswise into 3 pieces. Cover with damp towel and plastic wrap; refrigerate no longer than 24 hours. About 90 appetizers.

Watercress Triangles

- 40 *slices white or whole wheat sandwich bread*
- 2 *tablespoons dairy sour cream*
- 1/2 *teaspoon salt*
- 1/8 *teaspoon white pepper*
- 4 *packages (3 ounces each) cream cheese, softened*
- 2 *cups snipped watercress*

Trim crusts from bread. Mix sour cream, salt, pepper and cream cheese. Spread cheese mixture on 20 bread slices; sprinkle with watercress. Top with remaining bread slices. Cut sandwiches diagonally into 4 triangles. Cover with dampened towel; wrap with plastic wrap. Refrigerate no longer than 24 hours. About 80 appetizers.

Chicken-filled Puffs

Mini Puffs (below)
2 *cups finely chopped cooked chicken or 3 cans (6³⁄₄ ounces each) chicken, drained*
¹⁄₃ *cup mayonnaise or salad dressing*
1 *tablespoon finely chopped onion or ¹⁄₂ teaspoon instant minced onion*
1 *teaspoon ground ginger*
2 *teaspoons lemon juice*
¹⁄₂ *teaspoon salt*
¹⁄₄ *teaspoon pepper*
2 *stalks celery, finely chopped (about ¹⁄₂ cup)*

Prepare Mini Puffs. Mix remaining ingredients. Cover and refrigerate no longer than 24 hours.

Remove Mini Puffs from freezer; unwrap and let stand at room temperature until thawed, about 1 hour. Cut off tops of puffs with sharp knife; remove any filaments of soft dough. Fill each puff with rounded teaspoon chicken mixture; replace top. Refrigerate until serving time. 5 dozen appetizers.

Mini Puffs

1 *cup water*
¹⁄₂ *cup margarine or butter*
1 *cup all-purpose flour*
4 *eggs*

Heat oven to 400°. Heat water and margarine to rolling boil in 3-quart saucepan. Stir in flour. Stir vigorously over low heat until mixture forms a ball, about 1 minute; remove from heat. Beat in eggs, all at once; continue beating until smooth and glossy. Drop dough by slightly rounded teaspoonfuls onto ungreased cookie sheet. Bake until puffed, golden brown and dry, about 25 minutes. Cool on wire rack. Wrap, label and freeze no longer than 1 week.

Caviar Canapés, Watercress Triangles and Assorted Relish Tray

Caviar Canapés

20 *slices white sandwich bread*
¹⁄₃ *cup margarine or butter, softened*
2 *green onions, finely chopped*
2 *jars (2 ounces each) black or red caviar*

Cut 4 circles from each bread slice with 1¹⁄₂-inch round cutter. Place rounds on ungreased cookie sheet. Set oven control to broil and/or 550°. Broil bread rounds with tops 3 to 4 inches from heat until golden brown, about 1 minute; cool. Cover and store at room temperature no longer than 24 hours.

Mix margarine and onions; spread over toasted rounds. Top with caviar. Cover and refrigerate until serving time. 80 canapés.

Toasted Almond Wedding Cake

White Leaves (below)
Sugared Flowers (below)
Toasted Almond Cake (below)*
Chocolate Fruitcake (below)
Buttercream Decorator Frosting (page 112)
1 tube (7 ounces) marzipan or almond paste, if desired

Prepare White Leaves, Sugared Flowers, 2 recipes Toasted Almond Cake, the Chocolate Fruitcake and 2 recipes Buttercream Decorator Frosting.

Place 1 Toasted Almond Cake, top side down, on rectangular tray, or large serving plate. Spread top with 1 cup Buttercream Decorator Frosting; place remaining Toasted Almond Cake, top side up, on frosting. (Trim top of cake with serrated knife to make flat if necessary.) Shape ¾ of the marzipan into rectangle, about 4 × 2 inches. Place between 2 pieces waxed paper and roll into rectangle, 12½ × 8½ inches. (Trim to make edges even if necessary.) Carefully remove waxed paper from top. Lift remaining waxed paper with marzipan; invert and press onto top of cake. Remove waxed paper. Frost sides and top of cake.

Place a foil-covered cardboard rectangle, 8 × 4 inches, on center of frosted cake. Cut Chocolate Fruitcake into halves. Place one half, top side down, on cardboard on cake. Spread top with ⅓ cup frosting; place remaining half of cake, top side up, on frosting. (Trim top of cake with serrated knife to make flat if necessary.) Shape remaining marzipan into rectangle, 4 × 1 inch. Place between 2 pieces waxed paper and roll into rectangle, 8 × 4 inches. (Trim to make edges even if necessary.) Carefully remove waxed paper from top. Lift remaining waxed paper with marzipan; invert and press onto top of cake. Remove waxed paper. Frost sides and top of cake.

Place remaining frosting in decorating bag fitted with star tip #30. Pipe border around top edges, base and corners of cake. Arrange Sugared Flowers and White Leaves on cake as desired, using small amount of frosting on back of each to secure. Let cake stand at room temperature until frosting is set, about 1 hour. Cover cake with large box, or carefully tent aluminum foil over cake. Let stand at room temperature no longer than 24 hours.

Remove top tier of cake to later wrap, label and freeze for the first anniversary if desired. Make 2 cuts lengthwise and 11 cuts crosswise on remaining cake. 36 servings (about 2¾ × 1 inch each).

White Leaves

Wash and dry plastic or fresh ivy leaves of 4 different sizes from large to small, leaving about 1-inch stem attached to each leaf. Melt 4 squares (1 ounce each) vanilla-flavored candy coating as directed on package. Brush or spread candy coating about ⅛ inch thick evenly over back of leaves and just to edges. Refrigerate until firm, about 30 minutes. Carefully remove leaves from coating. Repeat until all coating is used. Place firm leaves in single layers in a box. Freeze no longer than 3 weeks, or refrigerate no longer than 3 days. About 8 dozen leaves.

Sugared Flowers

Fresh flowers (such as roses, violets, sweet peas, small orchids, carnations, bachelor buttons, daisies and mums)
1 egg white
1 teaspoon water
Granulated or superfine sugar

Wash and dry flowers. Trim stems of flowers to about 2 inches. Beat egg white and water just until foamy. Brush egg white mixture on flower petals with small, soft brush, separating petals to coat evenly. Sprinkle with sugar, shaking gently to remove excess if necessary. (Leaves of flowers also can be sugared in same way if desired.) Place flowers on aluminum foil-lined tray. Let stand uncovered at room temperature, turning once or twice a day, until dry, 1 to 3 days. Cover and store at room temperature.

NOTE: These flowers are for decoration only; they are not edible.

Toasted Almond Cake

2 cups all-purpose flour
½ cup sugar
¼ cup honey
¼ cup shortening
¼ cup margarine or butter, softened
¾ cup milk
3 teaspoons baking powder
1 teaspoon salt
1 teaspoon vanilla
½ teaspoon almond extract
2 eggs
½ cup chopped toasted almonds

Heat oven to 350°. Grease and flour rectangular pan, 13 × 9 × 2 inches. Beat all ingredients in large bowl on medium speed, scraping bowl constantly, 30 seconds. Beat on high speed, scraping bowl occasionally, 3 minutes. Spread in pan. Bake until wooden pick inserted in center comes out clean, 30 to 35 minutes. Cool 10 minutes; remove from pan. Cool completely. Cover tightly and store at room temperature no longer than 24 hours.

NOTE: To toast almonds, bake on ungreased cookie sheet in 350° oven, stirring occasionally, until golden brown, about 10 minutes.

*1 package golden pound cake mix can be substituted for each Toasted Almond Cake; prepare as directed except — add 2 tablespoons honey and ½ teaspoon almond extract with the water and stir ½ cup chopped toasted almonds into batter. Spread in greased and floured rectangular pan, 13 × 9 × 2 inches.

Bake until wooden pick inserted in center comes out clean, 35 to 40 minutes. Cool 10 minutes; remove from pan. Cool completely. Cover tightly and store at room temperature no longer than 24 hours.

Chocolate Fruitcake

1 cup all-purpose flour
1 cup sugar
1 teaspoon baking powder
½ teaspoon salt
¾ cup milk
¼ cup shortening
1 teaspoon vanilla
4 squares (1 ounce each) unsweetened chocolate, melted and cooled
1 egg
½ cup chopped candied pineapple
½ cup chopped candied cherries
½ cup chopped toasted almonds

Heat oven to 350°. Grease and flour square pan, 9 × 9 × 2 inches. Beat flour, sugar, baking powder, salt, milk, shortening and vanilla in small bowl on medium speed, scraping constantly, 2 minutes.

Add chocolate and egg; beat on medium speed, scraping bowl occasionally, 2 minutes. Stir in pineapple, cherries and almonds. Spread in pan. Bake until wooden pick inserted in center comes out clean, 40 to 45 minutes. Cool 10 minutes; remove from pan. Cool completely. Cover tightly and store at room temperature no longer than 24 hours.

Cutting the Toasted Almond Wedding Cake

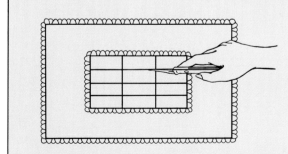

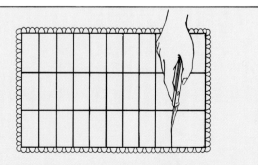

The top tier can be cut into 12 servings. Make 2 cuts crosswise and 3 cuts lengthwise.

Remove cardboard. Make 2 cuts lengthwise and 11 cuts crosswise to make 36 servings.

A Spring Tea

The Englishman is devoted to his tea and the ritual teatime. However for you, the afternoon tea is a time to use your prettiest china, your best silver or flatware and that special tablecloth. If you are a collector of china cups and saucers, now is the time to use them. You can mix the patterns, but just be sure that the cup and saucer match. Traditionally, tea should be served between four and four thirty in the afternoon, but anywhere between two and six is acceptable. However, a tea should not last longer than one hour.

Menu

12 servings

Citrus Cooler Punch*

Sandwich Loaf*

Coral Pinwheels*

Ambrosia Teacakes*

Fudge Meltaway Brownies*

Mints   Mixed Nuts

Tea*

***Recipe included**

About 2 months before buffet:
☐ Bake Coral Pinwheels; freeze.
☐ Bake Ambrosia Teacakes; freeze.

2 days before:
☐ Prepare Fudge Meltaway Brownies; refrigerate.
☐ Prepare Citrus Ice Ring for Citrus Cooler Punch; freeze.

1 day before:
☐ Prepare Sandwich Loaf; refrigerate.

About 45 minutes before serving:
☐ Arrange Coral Pinwheels and Ambrosia Teacakes on serving plates.

About 15 minutes before:
☐ Prepare Citrus Cooler Punch.
☐ Arrange Fudge Meltaway Brownies on serving plate.
☐ Arrange Mints and Mixed Nuts in serving container.
☐ Prepare Tea.

Citrus Cooler Punch

Citrus Ice Ring (right)
1 can (12 ounces) frozen lemonade concentrate, thawed
1 can (6 ounces) frozen orange juice concentrate, thawed
½ cup grenadine syrup, chilled
1 bottle (28 ounces) ginger ale, chilled

Prepare Citrus Ice Ring. Prepare concentrates as directed on cans. Mix lemonade, orange juice and grenadine syrup in large punch bowl; stir in ginger ale. Place Citrus Ice Ring, fruit side up, in punch bowl. 24 servings (about ½ cup each).

Citrus Ice Ring

Arrange small clusters of seedless green grapes, small whole strawberries, thin slices of lime, orange and lemon and, if desired, mint leaves in ring mold or bundt cake pan that fits into punch bowl. Pour water into mold to partially cover fruit; freeze. Add water to fill mold about ¾ full. Freeze until solid but no longer than 48 hours. To unmold, run cold water over inverted mold until ice ring releases.

Tea, Coral Pinwheels, Ambrosia Teacakes, Fudge Meltaway Brownies, Mixed Nuts, Sandwich Loaf, Mints, Coral Pinwheels, Ambrosia Teacakes, Fudge Meltaway Brownies and Citrus Cooler Punch

Sandwich Loaf

Fillings (below)
1 *loaf (1½ pounds) unsliced sandwich bread*
  Margarine or butter, softened
2 *packages (8 ounces each) cream cheese,*
  softened
½ *cup half-and-half*

Prepare fillings. Trim crust from loaf; cut loaf horizontally into 4 equal slices. Spread 3 slices with margarine. Place 1 slice on serving plate and spread evenly with Shrimp Salad Filling. Top with second slice and spread evenly with Cream Cheese-Pecan Filling. Top with third slice and spread evenly with Chicken-Bacon Filling. Top with unbuttered bread slice.

Mix cream cheese and half-and-half until smooth and of spreading consistency. Frost sides and top of loaf with cream cheese mixture. Refrigerate until set, about 30 minutes. Cover loaf and refrigerate at least 2½ hours but no longer than 24 hours. Garnish with slices of hard-cooked egg, slices of ripe olives and thin strips of green onion tops if desired.

Shrimp Salad Filling

2 *tablespoons finely chopped celery*
⅛ *teaspoon salt*
  Dash of pepper
3 *tablespoons mayonnaise or salad dressing*
1 *tablespoon lemon juice*
1 *hard-cooked egg, finely chopped*
1 *can (4¼ ounces) broken shrimp, rinsed and*
  drained.

Mix all ingredients thoroughly.

Cream Cheese-Pecan Filling

1 *cup finely chopped toasted pecans*
1 *package (3 ounces) cream cheese, softened*
1 *can (8¼ ounces) crushed pineapple, well*
  drained
2 *drops yellow food color, if desired*

Mix all ingredients thoroughly.

Chicken-Bacon Filling

6 *slices bacon, crisply fried and crumbled*
1 *cup finely chopped cooked chicken*
¼ *cup mayonnaise or salad dressing*
2 *tablespoons finely chopped green onions*
  (with tops)
1 *tablespoon finely snipped parsley*
¼ *teaspoon salt*

Mix all ingredients thoroughly.

Coral Pinwheels

1 *cup margarine or butter, softened*
½ *cup powdered sugar*
1 *teaspoon vanilla*
½ *teaspoon almond extract*
2¼ *cups all-purpose flour*
¼ *teaspoon salt*
¼ *teaspoon red food color*
7 *drops yellow food color*
  Granulated sugar

Mix margarine, powdered sugar, vanilla and almond extract. Stir in flour and salt. Divide dough into halves. Tint 1 half with food colors. Wrap and refrigerate doughs until firm, 1 to 2 hours.

Heat oven to 375°. For each pinwheel, shape 1 teaspoon dough from each half into 4-inch rope. For smooth, even strips, roll back and forth on lightly floured surface. Place 1 coral and 1 white strip side by side on ungreased cookie sheet. Press together lightly and shape into a coil. Repeat with remaining dough. Sprinkle pinwheels with granulated sugar. Bake until set but not brown, about 8 minutes. Remove from cookie sheet; cool. Wrap, label and freeze no longer than 2 months.

About 45 minutes before serving, remove Coral Pinwheels from freezer and unwrap. Arrange on serving plate; let stand uncovered at room temperature. About 3 dozen cookies.

Ambrosia Teacakes

1 cup margarine or butter, softened
½ cup powdered sugar
1 teaspoon vanilla
2¼ cups all-purpose flour
½ cup flaked coconut
1 tablespoon finely shredded orange peel
¼ teaspoon salt
  About 16 orange jellied candy slices, cut into thirds
  Powdered sugar
  Glaze (below)

Heat oven to 400°. Mix margarine, ½ cup powdered sugar and the vanilla. Stir in flour, coconut, orange peel and salt. (If dough is soft, cover and refrigerate until firm enough to shape.) Shape dough around each piece of orange candy.

Bake on ungreased cookie sheet until set but not brown, 8 to 9 minutes. Roll about half of the cookies in powdered sugar while warm. Cool; roll in powdered sugar again. Prepare Glaze; dip tops of remaining cookies into Glaze. Decorate some of the glazed cookies with flaked coconut if desired. Freeze cookies uncovered until firm, about 2 hours. Wrap, label and freeze no longer than 2 months.

About 45 minutes before serving, remove Ambrosia Teacakes from freezer and unwrap. Arrange on serving plate; let stand uncovered at room temperature. About 4 dozen cookies.

Glaze

1 cup powdered sugar
1 tablespoon plus 1½ teaspoons milk
1 teaspoon vanilla
2 drops yellow food color
1 drop red food color

Mix all ingredients until smooth and of desired consistency.

Fudge Meltaway Brownies

½ cup margarine or butter
1½ squares unsweetened chocolate
1¾ cups graham cracker crumbs
1 cup flaked coconut
½ cup chopped nuts
¼ cup granulated sugar
2 tablespoons water
1 teaspoon vanilla
2 cups powdered sugar
¼ cup margarine or butter, softened
3 tablespoons milk
1 teaspoon vanilla
1½ squares unsweetened chocolate

Heat ½ cup margarine and 1½ squares chocolate in 3-quart saucepan until melted; remove from heat. Stir in cracker crumbs, coconut, nuts, granulated sugar, water and 1 teaspoon vanilla. Press in aluminum foil-lined square pan, 9 × 9 × 2 inches. Refrigerate while making frosting.

Mix powdered sugar, ¼ cup margarine, the milk and 1 teaspoon vanilla; spread over chilled crumb mixture. Refrigerate 15 minutes. Heat 1½ squares chocolate until melted; spread evenly over frosting. Refrigerate 2 hours. Remove foil from pan; fold back foil. Cut into about 1½-inch squares before completely hard. Cover and refrigerate no longer than 48 hours. About 36 squares.

Tea

Fill ceramic teapot with rapidly boiling water; allow to stand a few minutes, then pour out. Heat cold water to a full rolling boil. Add tea or bags to the warm pot, allowing 1 teaspoon loose tea or 1 tea bag for each cup of tea desired. Pour boiling water over tea (¾ cup for each cup of tea); let stand 3 to 5 minutes. Judge the strength of the tea by the flavor; do not judge by the color. Stir once to ensure uniform strength. Strain tea or remove tea bags. Serve with sugar, milk and lemon slices.

Scones, Cinnamon Pastries, Finger Sandwiches, Dipped Fruits and Hot Tea

A High Tea

Menu

12 servings

Scones*

Finger Sandwiches*

Cinnamon Pastries*

Dipped Fruits*

Hot Tea*

*Recipe included

2 months before buffet:
- ☐ Bake Scones; freeze.

3 days before:
- ☐ Prepare Cinnamon Pastries for baking; refrigerate.

2 days before:
- ☐ Prepare tea concentrate for Hot Tea; refrigerate.

1 day before:
- ☐ Prepare Finger Sandwiches; refrigerate.
- ☐ Bake Cinnamon Pastries; store at room temperature.

4 hours before serving:
- ☐ Prepare Dipped Fruits; refrigerate.

About 30 minutes before:
- ☐ Heat Scones.

At serving time:
- ☐ Arrange Cinnamon Pastries on serving plate.
- ☐ Arrange Dipped Fruits on serving plate.
- ☐ Complete Hot Tea.

Scones

⅓ cup margarine, butter or shortening
1¾ cups all-purpose flour
3 tablespoons sugar
2½ teaspoons baking powder
½ teaspoon salt
1 egg, beaten
½ cup currants or raisins
4 to 6 tablespoons half-and-half
1 egg, beaten
Margarine or butter, softened
Strawberry preserves

Heat oven to 400°. Cut ⅓ cup margarine into flour, sugar, baking powder and salt until mixture resembles fine crumbs. Stir in 1 egg, the currants and just enough half-and-half so dough leaves side of bowl. Turn dough onto lightly floured surface. Knead lightly 10 times. Roll ½ inch thick.

Cut dough into 2-inch circles with floured cutter. Place on ungreased cookie sheet. Brush with 1 egg. Bake until golden, 10 to 12 minutes. Immediately remove from cookie sheet; cool 1 hour.

Freeze uncovered until completely frozen, at least 2 hours. Wrap in heavy-duty aluminum foil, label and freeze no longer than 2 months.

About 45 minutes before serving, remove from freezer and heat wrapped in 350° oven until warm, 30 to 35 minutes. Split scones; spread with margarine. Serve with strawberry preserves. 15 scones.

Finger Sandwiches

Smoked Fish Spread (below)
Olive-Nut Spread (below)
Margarine or butter, softened
12 slices day-old sandwich bread
Sliced almonds
Fresh dill or parsley
Sliced pimiento-stuffed olives or pimiento

Prepare Smoked Fish Spread and Olive-Nut Spread. Trim crusts from bread slices; spread with margarine. Spread half of the bread slices with Smoked Fish Spread and remaining bread slices with Olive-Nut Spread. Cut each slice into 3 pieces. Garnish fish sandwiches with almonds and dill. Garnish olive-nut sandwiches with olive slice.

Arrange sandwiches on serving tray or plate. Cover with dampened towel; wrap with plastic wrap. Refrigerate no longer than 24 hours. 36 sandwiches.

Smoked Fish Spread

4 ounces smoked fish, finely chopped
2 tablespoons finely chopped celery
2 teaspoons lemon juice
Dash of pepper
¼ cup mayonnaise or salad dressing
1 tablespoon finely chopped onion

Mix all ingredients. About 1 cup.

Olive-Nut Spread

1 package (3 ounces) cream cheese, softened
½ cup finely chopped nuts
¼ cup finely chopped pimiento-stuffed olives
2 tablespoons milk

Mix all ingredients. About 1 cup.

Cinnamon Pastries

1 cup margarine or butter
1½ cups all-purpose flour
½ cup dairy sour cream
3 tablespoons sugar
1 teaspoon ground cinnamon
3 tablespoons sugar
1 tablespoon water

Cut margarine into flour with pastry blender. Stir in sour cream. Cover and refrigerate at least 8 hours.

Mix 3 tablespoons sugar and the cinnamon. Divide dough into halves. Roll 1 half into rectangle, 20 × 7 inches, on sugared, well-floured cloth-covered board. Sprinkle with half of the sugar-cinnamon mixture. Roll up tightly, beginning at 7-inch side. Repeat with remaining dough and sugar-cinnamon mixture. Wrap and refrigerate at least 1 hour but no longer than 48 hours.

Heat oven to 350°. Cut rolls into ¼-inch slices with very sharp or electric knife. Place about 2 inches apart on ungreased cookie sheet. Mix 3 tablespoons sugar and the water; brush over cookies. Bake until golden brown, about 15 minutes; cool. Wrap loosely and store at room temperature no longer than 24 hours. About 4 dozen cookies.

NOTE: Cookies are easier to cut and retain their shape better if cut with an electric knife.

Dipped Fruits

1 package (6 ounces) semisweet chocolate chips
1 tablespoon shortening
12 large strawberries (with stems)
4 squares (2 ounces each) vanilla-flavored candy coating
24 dark sweet cherries (with stems)*
Granulated sugar

Heat chocolate chips and shortening over low heat, stirring occasionally, until melted. Dip each strawberry ¾ of the way into chocolate mixture (top of strawberry should be visible); place on waxed paper-covered cookie sheet.

Heat candy coating over low heat, stirring occasionally, until melted and smooth. Dip cherries into coating, allowing excess to drop off. Dip coated cherries into granulated sugar; place on waxed paper. Refrigerate uncovered until chocolate and coating are firm, at least 30 minutes but no longer than 4 hours. Serve in individual candy paper cups if desired. 36 pieces.

*24 large maraschino cherries (with stems) can be substituted for the dark sweet cherries; drain and pat dry. Continue as directed.

Hot Tea

Place 8 family-size tea bags or 2 ounces (¾ cup) loose tea in large heatproof container. Pour 5 cups boiling water over tea; steep 5 minutes. Remove tea bags or strain tea leaves. Cover and refrigerate no longer than 48 hours.

At serving time, mix 1 part tea concentrate and 3 parts boiling water; mix. Serve with lemon, milk, sugar and honey. 25 servings (about ⅔ cup each).

HIGH TEA

High tea, once the province of the English upper class, is becoming more popular in the United States where more restaurants now offer a high tea from three to six in the afternoon. Now, you can serve a high tea in your home to entertain your guests.

The tidbits should be tempting but not so heavy as to spoil appetites for dinner. Some popular high tea foods are scones, finger sandwiches, pastries and fruit. A pot of good brewed hot tea is essential — select from English, green, oolong, jasmine and many others.

A Dessert Buffet

Menu

24 servings

Brazil Nut Torte (page 36)

Cherry Squares*

Brandy Balls*

Raspberry Strips*

Coconut Meringues*

Chocolate Apricots (page 84)

Candied Citrus Peel*

Fresh Fruit

Mixed Nuts

Coffee   Tea

*****Recipe included**

---

1 week before buffet:
- ☐ Bake Raspberry Strips; freeze.
- ☐ Prepare Brandy Balls; refrigerate.
- ☐ Prepare Candied Citrus Peel; store at room temperature.

1 day before:
- ☐ Bake layers for Brazil Nut Torte; store at room temperature.
- ☐ Bake Cherry Squares; refrigerate.
- ☐ Bake Coconut Meringues; store at room temperature.
- ☐ Prepare Chocolate Apricots; refrigerate.

About 8 hours before serving:
- ☐ Complete Brazil Nut Torte; refrigerate.

About 45 minutes before:
- ☐ Arrange Fresh Fruit on serving plate.
- ☐ Arrange Candied Citrus Peel and Mixed Nuts in serving container.
- ☐ Prepare Coffee and Tea.
- ☐ Arrange Brandy Balls, Raspberry Strips, Coconut Meringues and Chocolate Apricots on serving plates.
- ☐ Cut Cherry Squares; arrange on serving plate.

Cherry Squares

1 cup all-purpose flour
⅓ cup margarine or butter, softened
¼ cup packed brown sugar
1 package (8 ounces) cream cheese, softened
¼ cup granulated sugar
2 teaspoons milk
½ teaspoon vanilla
1 egg
⅓ cup cut-up candied cherries

Heat oven to 350°. Mix flour, margarine and brown sugar. Press in ungreased square pan, 8×8×2 inches. Bake 10 minutes.

Beat remaining ingredients except cherries on low speed, scraping bowl constantly, 30 seconds. Beat on medium speed, scraping bowl occasionally, 1 minute. Stir in cherries. Spread over baked layer. Bake until edges are light brown, about 25 minutes; cool. Cover and refrigerate at least 2 hours but no longer than 24 hours. Cut into 1¼-inch squares. Store in refrigerator. About 3 dozen cookies.

Coconut Meringues, Chocolate Apricots, Raspberry Strips, Cherry Cheesecake Squares, Candied Citrus Peel and Brandy Balls

Raspberry Strips

    1 cup margarine or butter, softened
   ½ cup granulated sugar
   ½ cup packed brown sugar
    1 egg
    1 teaspoon vanilla
 2½ cups all-purpose flour
    1 teaspoon baking powder
   ½ cup raspberry jam
      Vanilla Glaze (below)

Mix margarine, sugars, egg and vanilla. Stir in flour and baking powder. (If dough is soft, cover and refrigerate at least 1 hour.)

Heat oven to 350°. Divide dough into 8 equal parts. Shape each part into strip, 8 × 1½ inches, on ungreased cookie sheet. Make slight indentation down center of each with handle of wooden spoon; fill with 1 measuring tablespoon jam. Bake until edges are light brown, 10 to 12 minutes; cool slightly. Prepare Vanilla Glaze; drizzle over strips. Cut diagonally into 1-inch pieces. Wrap, label and freeze no longer than 1 week.

About 20 minutes before serving, remove from freezer and unwrap. Thaw uncovered at room temperature. About 5 dozen cookies.

Vanilla Glaze

Beat 1 cup powdered sugar, ½ teaspoon vanilla and 2 to 3 teaspoons water until smooth and of desired consistency.

Coconut Meringues

4 egg whites
1¼ cups sugar
½ teaspoon vanilla
¼ teaspoon salt
2½ cups coconut

Heat oven to 325°. Beat egg whites in large bowl on high speed until foamy. Beat in sugar, 1 tablespoon at a time; continue beating until stiff and glossy. Do not underbeat. Stir in vanilla, salt and coconut. Drop mixture by heaping teaspoonfuls about 2 inches apart onto waxed paper-covered or lightly greased cookie sheet. Bake until set and delicate brown, about 20 minutes. Immediately remove from waxed paper; cool. Store in tightly covered container at room temperature no longer than 24 hours. About 3 dozen cookies.

Candied Citrus Peel

3 oranges
3 lemons
1½ cups sugar
¾ cup water
½ cup sugar

Cut peel of each orange and lemon into 4 sections with sharp knife. Remove peel carefully with fingers. Scrape white membrane from peel with spoon (back of peel will appear porous when membrane is removed). Cut peel lengthwise into strips about ¼ inch wide. Heat peel and enough water to cover to boiling in 1½-quart saucepan; reduce heat. Simmer uncovered 30 minutes; drain. Repeat simmering process.

Heat 1½ cups sugar and ¾ cup water to boiling in 1½-quart saucepan, stirring constantly, until sugar is dissolved. Add peel. Simmer uncovered, stirring occasionally, 45 minutes; drain in strainer. Roll peel in ½ cup sugar; spread on waxed paper to dry. Store in tightly covered container at room temperature no longer than 1 week. About 3 cups candies.

Brandy Balls

3 cups finely crushed vanilla wafers (about 75)
2 cups powdered sugar
1 cup finely chopped walnuts (about 4 ounces)
¼ cup cocoa
½ cup brandy
¼ cup light corn syrup
Granulated, powdered or colored sugar

Mix crushed vanilla wafers, powdered sugar, walnuts and cocoa. Stir in brandy and corn syrup. Shape mixture into 1-inch balls. Roll in granulated sugar. Refrigerate in tightly covered container no longer than 1 week. About 5 dozen candies.

DESSERT BUFFETS

Eating sweetmeats was a favorite pastime of the Elizabethans, and this love for sweets came across the ocean with the first new England settlers. Some of the descendants of the "dry sweetmeats" can be found in shops today: glacéed dried fruits, candied orange and lemon peel and such candies as gumdrops, lemon drops and creamy peppermint drops. There also are burnt almonds, sugar-coated almonds and marzipan fruits and vegetables. Add a variety of cookies, fresh fruit and a special cake or torte and you have a dessert buffet that your guests will not soon forget!

A Scandinavian Coffee Party

Menu
24 servings

Strawberry-Meringue Torte*

Kringler*

Marzipan Cream Puffs*

Cardamom Cookies*

Jam Sandwiches*

Spicy Ginger Cookies*

Coffee

*Recipe included

About 1 week before buffet:
- ☐ Bake Cardamom Cookies; freeze.
- ☐ Bake Jam Sandwiches; freeze.
- ☐ Bake Spicy Ginger Cookies; freeze.
- ☐ Bake cream puffs for Marzipan Cream Puffs; freeze.
- ☐ Bake meringue layers for Strawberry-Meringue Torte; freeze.

1 day before:
- ☐ Bake Kringler; store at room temperature.

About 4 hours before serving:
- ☐ Remove cream puffs from freezer.
- ☐ Complete Marzipan Cream Puffs; refrigerate until serving.

About 40 minutes before:
- ☐ Remove meringue layers from freezer. Complete Strawberry-Meringue Torte; refrigerate until serving.
- ☐ Remove Cardamom Cookies, Jam Sandwiches and Spicy Ginger Cookies from freezer; arrange on serving plates. Let stand at room temperature.

About 20 minutes before:
- ☐ Heat Kringler.
- ☐ Prepare Coffee.

Strawberry-Meringue Torte

    4 egg whites
  1/4 teaspoon cream of tartar
  1/2 teaspoon almond extract
    1 cup sugar
1 1/2 cups chilled whipping cream
    3 tablespoons sugar
1 1/2 cups sliced strawberries
    1 whole strawberry

Heat oven to 225°. Cover cookie sheet, 17 × 14 inches, with brown paper. Draw two 8-inch circles on paper. Beat egg whites and cream of tartar until foamy; add almond extract. Beat in 1 cup sugar, 1 tablespoon at a time; continue beating until stiff and glossy. Divide meringue mixture evenly between the 2 circles; spread evenly to fill each circle. Bake 1 1/2 hours. Turn off oven; leave meringues in oven 1 hour with door closed. Finish cooling meringues at room temperature. Carefully remove meringues from paper. Wrap, label and freeze no longer than 1 week.

Remove meringues from freezer. Beat whipping cream and 1/4 cup sugar in chilled 1-quart bowl until stiff. Spread 1 1/2 cups whipped cream on 1 meringue layer. Top with sliced strawberries and remaining meringue layer. Spread 1 1/2 cups whipped cream on top layer. Garnish with mint and strawberry. Refrigerate until serving time.

Kringler, Strawberry-Meringue Torte and Cardamom Cookies

Marzipan Cream Puffs

½ cup water
¼ cup margarine or butter
½ cup all-purpose flour
2 eggs
1 tube (7 ounces) marzipan or almond paste,
    cut into 24 slices
3 cups sweetened whipped cream
    Powdered sugar

Heat oven to 400°. Heat water and margarine to rolling boil in 1½-quart saucepan. Stir in flour. Stir vigorously over low heat until mixture forms a ball, about 1 minute; remove from heat. Beat in eggs, all at once; continue beating until smooth. Drop dough by rounded teaspoonfuls onto ungreased cookie sheet.

Bake until puffed and golden, 25 to 30 minutes. Cool away from draft. Cut off tops; pull out any filaments of soft dough. Wrap, label and freeze no longer than 1 week.

Remove puffs from freezer. Place 1 slice marzipan in bottom half of each puff; top with 2 tablespoons whipped cream and top half of puff. Sprinkle with powdered sugar. Refrigerate until serving time. 24 cream puffs.

Kringler

1 package active dry yeast
¼ cup warm water (105 to 115°)
½ cup lukewarm milk (scalded then cooled)
⅓ cup plus 1 tablespoon sugar
½ teaspoon salt
¼ cup margarine or butter, softened
1 egg, beaten
½ teaspoon ground cardamom
2¼ cups all-purpose flour
1 egg, beaten
¼ cup finely chopped walnuts
2 tablespoons sugar

Dissolve yeast in warm water in large bowl. Stir in milk, ⅓ cup plus 1 tablespoon sugar, the salt, margarine, 1 egg, cardamom and 1¼ cups of the flour. Beat until smooth. Mix in remaining flour. (Dough will be soft and sticky.) Cover; let rise in warm place until double, 1½ to 1¾ hours. (Dough is ready if indentation remains when touched.) Punch down dough; let rise about 1 hour.

Lightly grease cookie sheet, 15 × 10 inches. Turn dough onto lightly floured surface. (If necessary, work in additional flour to make dough easy to handle.) Shape dough into strand, 30 inches long. Twist strand in pretzel shape on cookie sheet (see below); let rise about 30 minutes.

Heat oven to 375°. Brush kringler with 1 egg; sprinkle with walnuts and 2 tablespoons sugar. Bake until golden brown, 25 to 30 minutes; cool. Wrap in aluminum foil and store at room temperature no longer than 24 hours. Before serving, heat foil-wrapped kringler in 350° oven until warm, about 20 minutes.

Shaping Kringler

Bring left end of strand over middle of strand forming a loop.

Bring right end of strand up and over first loop forming a pretzel shape.

Cardamom Cookies

½ cup sugar
½ cup shortening
1 egg
1⅔ cups all-purpose flour
½ cup chopped toasted almonds
1 teaspoon ground cardamom
1 teaspoon ground cinnamon
½ teaspoon baking powder
1 egg yolk
1 tablespoon water
About 42 blanched almonds

Mix sugar, shortening and egg. Stir in flour, chopped almonds, cardamom, cinnamon and baking powder.

Heat oven to 375°. Shape dough into 1-inch balls. Place on ungreased cookie sheet; flatten slightly. Mix egg yolk and water; brush over cookies. Top each with almond. Bake until golden brown, 10 to 12 minutes; cool. Wrap, label and freeze no longer than 1 week.

About 30 minutes before serving, remove from freezer and unwrap. Arrange on serving plate; let stand uncovered at room temperature until thawed. About 3½ dozen cookies.

NOTE: To toast almonds, bake on ungreased cookie sheet in 350° oven, stirring occasionally, until golden brown, about 10 minutes.

Jam Sandwiches

2 cups all-purpose flour
¾ cup margarine or butter, softened
⅓ cup sugar
½ teaspoon salt
2 eggs
Vanilla Glaze (page 126)
¼ cup raspberry jam

Heat oven to 375°. Mix flour, margarine, sugar, salt and eggs. Roll dough ⅛-inch thick on lightly floured surface. Cut into 2-inch circles, hearts or other decorative shapes. Place on ungreased cookie sheet. Bake until set, 8 to 10 minutes; cool. Prepare Vanilla Glaze. Put cookies together in pairs with jam in center; glaze with Vanilla Glaze. Wrap, label and freeze no longer than 1 week.

About 30 minutes before serving, remove from freezer and unwrap. Arrange on serving plate; let stand uncovered at room temperature until thawed. About 2 dozen cookies.

Spicy Ginger Cookies

½ cup packed brown sugar
½ cup molasses
2 tablespoons margarine or butter, softened
2 tablespoons shortening
1 egg
2½ cups all-purpose flour
¼ cup whipping cream
½ teaspoon baking soda
½ teaspoon ground ginger
½ teaspoon ground cinnamon
½ teaspoon grated orange peel
¼ teaspoon salt
¼ teaspoon ground cloves
¼ teaspoon ground allspice
Dash of white pepper

Mix brown sugar, molasses, margarine, shortening and egg. Stir in remaining ingredients. Cover and refrigerate at least 4 hours.

Heat oven to 375°. Roll dough ¼- to ⅛-inch thick on lightly floured cloth-covered board. Cut into 3-inch diamonds with floured cutter. Place 1 inch apart on lightly greased cookie sheet. Bake until no imprint remains when touched lightly, 8 to 10 minutes; cool. Wrap, label and freeze no longer than 1 week.

About 30 minutes before serving, remove from freezer and unwrap. Arrange on serving plate; let stand uncovered at room temperature until thawed. About 4½ dozen cookies.

Lunches

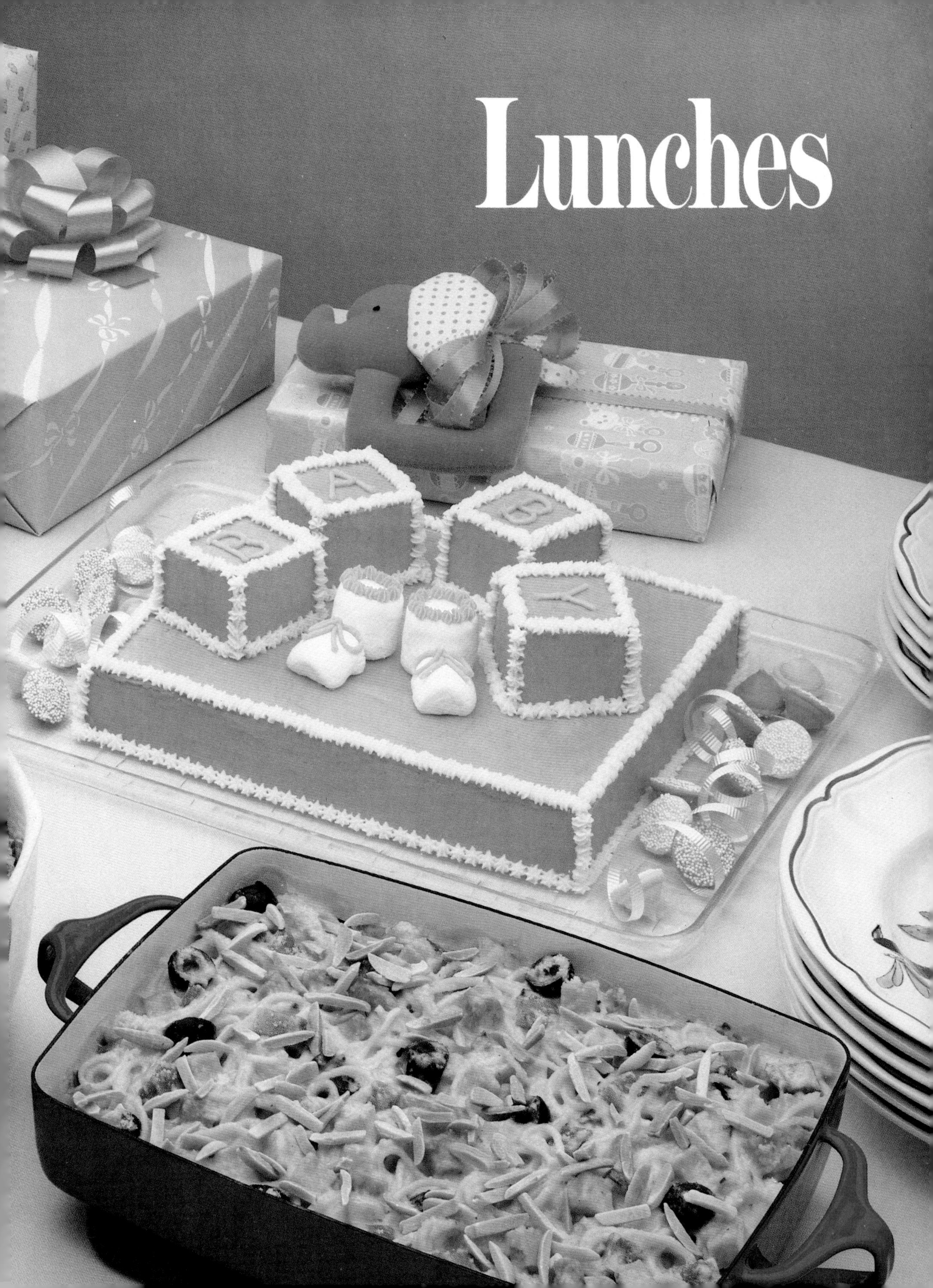

A Baby Shower Luncheon

Menu

12 servings

Strawberry Punch*

Pastel Mints

Mixed Nuts

**Turkey and Ham
Tetrazzini***

Tossed Green Salad

Crusty Bread

Baby Block Cake*

Coffee   Tea

***Recipe included**

---

1 day before buffet:
- ☐ Prepare Turkey and Ham Tetrazzini; refrigerate.
- ☐ Bake and decorate Baby Block Cake; cover and store at room temperature.

Several hours before serving:
- ☐ Prepare strawberry mixture for Strawberry Punch; refrigerate.

When guests arrive:
- ☐ Prepare Strawberry Punch; serve with Pastel Mints and Mixed Nuts.

About 45 minutes before serving:
- ☐ Bake Turkey and Ham Tetrazzini.

About 20 minutes before:
- ☐ Prepare Coffee and Tea.
- ☐ Heat Blue Cheese Bread.
- ☐ Prepare Tossed Green Salad.

A Baby Shower Luncheon

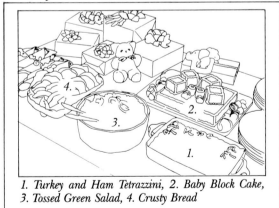

1. Turkey and Ham Tetrazzini, 2. Baby Block Cake,
3. Tossed Green Salad, 4. Crusty Bread

Strawberry Punch

1 pint strawberries, mashed
½ cup powdered sugar
½ cup almond-flavored liqueur
¼ cup lemon juice
1 quart strawberry ice cream, softened
*3 bottles (750 ml each) white catawba grape
    juice or dry white wine, chilled*
1 bottle (28 ounces) ginger ale, chilled
Whole strawberries with stems

Mix mashed strawberries, powdered sugar, liqueur and lemon juice. Cover and refrigerate at least 4 hours but no longer than 6 hours.

Stir together strawberry mixture and ice cream in punch bowl. Add wine and ginger ale; garnish with whole strawberries. 24 servings (about ½ cup each).

Turkey and Ham Tetrazzini

14 ounces uncooked spaghetti
2 cans (10¾ ounces each) condensed cream
    of mushroom soup
2 cans (10¾ ounces each) condensed cream
    of chicken soup
1½ cups milk
¼ cup dry white wine
4 cups cut-up cooked turkey or chicken
1 cup cut-up fully cooked smoked ham
1 medium green pepper, chopped (about 1 cup)
1 cup halved pitted ripe olives
1 cup grated Parmesan cheese
½ cup toasted slivered almonds

Cook spaghetti as directed on package; rinse under running cold water and drain. Mix 1 can mushroom soup, 1 can chicken soup, ¾ cup milk and 2 tablespoons wine in each of 2 ungreased 2-quart casseroles. Stir 2 cups turkey, ½ cup ham, half of the spaghetti, ½ cup green pepper and ½ cup olives into each; sprinkle each with ½ cup cheese. Cover and refrigerate no longer than 24 hours.

Bake uncovered in 375° oven until hot and bubbly, about 40 minutes. Sprinkle each with ¼ cup almonds.

NOTE: To toast almonds, bake on ungreased cookie sheet in 350° oven, stirring occasionally, until golden brown, about 10 minutes.

Shaping Marshmallow Booties

Cut 1 marshmallow into halves. Attach marshmallow half, cut side down, to whole marshmallows.

Baby Block Cake

1 prepared 13 × 9 × 2-inch cake (any flavor)
4½ cups powdered sugar
½ cup shortening
1 teaspoon vanilla
½ teaspoon almond extract
    About 3 tablespoons milk
3 drops blue food color
2 drops red food color
3 large white marshmallows

Cut a 2-inch wide strip from narrow end of cake. Cut strip into four 2-inch squares (see sketch). Freeze remaining cake and the 4 squares uncovered until firm, about 1 hour. (Freezing prevents crumbs from pulling out and into the frosting on cut edges.)

Mix powdered sugar and shortening. Stir in vanilla, almond extract and milk; beat until mixture is smooth and of desired consistency. Remove ⅓ cup frosting; stir in blue food color. Remove 1½ cups frosting; stir in red food color. Leave remaining frosting white.

Place large cake on plate; frost sides and top with pink frosting. Place the 4 squares, one at a time so they do not thaw before frosting, on cake; frost sides and tops of squares with remaining pink frosting.

Place white frosting in decorators' tube or bag fitted with star tip; pipe a border around large cake and up the 4 sides and around top and bottom edges of each of the 4 squares.

Place blue frosting in decorating bag fitted with writing tip. Make 1 letter on top of each of the 4 squares to spell BABY. Cut 1 marshmallow into halves. Attach marshmallow half to each whole marshmallow to make baby bootie, shaping marshmallow half slightly to resemble toe of bootie (see sketch). Moisten marshmallows with warm water, if necessary, to help them adhere. Make a border with blue frosting around top edge of each marshmallow bootie; make a frosting bow where mallows are attached. Place marshmallow booties on cake.

A Special Occasion Luncheon

Menu

8 servings

Chicken Fondue Bake*

Stuffed Tomato Salads*

Spiced Muffins*

Oranges in Syrup*

Coconut Thins*

Coffee   Tea

*Recipe included

Several days before buffet:
- ☐ Bake Coconut Thins; store at room temperature.

2 days before:
- ☐ Prepare Oranges in Syrup; refrigerate.

1 day before:
- ☐ Prepare Chicken Fondue Bake for baking; refrigerate.
- ☐ Prepare Stuffed Tomato Salads; refrigerate.

About 1 hour before serving:
- ☐ Bake Spice Muffins; remove from oven. Reduce oven temperature to 350°.
- ☐ Bake Chicken Fondue Bake.
- ☐ Prepare Coffee and Tea.

Chicken Fondue Bake

16 chicken thighs (about 4 pounds)
⅓ cup all-purpose flour
1 teaspoon salt
¼ teaspoon pepper
2 tablespoons margarine or butter
2 tablespoons vegetable oil
1 can (14 ounces) artichoke hearts, drained and cut into fourths
8 slices bacon, crisply fried and crumbled
   Fondue Sauce (right)
   Paprika

Remove skin and bones from chicken thighs. Mix flour, salt and pepper; coat chicken with flour mixture. Heat margarine and oil over medium heat in 12-inch skillet until margarine is melted. Cook half of the chicken, turning occasionally, until light brown, about 15 minutes. Repeat with remaining chicken. Arrange chicken in ungreased rectangular baking dish, 13 × 9 × 2 inches.

Place artichokes on chicken; sprinkle with bacon. Prepare Fondue Sauce; pour over bacon. Sprinkle with paprika. Cover and refrigerate no longer than 24 hours.

Bake uncovered in 350° oven until hot and bubbly, 30 to 35 minutes.

Fondue Sauce

3 tablespoons margarine or butter
3 tablespoons all-purpose flour
¼ teaspoon salt
   Dash of pepper
   Dash of ground nutmeg
1½ cups milk
⅓ cup dry white wine
1½ cups shredded Swiss cheese (6 ounces)

Heat margarine in 1½-quart saucepan until melted. Blend in flour, salt, pepper and nutmeg. Cook over low heat, stirring constantly, until smooth and bubbly; remove from heat. Stir in milk and wine. Heat to boiling, stirring constantly. Boil and stir 1 minute; remove from heat. Stir in cheese until melted.

Clockwise from top of plate: Spiced Muffin, Stuffed Tomato Salad and Chicken Fondue Bake

Stuffed Tomato Salads

8 large tomatoes, cut into halves
1 can (16 ounces) whole kernel corn, drained
1 small green pepper, chopped (about 1/2 cup)
1/4 cup sliced green onions
1/3 cup vegetable oil
2 tablespoons snipped parsley
2 tablespoons vinegar
1 teaspoon dried basil leaves
1/2 teaspoon salt

Remove pulp from each tomato half, leaving a 1/4-inch wall; chop enough pulp to measure 1/2 cup. Mix pulp with remaining ingredients. Fill tomatoes with corn mixture. Cover and refrigerate at least 3 hours but no longer than 24 hours.

Spice Muffins

2 cups buttermilk baking mix
1/2 cup chopped pecans
1/4 cup sugar
2/3 cup cold water or milk
1 teaspoon ground cinnamon
1 teaspoon ground allspice
1 egg
2 teaspoons sugar

Heat oven to 400°. Grease bottoms only of 12 medium muffin cups, 2½ × 1¼ inches. Mix baking mix, pecans, 1/4 cup sugar, the water, cinnamon, allspice and egg; beat vigorously 30 seconds. Fill muffin cups about 2/3 full. Sprinkle with 2 teaspoons sugar. Bake until golden brown, about 15 minutes. 12 muffins.

Oranges in Syrup

6 seedless oranges
1 cup water
2/3 cup sugar

Cut thin slivers of peel from 2 oranges with vegetable parer or sharp knife, being careful not to cut into white membrane. Cover peel with boiling water. Let stand 5 minutes; drain. Heat orange peel, water and sugar to boiling; reduce heat. Simmer uncovered until slightly thickened, 15 to 20 minutes; cool.

Pare oranges, cutting deep enough to remove all white membrane. Cut into slices. Pour syrup over slices. Cover and refrigerate at least 4 hours but no longer than 48 hours. Garnish with mint leaves if desired.

Coconut Thins

2 cups sugar
2 cups margarine or butter, softened
1 cup flaked coconut
1 teaspoon vanilla
3 cups all-purpose flour
1 teaspoon baking soda
1/2 teaspoon salt

Heat oven to 350°. Mix sugar, margarine, coconut and vanilla. Stir in remaining ingredients. Shape dough by rounded teaspoonfuls into balls. Place about 3 inches apart on ungreased cookie sheet. Flatten cookies with greased bottom of glass dipped in sugar. Bake until edges are golden brown, 8 to 10 minutes. Cool slightly before removing from cookie sheet; cool. Store in loosely covered container at room temperature no longer than 1 week. About 8 dozen cookies.

Marinated Onions with Cheese, Fresh Fruit Platter and Chicken and Shrimp Shells

A Bridal Shower Luncheon

Menu

12 servings

Sparkling Cranberry Punch*

Chicken and Shrimp Shells*

Marinated Onions with Cheese*

Fresh Fruit Platter

Ginger Ice Cream*

Wedding Teacakes*

Coffee   Tea

*Recipe included

1 month before buffet:
- ☐ Bake Wedding Teacakes; freeze.

2 days before:
- ☐ Prepare Ginger Ice Cream; freeze.

1 day before:
- ☐ Prepare chicken mixture for Chicken and Shrimp Shells; refrigerate.
- ☐ Prepare Marinated Onions with Cheese; refrigerate.
- ☐ Refrigerate cranberry juice cocktail, frozen lemonade concentrate and ginger ale for Sparkling Cranberry Punch.
- ☐ Scoop ice cream balls; freeze.

Several hours before serving:
- ☐ Bake patty shells for Chicken and Shrimp Shells.
- ☐ Assemble Fresh Fruit Platter; cover and refrigerate.

When guests arrive:
- ☐ Prepare Sparkling Cranberry Punch.

About 20 minutes before serving:
- ☐ Remove Wedding Teacakes from freezer.
- ☐ Complete Chicken and Shrimp Shells.
- ☐ Prepare Coffee and Tea.

At dessert time:
- ☐ Serve Ginger Ice Cream with Wedding Teacakes.

Sparkling Cranberry Punch

1 quart cranberry juice cocktail, chilled
1 can (6 ounces) frozen pink lemonade
    concentrate, thawed
2 quarts ginger ale or 2 bottles (750 ml each)
    champagne, chilled

Mix cranberry juice cocktail and lemonade concentrate in large punch bowl. Stir in ginger ale; serve immediately. 25 servings (about ½ cup each).

Chicken and Shrimp Shells

2 cups chicken broth
3 tablespoons cornstarch
1 package (8 ounces) cream cheese, softened
1 can (13 ounces) evaporated milk
3 cups cut-up cooked chicken or turkey
2 to 4 tablespoons snipped chives
1 can (about 4½ ounces) small shrimp, drained
1 can (4 ounces) mushroom stems and pieces,
    undrained
1 jar (2 ounces) diced pimientos, drained
2 packages (10 ounces each) frozen patty shells
    (12 shells)

Stir chicken broth gradually into cornstarch in 3-quart saucepan. Add cream cheese and milk. Heat to boiling, stirring constantly. Boil and stir 1 minute. Stir in chicken, chives, shrimp, mushrooms and pimientos. Cover and refrigerate no longer than 24 hours.

Bake patty shells as directed on package. Store uncovered at room temperature no longer than 4 hours. Heat chicken mixture, stirring occasionally, to boiling; reduce heat. Simmer uncovered until chicken and shrimp are hot, about 15 minutes. Serve chicken mixture with patty shells. Garnish with snipped chives or sprinkle with paprika if desired.

Marinated Onions with Cheese

1 cup olive or vegetable oil
¼ cup lemon juice
1½ teaspoons salt
1 teaspoon sugar
    Dash of pepper
    Dash of paprika
4 ounces blue cheese, crumbled
4 medium onions, thinly sliced

Shake oil, lemon juice, salt, sugar, pepper and paprika in tightly covered container. Sprinkle cheese over onions in glass or plastic bowl. Pour oil mixture over cheese and onions. Cover and refrigerate at least 4 hours but no longer than 24 hours.

Remove onions and cheese with slotted spoon; serve on lettuce leaves if desired.

NOTE: To crumble blue cheese, freeze first (it is easier to handle). After crumbling, wrap and freeze. Separate into pieces before sprinkling over onions.

Ginger Ice Cream

1 jar (2.7 ounces) crystallized ginger
½ cup sugar
¼ teaspoon salt
1 cup milk
3 egg yolks, beaten
1 tablespoon rum
2 cups chilled whipping cream

Place ginger in blender container. Cover and blend on medium-high speed, stopping blender occasionally to scrape sides, until a paste consistency, about 30 seconds.

For crank-type freezer: Mix sugar, salt, milk and egg yolks in saucepan. Cook over medium heat, stirring constantly, just until bubbles appear around edge; cool. Stir in rum, ginger and whipping cream. Pour into freezer can; put dasher in place. Cover and adjust crank.

Ginger Ice Cream

Place can in freezer tub. Fill freezer tub ⅓ full of ice; add remaining ice alternately with layers of rock salt (6 parts ice to 1 part rock salt). Turn crank until it turns with difficulty. Drain water from freezer tub. Remove lid from freezer can; take out dasher. Pack mixture down. Repack in ice and rock salt. Let ripen several hours. 1 quart.

For refrigerator: Mix sugar, salt, milk and egg yolks in saucepan. Cook over medium heat, stirring constantly, just until bubbles appear around edge; cool. Stir in rum and ginger. Pour into refrigerator tray. Freeze until mixture is mushy and partially frozen, ½ to 1 hour. Beat whipping cream until soft peaks form. Spoon partially frozen mixture into chilled bowl; beat until smooth. Fold in whipped cream. Pour into two refrigerator trays; cover to prevent crystals from forming. Freeze, stirring frequently during first hours, until firm, 3 to 4 hours. Keep trays covered with waxed paper to help prevent crystals from forming. 1 quart.

Wedding Teacakes

   1 cup margarine or butter, softened
  ½ cup powdered sugar
   1 teaspoon vanilla
2¼ cups all-purpose flour
  ¼ teaspoon salt
  ¾ cup finely chopped nuts
      Powdered sugar

Heat oven to 400°. Mix margarine, ½ cup powdered sugar and the vanilla. Stir in flour, salt and nuts. Shape dough into 1-inch balls.

Bake on ungreased cookie sheet until set but not brown, 8 to 9 minutes. Roll in powdered sugar while warm. Cool; roll in powdered sugar again. Wrap, label and freeze no longer than 1 month.

Remove cookies from freezer and unwrap. Arrange cookies on serving plate; let stand uncovered at room temperature until thawed, about 30 minutes. About 4 dozen cookies.

A Warm Weather Luncheon

Menu

10 servings

Layered Chicken Salad*

Ripe Olives Pickled Corn

Cornmeal Squares*

Toasted English Muffins

Fruit Fluff Dessert*

Iced Tea

Lemonade

*Recipe included

---

2 days before buffet:
- [ ] Prepare Fruit Fluff Dessert; refrigerate.

1 day before:
- [ ] Prepare Layered Chicken Salad; refrigerate.

4 hours before serving:
- [ ] Prepare Cornmeal Squares for baking; refrigerate.
- [ ] Prepare Iced Tea and Lemonade; refrigerate.
- [ ] Prepare fruit for Fruit Fluff Dessert; refrigerate.

About 20 minutes before:
- [ ] Bake Cornmeal Squares.
- [ ] Prepare Toasted English Muffins.
- [ ] Arrange Ripe Olives and Pickled Corn in serving containers.

At dessert time:
- [ ] Complete Fruit Fluff Dessert.

Layered Chicken Salad

Layered Chicken Salad

1 medium head lettuce, torn into bite-size pieces
    (about 7 cups)
1 can (20 ounces) white kidney beans, drained
1 small red onion, thinly sliced and separated
    into rings
3 cups cut-up cooked chicken or turkey
2 small zucchini, thinly sliced
1 cup shredded Monterey Jack or Cheddar cheese
    (4 ounces)
½ pound thinly sliced salami, cut into fourths
2 cups cherry tomatoes, cut into halves
2 cups mayonnaise or salad dressing
2 tablespoons prepared mustard
1 teaspoon prepared horseradish

Place about half of the lettuce in 5-quart glass bowl. Top with a layer of beans, onion, chicken, zucchini, cheese, salami, remaining lettuce and tomatoes. Mix mayonnaise, mustard and horseradish; spread over tomatoes, sealing to edge of bowl. Cover and refrigerate at least 8 hours but no longer than 24 hours.

Garnish with additional cherry tomatoes and parsley or watercress if desired.

Cornmeal Squares

1 tablespoon cornmeal
1½ cups buttermilk baking mix
½ cup cornmeal
½ cup milk
½ cup margarine or butter, softened
1 teaspoon cornmeal

Grease cookie sheet; sprinkle with 1 tablespoon cornmeal. Mix baking mix, ½ cup cornmeal and the milk with fork until soft dough forms. Pat dough on cookie sheet into rectangle, 10 × 8 inches. Cover and refrigerate no longer than 4 hours.

Heat oven to 450°. Bake until set, about 10 minutes. Brush with margarine and sprinkle with 1 teaspoon cornmeal. Cut into squares. Serve warm.

Fruit Fluff Dessert

2½ cups all-purpose flour
¼ cup sugar
½ teaspoon salt
⅓ cup firm margarine or butter
1 package (8 ounces) cream cheese, softened
¾ cup sugar
1 teaspoon vanilla
2 cups chilled whipping cream
2½ cups miniature marshmallows
5 cups fresh fruit (sliced bananas or
    strawberries, halved seedless grapes,
    pineapple chunks, raspberries or
    blueberries)

Mix flour, ¼ cup sugar and the salt. Cut in margarine until mixture is crumbly. Press in ungreased rectangular pan, 13 × 9 × 2 inches. Bake in 375° oven until light brown, about 20 minutes; cool.

Mix cream cheese, ¾ cup sugar and the vanilla in 4-quart bowl. Beat whipping cream in chilled bowl until stiff. Fold whipped cream and marshmallows into cream cheese mixture; spread over crust. Cover and refrigerate at least 8 hours but no longer than 48 hours.

Cut into about 2½-inch squares; serve with fruit. Refrigerate any remaining dessert.

DECORATIVE BUTTERS

Fancy cuts or shapes of butter are easy and can add that special touch to any buffet table.

- Cut a stick of firm butter into serving-size pieces. Dip a salad fork into warm water and pull the tines across the surface of the butter to form a wavy pattern.

- Use a melon baller, dipped in warm water, to scoop out balls of butter. Refrigerate or freeze until serving time.

- Cut a stick of firm butter into pats. Top each pat with a small piece of fresh herb, such as basil, mint or parsley, or watercress.

- Push softened butter through a decorating bag fitted with a decorating tip into serving size pieces. Refrigerate or freeze until firm.

A Teen Get-Together

3 days before buffet:
- ☐ Prepare Ice Bowl for Build-a-Sundae; freeze.

2 days before:
- ☐ Prepare Peanut Butter Bars; refrigerate.

1 day before:
- ☐ Scoop ice-cream balls for Build-a-Sundae; freeze.
- ☐ Prepare Carrot Sticks and Celery Sticks; cover with ice water and refrigerate.
- ☐ Prepare beef patties for Maxi Burger for baking; refrigerate.

About 30 minutes before serving:
- ☐ Bake beef patties for Maxi Burger.
- ☐ Unmold Ice Bowl; freeze.
- ☐ Place chips and vegetable sticks in serving containers.
- ☐ Serve Assorted Fruit Juices and Milk.

At dessert time:
- ☐ Complete Build-a-Sundae; serve with Peanut Butter Bars.

Maxi Burger

2   *pounds ground beef*
¼   *cup water*
1   *egg*
1½ *teaspoons salt*
¼   *teaspoon pepper*
6   *slices American processed cheese*
1   *round loaf unsliced bread, about 7 inches in diameter*
1   *cup shredded lettuce*
1   *medium tomato, thinly sliced*
    Hamburger pickles
1   *small onion, chopped (about ¼ cup)*
    Catsup
    Mustard

Mix ground beef, water, egg, salt and pepper; divide into halves. Spread each half in un-greased pie plate, 10 × 1½ inches, or shape into 9-inch patty in ungreased jelly roll pan, 15½ × 10½ × 1 inch. Cover and refrigerate no longer than 24 hours.

Bake uncovered in 350° oven until desired doneness (about 30 minutes for medium); drain off fat. Arrange cheese on top of one patty; return to oven just until soft, about 5 minutes.

Cut bread horizontally into 3 slices. Place plain beef patty on bottom slice; arrange lettuce and tomato on top. Place center bread slice on tomato; top with remaining patty. Top with pickles, onion, catsup and mustard. Place remaining bread slice on top; secure with eight 6-inch skewers. To serve, cut into wedges.

Maxi Burger

Peanut Butter Bars

1¼ cups creamy peanut butter
½ cup margarine or butter, softened
4 cups honey graham cereal, crushed
2 cups powdered sugar
1 tablespoon shortening
1 package (5.75 ounces) milk chocolate chips
    (about 1 cup)

Mix peanut butter and margarine in large bowl. Stir in cereal. Mix in powdered sugar, ⅓ at a time. Press mixture firmly in ungreased square pan, 9 × 9 × 2 inches.

Heat shortening in 1-quart saucepan over low heat until melted. Add chocolate chips. Heat over very low heat, stirring constantly, until chocolate chips are melted and mixture is smooth. Spread chocolate over mixture in pan. Cover and refrigerate until chilled, about 1 hour but no longer than 2 days.

Remove from refrigerator 10 minutes before serving. Cut into bars, about 2¼ × 1½ inches. Refrigerate any remaining bars. 24 bars.

PEANUT BUTTER CRUNCH CUPS: Press about 2 tablespoons cereal mixture in each of 24 to 30 small foil or paper baking cups.

Build-a-Sundae

Ice Bowl (below)
1 quart vanilla ice cream
1 quart chocolate ice cream
    Toppings (ice-cream sauces, chopped nuts,
    maraschino cherries, chocolate chips,
    bananas, granola, whipped topping)

Prepare Ice Bowl. Scoop ice cream into balls and place on chilled cookie sheet. Freeze uncovered no longer than 24 hours.

At serving time, place ice-cream balls in Ice Bowl; serve with several Toppings.

Ice Bowl

Place 1½-quart metal bowl in 3½-quart metal bowl. Holding small bowl down, pour water into large bowl until water between 2 bowls is about 1 inch wide. Fill small bowl with enough water to hold it down. Hold edges of bowls in place with 2 to 4 strips masking tape. Freeze at least 12 hours but no longer than 3 days.

To unmold, run small amount hot water into small bowl until it can be lifted out. Place large bowl in hot water for a few minutes; remove bowl from ice. Place Ice Bowl on plate or tray; return to freezer until serving time.

Chili con Carne, Assorted Relishes and Corn Muffin

A TV Sports Event Buffet

It is always more fun to watch a sports event on television with other sports enthusiasts. So invite some friends over and enjoy your favorite spectator sport along with good food. Start with chilled beverages and snacks during the program and top off the event with easy do-ahead Chili con Carne and warm Corn Muffins. Both you and your guests will sit back, relax and enjoy the event with Hot Fudge Sundae Cake and coffee.

Menu
8 servings

Chilled Beverages

Salted Nuts, Chips and Pretzels

Chili con Carne*

Corn Muffins*

Assorted Relishes

Hot Fudge Sundae Cake*

Coffee

***Recipe included**

2 days before buffet:
- ☐ Prepare Chili con Carne; refrigerate.

Several hours before serving:
- ☐ Prepare Assorted Relishes; cover with ice water and refrigerate.
- ☐ Scoop ice cream for Hot Fudge Sundae Cake; freeze.

When guests arrive:
- ☐ Serve beverages with Salted Nuts, Chips and Pretzels.

About 1 hour before serving:
- ☐ Bake Hot Fudge Sundae Cake; remove from oven. Increase oven temperature to 450°.

About 30 minutes before:
- ☐ Heat Chili con Carne.
- ☐ Bake Corn Muffins.
- ☐ Arrange Assorted Relishes in serving containers.
- ☐ Assemble Toppings for Chili con Carne.
- ☐ Prepare Coffee.

Chili con Carne

3 pounds beef boneless round steak, cut into
   1/2-inch cubes
3 tablespoons vegetable oil
1/2 cup snipped parsley
3 cups water
1 tablespoon paprika
1 tablespoon dried oregano leaves
2 teaspoons ground cumin
1 1/2 teaspoons salt
1 to 2 teaspoons dried crushed red pepper
3/4 teaspoon ground coriander
3 large cloves garlic, crushed
2 medium green peppers, chopped (about 2
   cups)
2 medium onions, chopped
1 large bay leaf, finely crushed
3 cans (10 1/2 ounces each) condensed beef
   broth
3 cans (15 1/2 ounces each) garbanzo beans,
   drained
   Toppings (below)

Cook and stir beef in oil in 4-quart Dutch oven over medium heat until light brown. Stir in remaining ingredients except beans and Toppings. Heat to boiling; reduce heat. Cover and simmer, stirring occasionally, 1 hour. Uncover and simmer, stirring occasionally, until mixture is thickened and beef is tender, about 45 minutes longer. Stir in beans. Cover and refrigerate no longer than 48 hours.

Remove excess fat from Chili con Carne. Heat chili to boiling; reduce heat. Cover and simmer, stirring occasionally, until beef is hot, about 20 minutes. Serve with Toppings.

Toppings

1 cup shredded Cheddar or Monterey Jack cheese
   (4 ounces)
1 cup dairy sour cream
1 medium avocado, chopped

Corn Muffins

1 1/2 cups cornmeal
1/2 cup all-purpose flour
1/4 cup shortening
1 1/2 cups buttermilk
2 teaspoons baking powder
1 teaspoon sugar
1 teaspoon salt
1/2 teaspoon baking soda
2 eggs

Heat oven to 450°. Grease 12 medium muffin cups, 2 1/2 × 1 1/4 inches. Mix all ingredients; beat vigorously 30 seconds. Fill cups about 7/8 full. Bake until golden brown, about 20 minutes. 12 muffins.

Hot Fudge Sundae Cake

Ice cream
1 cup all-purpose flour
3/4 cup granulated sugar
2 tablespoons cocoa
2 teaspoons baking powder
1/4 teaspoon salt
1/2 cup milk
2 tablespoons vegetable oil
1 teaspoon vanilla
1 cup chopped nuts, if desired
1 cup packed brown sugar
1/4 cup cocoa
1 3/4 cups hottest tap water

Scoop ice cream into 8 servings and place on chilled cookie sheet. Freeze uncovered no longer than 24 hours.

Heat oven to 350°. Stir together flour, granulated sugar, 2 tablespoons cocoa, the baking powder and salt in ungreased square pan, 9 × 9 × 2 inches. Mix in milk, oil and vanilla with fork until smooth. Stir in nuts. Spread evenly in pan. Sprinkle with brown sugar and 1/4 cup cocoa. Pour hot water over batter.

Bake 40 minutes. Let stand 15 minutes; spoon into individual dishes. Top with ice cream and spoon sauce over each serving.

A Southern-Style Buffet

Enjoy a southern lunch during the famous Kentucky Derby on the first Saturday of May. The next best thing to being there is watching it on television. So, no matter what part of the country you live in, turn on the television and serve traditional Mint Juleps. After the race, serve your guests pork sandwiches, grits and the renowned Louisville Pecan Pie.

Menu

10 servings

Mint Juleps*

Barbecued Pork Sandwiches*

Cheese Grits Casserole*

Cabbage Slaw

Louisville Pecan Pie*

Coffee   Tea

*Recipe included

1 or two days before buffet:
- ☐ Prepare mint mixture for Mint Juleps.

1 day before:
- ☐ Prepare pork mixture for Barbecued Pork Sandwiches; cover and refrigerate.
- ☐ Prepare Cheese Grits Casserole for baking; refrigerate.
- ☐ Bake Louisville Pecan Pie; refrigerate.

When guests arrive:
- ☐ Serve Mint Juleps.

About 1 hour before serving:
- ☐ Bake Cheese Grits Casserole.

About 20 minutes before:
- ☐ Complete Barbecued Pork Sandwiches.
- ☐ Prepare Coffee and Tea.
- ☐ Spoon Cabbage Slaw into serving dish.

Mint Juleps

Mint Juleps

½ cup sugar
½ cup water
2 cups mint leaves
  Crushed ice
  Bourbon

Heat sugar and water to boiling. Boil 5 minutes; cool. Place mint leaves in 1-quart container; pour syrup over mint leaves. Cover tightly and refrigerate at least 12 hours but no longer than 24 hours.

Strain mint mixture. For each Mint Julep, fill 12-ounce glass with crushed ice. Add 1½ teaspoons mint mixture and 2 ounces bourbon. Stir with an up-and-down action with long-handled spoon until frost forms on outside of glass. Serve with straw.

Barbecued Pork Sandwiches

4 pounds fresh pork boneless blade, Boston or
    arm picnic roast
  Salt and pepper
¼ cup packed brown sugar
¼ cup vinegar
¼ cup molasses
2 tablespoons dry mustard
1 tablespoon Worcestershire sauce
½ teaspoon salt
¼ teaspoon liquid smoke
¼ teaspoon red pepper sauce
2 cloves garlic, crushed
1 bottle (12 ounces) chili sauce
1 can (8 ounces) tomato sauce
10 hamburger buns

Place pork, fat side up, on rack in shallow roasting pan; sprinkle with salt and pepper. Insert meat thermometer so tip is in center of thickest part of pork and does not rest in fat.

Roast uncovered in 325° oven until thermometer registers 170°, about 2½ hours. Cool; shred into pieces with 2 forks. Heat remaining ingredients except hamburger buns to boiling in 3-quart saucepan. Cook, stirring occasionally, until thickened, about 20 minutes. Stir in shredded pork. Cover and refrigerate no longer than 24 hours.

Heat pork mixture to boiling over medium heat, stirring occasionally; reduce heat. Simmer uncovered until hot, about 15 minutes. Serve pork mixture with buns.

Cheese Grits Casserole

5 cups water
1½ cups quick-cooking grits
2 cups shredded Cheddar cheese (8 ounces)
¼ cup margarine or butter
1 teaspoon salt
¼ teaspoon red pepper sauce
2 cloves garlic, crushed
3 eggs, slightly beaten

Heat water to boiling in 3-quart saucepan. Gradually stir in grits. Heat to boiling; reduce heat. Cook uncovered, stirring occasionally, until thick, about 5 minutes. Stir in cheese, margarine, salt, pepper sauce and garlic. Stir about ¼ of the hot mixture into eggs; stir into remaining hot mixture in saucepan. Spread in ungreased rectangular baking dish, 11 × 7 × 1½ inches. Cover and refrigerate no longer than 24 hours.

Bake uncovered in 350° oven until firm and cracks feel dry, 55 to 60 minutes.

Louisville Pecan Pie

  Pastry for 9-inch one-crust pie
½ cup sugar
¼ cup margarine or butter, melted
1 cup dark corn syrup
¼ cup bourbon
1 teaspoon vanilla
¼ teaspoon salt
3 eggs
1 package (6 ounces) semisweet chocolate chips
1 cup pecan halves or pieces

Heat oven to 375°. Prepare pastry. Beat sugar, margarine, corn syrup, bourbon, vanilla, salt and eggs with hand beater. Stir in chocolate chips and pecans. Pour into pastry-lined pie plate. Cover edge with 2- to 3-inch strip of aluminum foil to prevent excessive browning; remove foil last 10 minutes of baking. Bake until set, 40 to 45 minutes; cool. Cover and refrigerate no longer than 24 hours.

Serve with sweetened whipped cream if desired. Refrigerate any remaining pie.

Waldorf Cabbage Salad, Cauliflower and Peas and Impossible Ham Pie

A Back-to-School Lunch

Be the first to launch an annual event — a back-to-school lunch. On the day when all children in the neighborhood return to school, invite their parents to share a good lunch and conversation on your first quiet afternoon since school was out in the spring. They'll all appreciate your thoughtfulness.

Menu

12 servings

Impossible Ham Pie*

Cauliflower and Peas

Waldorf Cabbage Salad*

Brandied Peach Shortcake*

Coffee   Tea

***Recipe included**

Several days before buffet:
- ☐ Prepare peaches for Brandied Peach Shortcake; refrigerate.

1 day before:
- ☐ Prepare cabbage and Creamy Dressing for Waldorf Cabbage Salad; refrigerate.
- ☐ Prepare ham mixture for Impossible Ham Pie; refrigerate.

About 45 minutes before serving:
- ☐ Bake Impossible Ham Pie.

About 15 minutes before:
- ☐ Cook Cauliflower and Peas.
- ☐ Complete Waldorf Cabbage Salad.
- ☐ Prepare Coffee and Tea.

At dessert time:
- ☐ Complete Brandied Peach Shortcake.

Impossible Ham Pie

4 cups cut-up fully cooked smoked ham
2 cans (4 ounces each) mushroom stems and
    pieces, drained
1 jar (2 ounces) diced pimientos, drained
⅔ cup sliced green onions (with tops)
2 cups shredded natural Swiss cheese (8
    ounces)
3 cups milk
1½ cups buttermilk baking mix
6 eggs

Divide ham, mushrooms, pimientos, onions
and cheese between 2 lightly greased pie
plates, 10 × 1½ inches. Cover and refrigerate
no longer than 24 hours.

Beat remaining ingredients with hand beater
until smooth. Divide mixture between pie
plates. Bake in 400° oven until golden brown
and knife inserted halfway between center
and edge comes out clean, 30 to 35 minutes.
Let stand 5 minutes before cutting. Garnish
with green onions and pimientos if desired.
Refrigerate any remaining pie.

Waldorf Cabbage Salad

Creamy Dressing (right)
1 head green cabbage (about 2 pounds), coarsely
    shredded (about 8 cups)
½ cup coarsely chopped walnuts
2 apples
2 cups seedless grapes

Prepare Creamy Dressing. Place cabbage in
plastic bag. Fasten bag and refrigerate no
longer than 24 hours.

Toss cabbage and walnuts with dressing.
Spoon into serving bowl or onto large plate.
Cut apples into thin slices. (To prevent apples
from discoloring, sprinkle with fruit protector
or lemon juice.) Arrange apples and grapes on
cabbage mixture.

Creamy Dressing

1 cup mayonnaise or salad dressing
2 tablespoons sugar
2 tablespoons lemon juice
1 tablespoon milk
½ teaspoon salt

Mix all ingredients. Cover and refrigerate at
least 1 hour but no longer than 24 hours.

Brandied Peach Shortcake

1 can (29 ounces) sliced peaches
½ cup brandy
1 cup whipping cream
2 tablespoons powdered sugar
1 teaspoon brandy
1 prepared white angel food cake

Drain peaches, reserving 2 cups syrup. Place
peaches in glass bowl or jar. Heat reserved
syrup and ½ cup brandy to boiling; pour over
peaches. Cover and refrigerate at least 24
hours but no longer than 2 weeks.

Beat whipping cream, powdered sugar and 1
teaspoon brandy in chilled bowl until stiff.
Serve cake with peaches and whipped cream.

An Election Day Luncheon

Menu

8 servings

Rice-Sausage Casserole*

Braised Celery and Tomatoes*

Tossed Green Salad

Croissants

Fruit Tart (page 24)

Coffee   Tea

*Recipe included

1 day before buffet:
- ☐ Prepare Rice-Sausage Casserole for baking; refrigerate.
- ☐ Prepare greens for Tossed Salad; refrigerate.
- ☐ Prepare Fruit Tart; refrigerate.

About 1 hour before serving:
- ☐ Bake Rice-Sausage Casserole.

About 15 minutes before:
- ☐ Prepare Coffee and Tea.
- ☐ Cook Braised Celery and Tomatoes.
- ☐ Arrange Croissants in serving container.
- ☐ Complete Tossed Green Salad.

At dessert time:
- ☐ Serve Fruit Tart

Rice-Sausage Casserole

- 2 *pounds bulk pork sausage*
- 1 *medium onion, chopped (about ½ cup)*
- 2 *cups cooked wild rice*
- 2 *cups cooked white rice*
- ½ *cup shredded Swiss cheese (2 ounces)*
- 1½ *cups milk*
- 1 *small green pepper, chopped (about ½ cup)*
- 1 *can (10¾ ounces) condensed cream of chicken soup*
- 1 *can (4 ounces) mushroom stems and pieces, drained*
- 1 *jar (2 ounces) diced pimientos, drained*
- ¼ *cup toasted sliced almonds*

Cook and stir sausage and onion in 4-quart Dutch oven until sausage is brown; drain. Stir in wild rice, white rice, cheese, milk, green pepper, soup, mushrooms and pimientos. Pour into ungreased 3-quart casserole. Cover and refrigerate no longer than 24 hours.

Bake covered in 350° oven until center is bubbly, about 1 hour; stir. Sprinkle with almonds. Garnish with green pepper rings if desired.

Braised Celery and Tomatoes

- 6 *stalks celery, cut diagonal into 1-inch pieces*
- 1 *small onion, thinly sliced*
- ¼ *cup margarine or butter*
- ¼ *cup water*
- 1 *teaspoon instant chicken bouillon*
- 1 *pint cherry tomatoes, cut into halves*

Cook and stir celery and onion in margarine in 10-inch skillet over medium heat until celery is crisp-tender, about 5 minutes. Add water and bouillon (dry). Heat to boiling; reduce heat. Simmer uncovered until celery is tender, about 5 minutes. Add cherry tomatoes. Cook until heated through, about 3 minutes.

A Bridge Luncheon

Menu

8 servings

Shrimp Bisque*

Puff Sandwich Loaf*

Melon Compotes*

Sugar Cookies

*Recipe included

Several hours before serving:
- ☐ Scoop sherbet for Melon Compotes; freeze.
- ☐ Prepare melon for Melon Compotes; cover and refrigerate.

About 20 minutes before:
- ☐ Bake Puff Sandwich Loaf.
- ☐ Heat Shrimp Bisque.

At dessert time:
- ☐ Complete Melon Compotes; serve with Sugar Cookies.

Shrimp Bisque

2 cups half-and-half
2 cans (11 ounces each) condensed tomato bisque
½ cup dry white wine
1 can (4½ ounces) small shrimp, drained

Heat half-and-half and bisque just to boiling in 3-quart saucepan over medium heat. Stir in wine and shrimp. Heat until hot (do not boil).

Puff Sandwich Loaf

2½ cups buttermilk baking mix
1½ cups mayonnaise or salad dressing
½ teaspoon salt
2 eggs
4 cups shredded Swiss cheese (16 ounces)
2 avocados, chopped
1 medium zucchini, chopped
1 loaf (1 pound) French bread
1 cup alfalfa sprouts

Mix baking mix, mayonnaise, salt and eggs. Stir in cheese, avocados and zucchini. Cut bread crosswise into halves; cut each half lengthwise into halves. Divide cheese mixture among bread pieces, spreading evenly to edges.

Heat oven to 450°. Bake on ungreased cookie sheet until puffy and golden brown, about 12 minutes. Cut each piece diagonally into slices, keeping slices together to retain shape of bread. Sprinkle with alfalfa sprouts.

Melon Compotes

2 pints sherbet
6 cups melon balls or pieces
2 cups sparkling white catawba grape juice or ginger ale, chilled

Scoop sherbet into 8 servings and place on chilled cookie sheet. Freeze uncovered no longer than 6 hours.

Divide melon balls among 8 individual dishes. Top each with sherbet; pour ¼ cup grape juice over top.

Quiche Lorraine, Herbed Broccoli and Mushrooms, Watermelon Pickles, and Spiced Apple Rings

A Committee Meeting Luncheon

Menu

12 servings

Quiche Lorraine*

Herbed Broccoli and Mushrooms*

Spiced Apple Rings

Watermelon Pickles

Ambrosia Fruit Bowl*

Sugar Cookies

Coffee   Tea

*Recipe included

1 day before buffet:
- ☐ Prepare Quiche Lorraine for baking; refrigerate.
- ☐ Toast coconut for Ambrosia Fruit Bowl; store at room temperature.

Several hours before serving:
- ☐ Prepare Ambrosia Fruit Bowl; refrigerate.

About 1 hour before:
- ☐ Bake Quiche Lorraine.

About 20 minutes before:
- ☐ Cook broccoli for Herbed Broccoli and Mushrooms.
- ☐ Prepare Coffee and Tea.

At serving time:
- ☐ Arrange Spiced Apple Rings and Watermelon Pickles in serving containers.
- ☐ Complete Herbed Broccoli and Mushrooms.

At dessert time:
- ☐ Sprinkle Ambrosia Fruit Bowl with coconut; serve with Sugar Cookies.

Herbed Broccoli and Mushrooms

3 packages (10 ounces each) frozen broccoli
   *spears**
¼ cup margarine or butter
1 tablespoon instant chicken bouillon
1 teaspoon dried basil leaves
1 teaspoon dry mustard
½ teaspoon dried thyme leaves
8 ounces mushrooms, sliced (about 3 cups)

Cook broccoli as directed on package except use 4-quart Dutch oven; drain. Heat margarine, chicken bouillon (dry), basil, mustard and thyme in 10-inch skillet over medium heat, stirring constantly, until hot and smooth. Add mushrooms. Cook and stir until mushrooms are hot, about 5 minutes. Spoon mushroom mixture over broccoli.

*4½ pounds fresh broccoli, cooked and drained, can be substituted for the frozen broccoli spears.

Ambrosia Fruit Bowl

1 large pineapple, cut into 1-inch pieces
6 oranges, pared and sectioned
½ cup powdered sugar
¼ cup orange-flavored liqueur
1 cup toasted flaked coconut

Mix pineapple and oranges; toss with powdered sugar and liqueur until evenly coated. Cover and refrigerate at least 2 hours. Sprinkle with coconut.

NOTE: To toast coconut, heat oven to 350°. Spread coconut evenly in ungreased shallow pan. Toast, stirring frequently, until golden brown, about 8 minutes.

Quiche Lorraine

1 pound bacon, crisply fried and crumbled
2 cups shredded natural Swiss cheese (8 ounces)
⅔ cup finely chopped onion
2 9-inch unbaked pie shells
8 eggs
4 cups half-and-half
1 teaspoon salt
½ teaspoon pepper
¼ teaspoon ground red pepper

Divide bacon, cheese and onion between pastry-lined pie plates. Cover with plastic wrap and refrigerate no longer than 24 hours. Beat eggs slightly; beat in remaining ingredients. Cover and refrigerate no longer than 24 hours.

Stir egg mixture; divide between pie plates. Heat oven to 425°. Bake uncovered 15 minutes. Reduce oven temperature to 300°. Bake until knife inserted halfway between center and edge comes out clean, 30 to 40 minutes. Let stand 10 minutes before cutting.

Cod with Cucumber Sauce, Beet-Potato Salad, Sliced Liver Sausage, Havarti Cheese, and Rye Bread

A Scandinavian Luncheon Buffet

Menu

8 servings

Cod with Cucumber Sauce*

Beet-Potato Salad*

Havarti Cheese

Sliced Liver Sausage

Rye Bread or Lefse

Fruit Soup*

Coffee

***Recipe included**

1 day before buffet:
- ☐ Prepare Cod with Cucumber Sauce; refrigerate.
- ☐ Prepare Beet-Potato Salad; refrigerate.
- ☐ Prepare Fruit Soup; refrigerate.

About 2 hours before serving:
- ☐ Remove Havarti Cheese from refrigerator; let stand at room temperature.

About 30 minutes before:
- ☐ Prepare Coffee.
- ☐ Arrange Sliced Liver Sausage and Rye Bread in serving containers.

At dessert time:
- ☐ Serve Fruit Soup.

Cod with Cucumber Sauce

2 pounds cod fillets
2 teaspoons salt
   Cucumber Sauce (below)

If fish fillets are large, cut into 8 serving pieces. Heat 1½ inches water and salt to boiling in 12-inch skillet; reduce heat. Arrange fish in single layer in skillet. Simmer uncovered until fish flakes easily with a fork, 8 to 10 minutes. Remove fish with slotted spoon. Cover and refrigerate no longer than 24 hours. Prepare Cucumber Sauce; serve with fish.

Cucumber Sauce

Cut 1 medium cucumber lengthwise into halves; remove seeds and coarsely chop. Mix cucumber, 2 cups mayonnaise or salad dressing and 1 teaspoon dried dill weed. Cover and refrigerate no longer than 24 hours.

Beet-Potato Salad

4 medium potatoes, cooked and cut into cubes
   (about 4 cups)
1 jar (16 ounces) sliced pickled beets, drained
   and cut into ¼-inch strips
2 small dill pickles, chopped
1 apple, coarsely chopped
1 small onion, chopped (about ¼ cup)
¼ cup vinegar
2 tablespoons sugar
2 tablespoons water
⅛ teaspoon pepper
   Dairy sour cream

Place potatoes, beets, pickles, apple and onion in glass or plastic bowl. Mix vinegar, sugar, water and pepper; pour over potato mixture and toss lightly. Cover and refrigerate, stirring occasionally, at least 2 hours but no longer than 24 hours. Garnish with sour cream.

Fruit Soup

1 package (about 12 ounces) mixed dried fruit
   such as prunes, apricots, peaches, pears,
   raisins (2 cups)
1½ cups water
1½ cups grape juice or cranberry juice cocktail
2 tablespoons quick-cooking tapioca
¼ teaspoon salt
½ cup sugar
3- inch cinnamon stick
2 or 3 thin slices lemon, if desired
1 can (8 ounces) pitted dark sweet cherries,
   undrained

Heat all ingredients except cherries to boiling in 3-quart saucepan, stirring occasionally; reduce heat. Cover and simmer until fruit is tender, 30 to 40 minutes. Stir in cherries. Cover and refrigerate no longer than 24 hours.

Fruit Soup

Crab Louis in Puff Bowl

A Fall Luncheon Buffet

Menu

8 servings

Hot Consommé*

Crab Louis in Puff Bowl*

Marinated Cucumbers*

Grapes in Sour Cream*

Coffee   Tea

*Recipe included

About 1 week before buffet:
- ☐ Prepare Puff Bowl for Crab Louis in Puff Bowl; freeze.

2 days before:
- ☐ Prepare Marinated Cucumbers; refrigerate.

1 day before:
- ☐ Prepare crab mixture for Crab Louis in Puff Bowl; refrigerate.

About 4 hours before serving:
- ☐ Prepare Grapes in Sour Cream; refrigerate.

About 1 hour before:
- ☐ Remove Puff Bowl from freezer; heat.

About 15 minutes before:
- ☐ Prepare Coffee and Tea.
- ☐ Prepare Hot Consommé.
- ☐ Complete Crab Louis in Puff Bowl.
- ☐ Spoon Marinated Cucumbers into serving dish.

Crab Louis in Puff Bowl

Puff Bowl (below)
½ cup mayonnaise or salad dressing
½ cup catsup
3 tablespoons vegetable oil
1 tablespoon vinegar
1 green onion, thinly sliced (with top)
2 dashes of Worcestershire sauce
3 drops red pepper sauce
3 packages (6 ounces each) frozen crabmeat,
  thawed*
2 cups shredded lettuce
1 avocado, sliced

Prepare Puff Bowl. Mix mayonnaise, catsup, oil, vinegar, onion, Worcestershire sauce, pepper sauce and crabmeat. Cover and refrigerate no longer than 24 hours.

Remove Puff Bowl from freezer and unwrap; place on ungreased cookie sheet. Heat in 400° oven until crisp, about 8 minutes; cool. Fill with shredded lettuce; top with crabmeat mixture. Garnish with avocado wedges. To serve, cut into 8 wedges.

Puff Bowl

½ cup water
¼ cup margarine or butter
½ cup all-purpose flour
⅛ teaspoon salt
2 eggs

Heat oven to 400°. Grease pie plate, 9 × 1¼ inches. Heat water and margarine to rolling boil in 1½-quart saucepan. Stir in flour and salt. Stir vigorously over low heat until mixture forms a ball, about 1 minute; remove from heat. Cool 10 minutes. Beat in eggs, all at once; continue beating until smooth. Spread dough evenly in pie plate, building up edge slightly. Bake until puffed and dry in center, 45 to 60 minutes; cool. Wrap, label and freeze no longer than 1 week.

*3 cans (6 ounces each) crabmeat, drained and cartilage removed, or 3 cans (6½ ounces each) tuna, drained, can be substituted for the frozen crabmeat.

Marinated Cucumbers

½ cup vinegar
½ cup water
2 tablespoons sugar
¼ teaspoon salt
2 medium cucumbers, thinly sliced
1 small onion, thinly sliced

Mix vinegar, water, sugar and salt. Toss with cucumbers and onion in glass or plastic bowl. Cover and refrigerate, stirring occasionally, at least 2 hours but no longer than 48 hours. Drain before serving.

Grapes in Sour Cream

⅓ cup packed brown sugar
⅔ cup dairy sour cream
4 cups seedless grapes
2 tablespoons packed brown sugar

Mix ⅓ cup brown sugar and the sour cream. Toss with grapes. Cover and refrigerate no longer than 4 hours. Sprinkle with 2 tablespoons brown sugar.

Hot Consommé

Heat 2 cans (13 ounces each) clear consommé and 2 cans (13 ounces each) red consommé to boiling; remove from heat. Stir in ½ cup dry white wine. 8 servings (about ¾ cup each).

A Build-a-Salad Buffet

This is a lunch that can be light or hearty — let guests determine for themselves which way to go. They can build their own salad of crisp vegetables with a sprinkle of bacon or sunflower seeds and top them with Cucumber Dressing or oil and vinegar dressing. Breadsticks can add crunch, and the lunch can end with a serving of cut-up fresh fruit. Or, if after eating a salad for lunch you feel you deserve a richer dessert, finish the meal with Fruit Fluff Dessert, which looks light but is rich with cream cheese and whipping cream. For the hearty appetite, compose a substantial salad and top it off with a Raisin-Bran Muffin and the Fruit Fluff Dessert. Here is a buffet where guests can truly make their own choices.

Menu

10 servings

Build-Your-Own Salad*

Blue Cheese Dressing*

Cucumber Dressing*

French Dressing*

Oil and Vinegar

Hard Rolls

Breadsticks

Raisin-Bran Muffins*

Fruit Fluff Dessert
(page 143)

Iced Coffee*

Iced Tea*

*Recipe included

About 1 week before buffet:
- ☐ Prepare Blue Cheese Dressing and French Dressing; refrigerate.

About 4 days before:
- ☐ Prepare batter for Raisin-Bran Muffins; refrigerate.

2 days before:
- ☐ Prepare Fruit Fluff Dessert; refrigerate.
- ☐ Prepare Cucumber Dressing; refrigerate.

1 day before:
- ☐ Prepare salad mixture, Vegetables, Toppers and Sprinklers for Build-Your-Own Salad; refrigerate perishable items.
- ☐ Prepare coffee cubes for Iced Coffee; freeze. Prepare tea for Iced Tea; refrigerate.

Several hours before serving:
- ☐ Prepare fruit for Fruit Fluff Dessert; cover and refrigerate.

About 30 minutes before:
- ☐ Bake Raisin-Bran Muffins.
- ☐ Remove Blue Cheese Dressing from refrigerator.
- ☐ Pour Oil and Vinegar into serving containers.
- ☐ Complete Build-Your-Own Salad.
- ☐ Arrange Hard Rolls, Breadsticks and Raisin-Bran Muffins in serving containers.
- ☐ Complete Iced Coffee and Iced Tea.

At dessert time:
- ☐ Arrange Fruit Fluff Dessert on serving plates; serve with fruit.

Build-Your-Own Salad

12 cups bite size pieces mixed salad greens
3 cups shredded red cabbage

Vegetables

2 cups sliced mushrooms
2 cups cauliflowerets
2 cups broccoli flowerets
2 cups bean or alfalfa sprouts
1 cup sliced green onions (with tops)
1 cup shredded carrots
1 pint cherry tomatoes
1 medium cucumber, thinly sliced
1 can (16 ounces) garbanzo beans, drained
1 can (16 ounces) sliced beets, drained
1 jar (16 ounces) pickled mixed vegetables, drained

Toppers

8 ounces fully cooked smoked ham, cut into ¼-inch strips
8 ounces cooked turkey, cut into ¼-inch strips
1 cup shredded Cheddar cheese (4 ounces)
1 cup shredded Swiss cheese (4 ounces)
4 hard-cooked eggs, chopped

Sprinklers

2 cups seasoned croutons
½ cup sunflower nuts
8 slices bacon, crisply fried and crumbled

Mix salad greens and cabbage; place in large plastic bag. Fasten bag and refrigerate no longer than 24 hours.

Place salad mixture in large salad bowl or bowls on buffet table. Choose 4 or more Vegetables. Place Vegetables, Toppers and Sprinklers in containers on buffet table.

Blue Cheese Dressing

¾ cup crumbled blue cheese
1 package (3 ounces) cream cheese, softened
½ cup mayonnaise or salad dressing
⅓ cup half-and-half

Reserve ⅓ cup blue cheese. Beat remaining blue cheese and cream cheese on low speed. Add mayonnaise and half-and-half; beat on medium speed until creamy. Stir in reserved blue cheese. Cover and refrigerate at least 3 hours but no longer than 1 week. Remove from refrigerator about 30 minutes before serving. Stir before serving. 1⅔ cups dressing.

NOTE: To crumble blue cheese, freeze first (it is easier to handle and remains in separate pieces). After crumbling, wrap and freeze. Separate into pieces before adding to dressing.

Buffet Napkin Fold

Place napkin, folded into halves, with the open edge at top and folded edge at bottom.

Fold the top edge down to folded edge at bottom; turn napkin over.

Fold left edge into center of napkin; fold left side over 2 more times to form a pocket to place silverware in.

Build-Your-Own Salad,

French Dressing

1   cup olive or vegetable oil or combination
1/4 cup vinegar
1/4 cup lemon juice
1   teaspoon salt
1/2 teaspoon dry mustard
1/2 teaspoon paprika

Shake all ingredients in tightly covered jar.
Refrigerate at least 2 hours but no longer than
1 week. Shake before serving. 1½ cups dressing.

Cucumber Dressing

1   carton (8 ounces) plain yogurt (1 cup)
1/2 cup seeded finely chopped cucumber
1/2 cup buttermilk
1   teaspoon instant minced onion
1/2 teaspoon salt
1/4 teaspoon dried dill weed
1/8 teaspoon pepper
1   clove garlic, crushed

Shake all ingredients in tightly covered jar.
Refrigerate at least 2 hours but no longer than
48 hours. Shake before serving. About 1⅔
cups dressing.

Blue Cheese Dressing, French Dressing, Cucumber Dressing, Oil and Vinegar, Hard Rolls, Breadsticks and Raisin-Bran Muffins

Raisin-Bran Muffins

1 cup whole bran cereal
1 cup buttermilk
1 egg
1/4 cup vegetable oil
1 cup all-purpose flour
1/2 cup raisins
1/3 cup packed brown sugar
1 teaspoon baking powder
1 teaspoon baking soda
1/2 teaspoon salt

Mix cereal and buttermilk; let stand until buttermilk is absorbed, about 3 minutes. Beat in egg and oil. Add remaining ingredients; mix until flour is moistened. Cover tightly and refrigerate no longer than 4 days.

Heat oven to 400°. Grease bottoms only of 12 medium muffin cups, 2½ × 1¼ inches. Fill muffin cups about ⅔ full. Bake until golden brown, 15 to 20 minutes. Immediately remove from pan. 12 muffins.

Iced Coffee

Prepare medium coffee (2 level tablespoons ground coffee to ¾ cup water); cool. Pour into ice cube trays; freeze no longer than 24 hours. Pour freshly brewed medium coffee over coffee cubes in pitcher. Serve with sugar and cream or whipped cream if desired.

Iced Tea

Use 2 teaspoons loose tea or 2 tea bags for each cup of cold water. Place tea in glass container; add water. Cover and refrigerate at least 24 hours. Serve over ice with sugar, cream and lemon if desired.

Breakfasts & Brunches

A Fall Brunch

Menu

12 servings

Hot Orange Cider*

Ham and Cheese Pies*

Dilled Vegetables*

Fresh Pineapple Spears

Swirl Coffee Cake*

Coffee   Tea

***Recipe included**

1 day before buffet:

☐ Prepare Ham and Cheese Pies for baking; refrigerate.
☐ Prepare orange juice for Hot Orange Cider; refrigerate.
☐ Prepare carrots for Dilled Vegetables; cover with ice water and refrigerate. Prepare zucchini, onions and peppers; fasten securely in plastic bag and refrigerate.
☐ Bake Swirl Coffee Cake; store at room temperature.

About 1 hour 30 minutes before serving:

☐ Prepare Fresh Pineapple Spears; refrigerate.
☐ Bake Ham and Cheese Pies.

About 30 minutes before:

☐ Drain carrots; prepare Dilled Vegetables.
☐ Heat Swirl Coffee Cake; drizzle with Glaze.
☐ Prepare Coffee and Tea.
☐ Prepare Hot Orange Cider.

A Fall Brunch

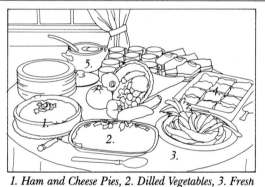

1. Ham and Cheese Pies, 2. Dilled Vegetables, 3. Fresh Pineapple Spears, 4. Swirl Coffee Cake, 5. Hot Orange Cider

Ham and Cheese Pies

2 cups shredded sharp Cheddar cheese (8 ounces)
2 packages (2.5 ounces each) sliced smoked ham, chopped, or 1⅓ cups cut-up cooked ham
8 eggs, slightly beaten
4 cups milk
¼ cup sliced green onions (with tops)
1 teaspoon dried tarragon leaves
1 teaspoon dry mustard
½ teaspoon salt
⅛ teaspoon ground red pepper
4 cups unseasoned croutons

Divide cheese and ham between 2 ungreased pie plates, 10 × 1½ inches. Mix remaining ingredients except croutons; divide egg mixture between pie plates. Cover and refrigerate no longer than 24 hours.

Heat oven to 325°. Sprinkle 2 cups croutons over egg mixture in each pie plate. Bake uncovered until knife inserted 1 inch from edge comes out clean, 50 to 55 minutes (do not overbake). Let stand 10 minutes before serving. Refrigerate any remaining pie.

Hot Orange Cider

1 can (12 ounces) frozen orange juice
   concentrate
1½ quarts apple cider
½ cup rum, if desired
1 orange, cut into 12 slices

Prepare orange juice as directed on can. Heat orange juice and apple cider over low heat just to boiling. Pour about 1 cup orange juice mixture into each mug. Stir in 2 teaspoons rum; top with orange slice. Garnish with stick cinnamon if desired.

HOT CRANAPPLE CIDER: Substitute 1 can (12 ounces) frozen cranberry juice cocktail concentrate. Prepare as directed above.

Dilled Vegetables

6 medium carrots, cut into ¼-inch slices (about
   3 cups)
4 small zucchini, cut crosswise and then
   lengthwise into fourths
2 medium onions, cut into ¼-inch slices
2 medium green peppers, cut into ¼-inch strips
¼ cup margarine or butter, melted
1 tablespoon lemon juice
½ teaspoon dried dill weed
½ teaspoon dry mustard
¼ teaspoon pepper

Heat 1 inch salted water (½ teaspoon salt to 1 cup water) to boiling in 4-quart Dutch oven. Add carrots. Heat to boiling; reduce heat. Cover and simmer until crisp-tender, about 10 minutes. Add zucchini, onions and green peppers. Heat to boiling; reduce heat. Cover and simmer until zucchini are tender, 5 to 8 minutes; drain. Mix remaining ingredients; toss with vegetables.

Swirl Coffee Cake

1½ cups sugar
½ cup margarine or butter, softened
½ cup shortening
1½ teaspoons baking powder
1 teaspoon vanilla
1 teaspoon almond extract
4 eggs
3 cups all-purpose flour
1 can (21 ounces) cherry, apricot or blueberry
   pie filling
Glaze (below)

Heat oven to 350°. Generously grease jelly roll pan, 15½ × 10½ × 1 inch, or 2 square pans, 9 × 9 × 2 inches. Blend sugar, margarine, shortening, baking powder, vanilla, almond extract and eggs in large bowl on low speed, scraping bowl constantly. Beat on high speed, scraping bowl occasionally, 3 minutes. Stir in flour. Spread ⅔ of the batter in jelly roll pan or ⅓ in each square pan. Spread pie filling over batter. Drop remaining batter by tablespoonfuls onto pie filling.

Bake until light golden brown, about 45 minutes. Cover and store at room temperature.

Heat covered in 325° oven until warm, about 10 minutes. Prepare Glaze; drizzle over warm coffee cake. Cut cake in jelly roll pan into 3-inch squares; cut cake in square pans into 2¾-inch squares.

Glaze

Mix 1 cup powdered sugar and 1 to 2 tablespoons milk until mixture is smooth and desired consistency.

A Before-Skiing Brunch

Menu
12 servings

Hot Orange Cider (page 167)

Creamed Eggs and Corn Bread*

Oven Bacon*

Mushroom Tossed Salad*

Coffee

*Recipe included

1 day before buffet:
- ☐ Prepare egg mixture for Creamed Eggs and Corn Bread; refrigerate.
- ☐ Prepare greens and slice mushrooms for Mushroom Tossed Salad; refrigerate.
- ☐ Bake Oven Bacon; refrigerate
- ☐ Prepare Hot Orange Cider; refrigerate.

About 40 minutes before serving:
- ☐ Bake Corn Bread for Creamed Eggs and Corn Bread.

About 15 minutes before:
- ☐ Heat Oven Bacon.
- ☐ Heat egg mixture for Creamed Eggs and Corn Bread.
- ☐ Prepare Coffee.
- ☐ Complete Mushroom Tossed Salad.
- ☐ Complete Hot Orange Cider.

Creamed Eggs and Corn Bread, Mushroom Tossed Salad and Oven Bacon

Creamed Eggs and Corn Bread

    1 large onion, chopped (about ¾ cup)
    ⅓ cup margarine or butter
    ⅓ cup all-purpose flour
    2 teaspoons dry mustard
    1½ teaspoons salt
    ¼ teaspoon pepper
    3½ cups milk
    2 cups shredded Cheddar cheese (8 ounces)
    1 package (10 ounces) frozen green peas
    12 hard-cooked eggs, sliced
    1 can (2.2 ounces) sliced ripe olives (about
        ½ cup)
        Corn Bread (below)

Cook and stir onion in margarine in 3-quart saucepan over medium heat until onion is tender, about 5 minutes. Stir in flour, mustard, salt and pepper. Cook over low heat, stirring constantly, until bubbly; remove from heat. Stir in milk. Heat to boiling, stirring constantly. Boil and stir 1 minute. Add cheese; cook and stir until cheese is melted. Rinse peas under running cold water to separate; drain. Stir peas, eggs and olives into cheese sauce. Cover and refrigerate no longer than 24 hours.

Prepare Corn Bread. Cover cheese sauce-egg mixture and heat over medium-low heat, stirring occasionally, until hot, about 25 minutes. Cut warm bread into 12 pieces; serve with cheese sauce-egg mixture.

Corn Bread

    1½ cups cornmeal
    ½ cup all-purpose flour
    2 teaspoons baking powder
    1 teaspoon sugar
    1 teaspoon salt
    ½ teaspoon baking soda
    ¼ cup shortening
    1½ cups buttermilk
    2 eggs

Heat oven to 450°. Mix all ingredients; beat vigorously 30 seconds. Pour into greased square pan, 9 × 9 × 2 inches. Bake until top springs back when touched lightly in center, about 20 minutes.

Oven Bacon

Place 24 slices bacon (about 1 pound) on rack in broiler pan and on wire rack in jelly roll pan, 15 × 10 × 1 inch (do not overlap slices). Bake in 400° oven, without turning, until light brown, 15 to 20 minutes. Cool slightly; remove from racks. Cover and refrigerate no longer than 24 hours.

Heat oven to 450°. Place bacon slices in jelly roll pan, 15½ × 10½ × 1 inch. Bake until hot and crisp, about 5 minutes.

Mushroom Tossed Salad

    12 ounces spinach, torn into bite-size pieces
    ½ medium head lettuce, torn into bite-size pieces
    ¼ cup wine vinegar
    1 teaspoon salt
    ⅛ teaspoon pepper
    2 cloves garlic, crushed
    8 ounces mushrooms, sliced (about 3 cups)
    1 can (8 ounces) sliced water chestnuts, drained
    ½ cup vegetable oil
    2 cups seasoned croutons

Place spinach and lettuce in large plastic bag. Fasten bag securely and refrigerate no longer than 24 hours.

Mix vinegar, salt, pepper and garlic; toss with mushrooms and let stand at least 20 minutes. Add mushroom mixture, water chestnuts and oil to greens in bag. Fasten bag securely and shake until leaves glisten. Place in serving bowl; sprinkle with croutons.

An Easter Morning Brunch

Menu

8 servings

Mimosa*

Eggs with Vegetables*

Sausage Ring*

Hot Cross Buns

Lemon Roll with Strawberries*

Coffee   Tea

*Recipe included

1 day before buffet:
- ☐ Bake and assemble Lemon Roll; refrigerate.
- ☐ Prepare Sausage Ring for baking; refrigerate.
- ☐ Refrigerate champagne for Mimosa.
- ☐ Prepare green peppers and onions for Eggs with Vegetables; cover and refrigerate.

About 1 hour before serving:
- ☐ Bake Sausage Ring.
- ☐ Squeeze orange juice for Mimosa; cover and refrigerate.

About 45 minutes before:
- ☐ Prepare strawberries for Lemon Roll. Garnish Lemon Roll and refrigerate.

About 20 minutes before:
- ☐ Arrange Hot Cross Buns in serving container.
- ☐ Prepare Eggs with Vegetables.
- ☐ Prepare Coffee and Tea.

At serving time:
- ☐ Prepare Mimosa.

Mimosa

⅓ cup sugar
2⅔ cups fresh orange juice, chilled
2 bottles (750 ml each) champagne, chilled
8 orange slices
8 mint sprigs

Place sugar and orange juice in blender container. Cover and blend on medium speed until foamy, about 15 seconds. Pour ⅓ cup into each of 8 tall glasses; add about 1 cup champagne to each. Garnish with orange slice and mint sprig.

Eggs with Vegetables

2 medium green peppers, cut into ¼-inch strips
2 medium onions, sliced
2 cloves garlic, crushed
1 teaspoon salt
1 teaspoon dried basil leaves
½ teaspoon dried thyme leaves
3 tablespoons margarine or butter
4 medium tomatoes, coarsely chopped
1 can (8 ounces) sliced water chestnuts, drained
16 eggs
¾ cup milk
2 teaspoons salt
⅛ teaspoon pepper

Cook green peppers, onions, garlic, 1 teaspoon salt, the basil and thyme in 1 tablespoon of the margarine in 10-inch skillet over medium heat, stirring occasionally, until green peppers are crisp-tender, about 8 minutes.

Add tomatoes and water chestnuts. Heat until hot, about 2 minutes. Remove vegetables from skillet with slotted spoon; keep warm. Drain excess liquid from skillet.

Heat remaining margarine in same skillet over medium heat until hot enough to sizzle a drop of water. Mix remaining ingredients; pour into skillet. As egg mixture begins to set at bottom and side, gently lift cooked portions with spatula so that thin, uncooked portion can flow to bottom. Avoid constant stirring. Cook until eggs are thickened throughout but still moist, 3 to 5 minutes. Serve immediately with vegetables.

Sausage Ring

2 pounds bulk pork sausage
1 cup soft bread crumbs
1/4 cup snipped parsley
1/2 teaspoon ground sage
2 eggs, slightly beaten
1 small onion, chopped (about 1/4 cup)

Mix all ingredients. Press lightly in ungreased 6-cup ring mold. Cover and refrigerate no longer than 24 hours.

Unmold sausage mixture on rack in shallow baking pan; cover loosely with aluminum foil. Bake in 350° oven 30 minutes; remove foil. Bake until done, about 30 minutes longer.

Lemon Roll with Strawberries

3 eggs
1 cup granulated sugar
1/3 cup water
1 teaspoon vanilla
3/4 cup all-purpose flour
1 teaspoon baking powder
1/4 teaspoon salt
   Powdered sugar
   Clear Lemon Filling (right)
2 pints strawberries

1/4 cup granulated sugar
1 kiwi fruit, sliced
   Mint leaves

Heat oven to 375°. Line jelly roll pan, 15½ × 10½ × 1 inch, with aluminum foil or waxed paper; grease generously. Beat eggs in small bowl on high speed until very thick and lemon colored, about 5 minutes. Pour eggs into large bowl. Beat in 1 cup granulated sugar gradually. Beat in water and vanilla on low speed. Add flour, baking powder and salt gradually, beating just until batter is smooth. Pour into pan, spreading batter to corners.

Bake until wooden pick inserted in center comes out clean, 12 to 15 minutes. Immediately loosen cake from edges of pan; invert on towel sprinkled with powdered sugar. Carefully remove foil; trim off stiff edges of cake if necessary. Roll hot cake and towel from narrow end. Cool on wire rack. Prepare Clear Lemon Filling; cool. Unroll cake; remove towel. Spread cake with Clear Lemon Filling. Roll up; refrigerate no longer than 24 hours.

Reserve 8 medium strawberries; slice remaining strawberries. Sprinkle sliced strawberries with 1/4 cup granulated sugar; let stand 1 hour. Sprinkle roll with powdered sugar. Garnish with reserved strawberries, kiwi slices and mint leaves. Serve sliced strawberries with roll.

Clear Lemon Filling

3/4 cup sugar
3 tablespoons cornstarch
1/4 teaspoon salt
3/4 cup water
1 tablespoon margarine or butter
1 teaspoon grated lemon peel
1/3 cup lemon juice

Mix sugar, cornstarch and salt in saucepan. Stir in water gradually. Cook, stirring constantly, until mixture thickens and boils. Boil and stir 1 minute; remove from heat. Stir in margarine and lemon peel. Stir in lemon juice gradually and, if desired, 4 drops yellow food color. If filling is too soft, refrigerate until set.

Oven Scrambled Eggs, Melon and Ham Platter and Orange Rolls

A Patio Brunch

Menu

12 servings

Melon and Ham Platter*

Oven Scrambled Eggs*

Orange Rolls*

Coffee   Tea

***Recipe included**

---

4 days before buffet:
- ☐ Prepare Sweet Roll Dough for Orange Rolls; refrigerate.

1 day before:
- ☐ Prepare Oven Scrambled Eggs for baking; refrigerate.

Several hours before serving:
- ☐ Bake Orange Rolls.
- ☐ Prepare Melon and Ham Platter; refrigerate.

About 30 minutes before:
- ☐ Bake Oven Scrambled Eggs.
- ☐ Prepare Coffee and Tea.

Melon and Ham Platter

1 *cantaloupe*
1 *honeydew melon*
24 *thin slices smoked fully cooked ham*
2 *lemons, cut into wedges*

Cut melons lengthwise into halves; remove seeds. Cut each half into 6 wedges; pare. Arrange melon wedges on platter. Roll up slices of ham; place around melon. Garnish with lemon wedges. Cover and refrigerate no longer than 4 hours.

Oven Scrambled Eggs

¼ *cup margarine or butter, melted*
18 *eggs*
1 *cup milk*
1½ *teaspoons salt*
¼ *to ½ teaspoon pepper*

Pour margarine into rectangular pan, 13 × 9 × 2 inches; tilt pan to coat bottom. Beat remaining ingredients with rotary beater. Pour into pan. Cover and refrigerate no longer than 24 hours.

Bake uncovered in 350° oven, stirring frequently, until eggs are thickened throughout but still moist, about 30 minutes.

MORNING ENTERTAINING

Breakfast and brunch buffets can be as festive or luxurious as evening entertaining. Morning entertaining on weekends is becoming more popular with the working group. You can entertain and still have the remainder of the day and evening to run errands, attend classes or enjoy other weekend events.

Unless your party precedes some other planned event, your guests may not be in a hurry to depart. So be prepared by having lots of coffee and plenty of beverages to carry them through a relaxing afternoon.

Orange Rolls

Sweet Roll Dough (below)
¼ *cup margarine or butter, softened*
1 *tablespoon plus 1 teaspoon grated orange peel*
3 *tablespoons orange juice*
2¼ *cups powdered sugar*

Prepare Sweet Roll Dough. Mix remaining ingredients until smooth and creamy. Punch down dough; divide into halves.

Roll one half into rectangle, 12 × 7 inches, on lightly floured surface; spread with ½ cup of the orange mixture. Roll up tightly, beginning at 12-inch side. Pinch edge of dough into roll to seal well. Stretch roll to make even. Cut into twelve 1-inch slices. Place in one end of greased rectangular pan, 13 × 9 × 2 inches. Repeat with remaining dough; place in same pan. (Reserve remaining orange mixture.) Let rise until double, about 40 minutes.

Heat oven to 375°. Bake until golden brown, 20 to 25 minutes. Frost with reserved orange mixture while warm. 2 dozen rolls.

Sweet Roll Dough

1 *package active dry yeast*
½ *cup warm water (105 to 115°)*
½ *cup lukewarm milk (scalded then cooled)*
⅓ *cup sugar*
⅓ *cup shortening, or margarine or butter, softened*
1 *teaspoon salt*
1 *egg*
3½ *to 4 cups all-purpose flour*

Dissolve yeast in warm water in large bowl. Stir in milk, sugar, shortening, salt, egg and 2 cups of the flour. Beat until smooth. Mix in enough of the remaining flour to make dough easy to handle. Turn dough onto lightly floured surface; knead until smooth and elastic, about 5 minutes. Place in greased bowl; turn greased side up. Cover and refrigerate no longer than 4 days.

A Winter Brunch

Menu

12 servings

Oven Omelet*

Canadian-style Bacon*

Sautéed Cherry Tomatoes*

Spinach-Mushroom Salad*

Assorted Danish Pastries

Winter Fruit Compote*

Coffee   Tea

***Recipe included**

2 days before buffet:
- ☐ Prepare Winter Fruit Compote except for oranges; refrigerate.

1 day before:
- ☐ Prepare Canadian-style Bacon for baking; refrigerate.
- ☐ Prepare spinach and mushrooms for Spinach-Mushroom Salad; refrigerate.

About 45 minutes before serving:
- ☐ Bake Oven Omelet.
- ☐ Bake Canadian-style Bacon.

About 15 minutes before:
- ☐ Complete Winter Fruit Compote; let stand at room temperature.
- ☐ Arrange Danish Pastries on serving tray.
- ☐ Cook Sautéed Cherry Tomatoes.
- ☐ Complete Spinach-Mushroom Salad.
- ☐ Prepare Coffee and Tea.

Winter Fruit Compote

Oven Omelet

1/4 cup margarine or butter
18 eggs
1 cup dairy sour cream
1 cup milk
2 teaspoons salt
1/4 cup chopped green onions (with tops)

Heat oven to 325°. Heat margarine in rectangular baking dish, 13 × 9 × 2 inches, in oven until melted. Tilt dish to coat bottom. Beat eggs, sour cream, milk and salt until blended. Stir in onions. Pour into dish.

Bake until eggs are set but moist, about 35 minutes. Cut into serving pieces. Garnish with parsley if desired.

Canadian-style Bacon

Cut 1 pound Canadian-style bacon into twenty-four 1/8-inch slices; reassemble into roll on 18 × 12-inch piece of aluminum foil. Pour 1/4 cup maple-flavored syrup over roll. Wrap and refrigerate no longer than 24 hours.

Place foil package in baking pan, 9 × 9 × 2 inches. Bake in 325° oven until bacon is hot, about 35 minutes.

Sautéed Cherry Tomatoes

1/4 cup margarine or butter
2 tablespoons water
1 tablespoon honey
2 pints cherry tomatoes
1/4 cup snipped parsley
1/2 teaspoon dried basil leaves.

Heat margarine in 12-inch skillet until melted; stir in water and honey. Add tomatoes. Cook and stir over medium heat until skins begin to split, about 3 minutes. Carefully toss with parsley and basil.

Spinach-Mushroom Salad

10 cups bite-size pieces spinach (about 10 ounces)
1/4 cup tarragon or wine vinegar
1 teaspoon salt
1/8 teaspoon pepper
2 cloves garlic, crushed
12 ounces mushrooms, sliced (about 4 cups)
1/3 cup vegetable oil

Place spinach in large plastic bag; fasten and refrigerate. Mix vinegar, salt, pepper and garlic; toss with mushrooms. Cover and refrigerate no longer than 24 hours.

Add oil to spinach in bag. Fasten bag securely and shake until leaves glisten. Add mushroom mixture. Shake until mixed.

Winter Fruit Compote

2 jars (17 ounces each) figs, drained (reserve syrup)
2 jars (16 ounces each) prunes, drained (reserve syrup)
3-inch stick cinnamon
8 whole cloves
3 oranges, pared and cut into thin slices

Heat reserved syrups, cinnamon and cloves to boiling; boil 5 minutes. Add figs and prunes. Cover and refrigerate no longer than 2 days.

Remove cinnamon and cloves. Heat to boiling; reduce heat. Simmer until fruit is warm, about 3 minutes; remove from heat. Stir in orange slices. Serve warm.

A Holiday Break Gathering

The perfect time to have a brunch is during the holidays. It is an occasion to invite a few friends or relatives for a quiet, relaxing visit. Many people have eaten more than their share during holiday meals so a large platter of fresh seasonal fruit and a baked egg casserole with low-calorie crab is just the answer. Serve warm milk with coffee and your guests can have either plain coffee or Café au Lait.

Menu

8 servings

Crab Scramble Casserole*

Fruit Platter*

Danish Puff*

Café au Lait*

***Recipe included**

1 day before buffet:
- ☐ Bake Danish Puff; store at room temperature.
- ☐ Prepare Crab Scramble Casserole for baking; refrigerate.

About 3 hours before serving:
- ☐ Assemble Fruit Platter; refrigerate.

About 1 hour before:
- ☐ Bake Crab Scramble Casserole.

About 30 minutes before:
- ☐ Prepare coffee for Café au Lait.

At serving time:
- ☐ Heat milk. Have guests pour their own Café au Lait.

Crab Scramble Casserole

¼ cup margarine or butter, melted
12 eggs
½ cup milk
1 teaspoon salt
½ teaspoon white pepper
½ teaspoon dried dill weed
1 can (7½ ounces) crabmeat, drained and cartilage removed
1 package (8 ounces) cream cheese, cut into ½-inch cubes
Paprika

Pour margarine into square baking dish, 8 × 8 × 2 inches; tilt dish to coat bottom. Beat eggs, milk, salt, pepper and dill weed; stir in crabmeat and cheese. Pour into dish. Cover and refrigerate no longer than 24 hours.

Heat oven to 350°. Sprinkle with paprika. Bake uncovered until center is set, 40 to 45 minutes.

Fruit Platter

3 oranges, pared and cut into slices
2 grapefruit, pared and sectioned
2 kiwi fruit, pared and sliced
1 jar (17 ounces) figs, drained
1 jar (16 ounces) stewed prunes, drained
Lettuce leaves

Arrange fruits on lettuce leaves. Cover and refrigerate no longer than 3 hours.

Counterclockwise from top: Café au Lait, Fruit Platter, Crab Scramble Casserole and Danish Puff

Danish Puff

½ cup margarine or butter, softened
1 cup all-purpose flour
2 tablespoons water
½ cup margarine or butter
1 cup water
1 teaspoon almond extract
1 cup all-purpose flour
3 eggs
Vanilla Glaze (below)
½ cup sliced almonds

Heat oven to 350°. Cut ½ cup margarine into 1 cup flour. Sprinkle 2 tablespoons water over mixture; mix with fork. Gather into ball; divide into halves. Pat each half into strip, 12 × 3 inches, on ungreased cookie sheet (strips should be about 3 inches apart).

Heat ½ cup margarine and 1 cup water to rolling boil; remove from heat. Quickly stir in almond extract and 1 cup flour. Stir vigorously over low heat until mixture forms a ball, about 1 minute; remove from heat. Add eggs; beat until smooth. Spread half of the topping evenly over each strip. Bake until topping is crisp and nicely browned, about 1 hour; cool (topping will shrink and fall, forming custardy top). Prepare Vanilla Glaze; spread over topping and sprinkle each with ¼ cup almonds. Cover and store at room temperature no longer than 24 hours. 2 coffee cakes.

Vanilla Glaze

1½ cups powdered sugar
2 tablespoons margarine or butter, softened
1½ teaspoons vanilla
1 to 2 tablespoons warm water

Mix all ingredients until glaze is of desired consistency.

Café au Lait

Prepare coffee, using 1½ cups ground coffee and 6 cups water. Heat 6 cups milk. Pour equal amounts of hot coffee and hot milk simultaneously from separate pots into each cup. 16 servings (¾ cup each).

Eggs Benedict Casserole and Basil Tomatoes

A Special Occasion Brunch

Eggs Benedict, a popular egg dish, can be ideal for brunch. However, poaching eggs and keeping the sauce hot and smooth is difficult when serving a group. Eggs Benedict Casserole is an easy answer. It can be prepared ahead and just heated in the oven after guests arrive. Served with toasted English muffins, it tastes like Eggs Benedict itself.

Menu

10 servings

Eggs Benedict Casserole*

Basil Tomatoes*

Tossed Fruit Salad*

English Muffins

Strawberry Preserves

Assorted Danish Pastries

Coffee   Tea

*Recipe included

2 days before buffet:
- ☐ Prepare Lime-Honey Dressing for Tossed Fruit Salad; refrigerate.

1 day before:
- ☐ Prepare Eggs Benedict Casserole for baking; refrigerate.
- ☐ Prepare Basil Tomatoes for baking; refrigerate.
- ☐ Prepare Tossed Fruit Salad; refrigerate.

About 45 minutes before serving:
- ☐ Bake Eggs Benedict Casserole.

About 25 minutes before:
- ☐ Bake Basil Tomatoes.
- ☐ Prepare Coffee and Tea.
- ☐ Toast English Muffins. Place muffins and Assorted Danish Pastries on serving tray.
- ☐ Place Strawberry Preserves in serving container.
- ☐ Complete Tossed Fruit Salad.

Eggs Benedict Casserole

2½ cups cut-up fully cooked smoked ham
10 eggs
¼ teaspoon pepper
   Mornay Sauce (below)
 1 cup crushed corn flake cereal (about 2 cups
   uncrushed)
¼ cup margarine or butter, melted

Sprinkle ham in ungreased rectangular baking dish, 13 × 9 × 2 inches. Heat water (1½ to 2 inches) to boiling; reduce to simmer. Break egg into measuring cup or saucer; holding cup or saucer close to water's surface, slip egg into water. Cook until egg is just set, about 3 minutes. Remove from water with slotted spoon; place on ham. Repeat with remaining eggs (place eggs in 2 rows on ham). Sprinkle eggs with pepper. Prepare Mornay Sauce; pour over eggs. Toss cereal with margarine; sprinkle over sauce in rectangle around each egg. Cover and refrigerate no longer than 24 hours.

Bake uncovered in 350° oven until hot and bubbly, 35 to 40 minutes. Garnish each serving with a piece of ripe olive if desired.

Mornay Sauce

¼ cup margarine or butter
¼ cup all-purpose flour
½ teaspoon salt
⅛ teaspoon ground nutmeg
2½ cups milk
1½ cups shredded Gruyère or Swiss cheese (6
   ounces)
½ cup grated Parmesan cheese

Heat margarine in 2-quart saucepan over low heat until melted. Blend in flour, salt and nutmeg. Cook over low heat, stirring constantly, until smooth and bubbly; remove from heat. Stir in milk. Heat to boiling, stirring constantly. Boil and stir 1 minute. Add Gruyère and Parmesan cheese; cook and stir until cheese is melted and mixture is smooth.

Basil Tomatoes

 5 medium tomatoes, cut into ¼-inch slices
 1 small onion, chopped (about ¼ cup)
¼ cup margarine or butter, melted
 1 teaspoon salt
½ teaspoon dried basil leaves
⅛ teaspoon pepper
 2 tablespoons snipped parsley

Arrange tomato slices, overlapping slightly, in ungreased square baking dish, 8 × 8 × 2 inches, or shallow round baking dish. Sprinkle with onion. Mix margarine, salt, basil and pepper; drizzle over vegetables. Cover and refrigerate no longer than 24 hours.

Bake uncovered in 350° oven until tomatoes are hot, 15 to 20 minutes. Sprinkle with parsley.

Tossed Fruit Salad

   Lime-Honey Dressing (below)
 3 grapefruit
 8 cups bite-size pieces salad greens
 2 large apples
½ cup coarsely chopped walnuts

Prepare Lime-Honey Dressing. Pare and section grapefruit; reserve juice and refrigerate. Place grapefruit sections and salad greens in large plastic bag. Fasten bag and refrigerate no longer than 24 hours.

Cut up apples. Toss with reserved grapefruit juice; drain. Add apples to salad greens. Fasten bag securely and shake until well mixed. Pour into serving bowl; sprinkle with walnuts. Serve with Lime-Honey Dressing.

Lime-Honey Dressing

½ cup lime juice
⅓ cup honey
⅓ cup vegetable oil
 1 teaspoon poppy or celery seed

Shake all ingredients in tightly covered container; refrigerate no longer than 48 hours.

Gnocchi, Italian Sausage Skillet, Whole Green Beans and Panettone

An Italian-Style Brunch

Menu

8 servings

Gnocchi*

Italian Sausage Skillet*

Whole Green Beans

Peaches and Raspberries

Panettone*

Espresso

***Recipe included**

2 days before buffet:
- ☐ Prepare Gnocchi for baking; refrigerate.

1 day before:
- ☐ Bake Panettone; store at room temperature.

About 45 minutes before serving:
- ☐ Bake Gnocchi.
- ☐ Prepare Italian Sausage Skillet.

About 30 minutes before:
- ☐ Prepare Espresso.
- ☐ Heat Panettone.
- ☐ Cook Whole Green Beans.
- ☐ Place Peaches and Raspberries in serving containers.

Gnocchi

2 cups milk
2 cups white cornmeal
2 tablespoons margarine or butter
4 eggs, well beaten
3/4 teaspoon salt
1/4 cup margarine or butter, melted
3/4 cup grated Parmesan cheese

Heat milk to scalding in 3-quart saucepan; reduce heat. Sprinkle cornmeal slowly into hot milk, stirring constantly. Cook, stirring constantly, until thick, about 3 minutes (spoon will stand upright in mixture); remove from heat. Add 2 tablespoons margarine, the eggs and salt; beat until smooth. Spread in greased rectangular pan, 13 × 9 × 2 inches; cool. Cover and refrigerate until firm, at least 4 hours.

Cut cornmeal mixture into 1½-inch squares or circles. (Dip knife in cold water to prevent sticking.) Overlap squares in ungreased rectangular pan, 13 × 9 × 2 inches, or shallow baking dish. Drizzle with ¼ cup margarine; sprinkle with cheese. Cover and refrigerate no longer than 48 hours.

Bake uncovered in 350° oven until hot, about 30 minutes. Set oven control to broil and/or 550°. Broil with tops 2 to 3 inches from heat until golden brown, about 3 minutes.

Italian Sausage Skillet

2 pounds Italian sausage, cut into 1-inch slices
1 tablespoon olive or vegetable oil
4 ounces mushrooms, sliced
1 large red onion, cut into halves and each half cut into 1/8-inch slices
1 medium green pepper, chopped (about 1 cup)

Cook sausage in oil in 12-inch skillet over medium heat until brown and no longer pink inside, 20 to 25 minutes. Add mushrooms and onion; reduce heat. Cover and simmer, stirring occasionally, until vegetables are tender, about 10 minutes. Add green pepper. Cover and simmer until green pepper is tender, about 5 minutes.

Panettone

1 package active dry yeast
½ cup warm water (105 to 115°)
¼ cup sugar
¼ cup margarine or butter, softened
2 eggs
½ teaspoon salt
½ teaspoon grated lemon peel
½ teaspoon vanilla
2½ to 3 cups all-purpose flour
¼ cup golden raisins
¼ cup chopped citron
¼ cup pine nuts or chopped walnuts, if desired
   Margarine or butter, softened

Dissolve yeast in warm water in large bowl. Stir in sugar, ¼ cup margarine, the eggs, salt, lemon peel, vanilla and 1½ cups of the flour. Beat until smooth. Stir in raisins, citron, pine nuts and enough remaining flour to make dough easy to handle.

Turn dough onto lightly floured surface; knead until smooth and elastic, about 5 minutes. Place in greased bowl; turn greased side up. Cover; let rise in warm place until double, 1½ to 2 hours. (Dough is ready if indentation remains when touched.)

Punch down dough. Shape into round loaf, about 7 inches in diameter. Place loaf in greased round pan, 8 × 1½ inches. Cut a cross ½ inch deep on top of loaf. Generously grease 1 side of a strip of heavy brown paper, about 25 × 4 inches. Fit around inside of pan, forming a collar; fasten with paper clip. Let rise until double, about 1 hour.

Heat oven to 350°. Bake loaf until golden brown, 35 to 45 minutes; remove paper. Brush top of loaf with margarine; cool on wire rack. Wrap in aluminum foil; store at room temperature no longer than 24 hours.

Heat wrapped bread in 350° oven until warm, about 15 minutes.

An Oven Pancake Breakfast

Menu
8 servings

Soufflé Apple Pancake*

Walnut Butter*

Pork Sausage Links

Pineapple and Blueberries

Spiced Tea*

*Recipe included

1 week before buffet:
- ☐ Prepare mix for Spiced Tea; store at room temperature.

2 days before:
- ☐ Prepare Walnut Butter; refrigerate.

About 1 hour before serving:
- ☐ Remove Walnut Butter from refrigerator; let stand at room temperature.
- ☐ Prepare Pineapple and Blueberries; refrigerate.
- ☐ Bake Soufflé Apple Pancake.
- ☐ Cook Pork Sausage Links.
- ☐ Complete Spiced Tea.

Soufflé Apple Pancake

6 *eggs, separated*
½ *cup sugar*
¾ *cup buttermilk baking mix*
½ *cup milk*
1 *teaspoon vanilla*
2 *tablespoons lemon juice*
3 *cups finely chopped pared apples*
¼ *cup margarine or butter*
1 *tablespoon sugar*
¼ *teaspoon ground cinnamon*
　 Maple syrup

Beat egg whites in large bowl until foamy. Beat in ½ cup sugar, 1 tablespoon at a time; continue beating until stiff and glossy. Beat egg yolks in small bowl until light and lemon colored. Beat in baking mix, milk and vanilla. Sprinkle lemon juice over apples; stir into egg yolk mixture. Fold egg whites into egg yolk mixture. Heat margarine in rectangular pan, 13×9×2 inches, in 375° oven until melted. Pour batter into pan. Mix 1 tablespoon sugar and the cinnamon; sprinkle over batter. Bake until knife inserted in center comes out clean, about 30 minutes. Serve with maple syrup and Walnut Butter (right).

Walnut Butter

Beat 1 cup margarine or butter, softened, and ¼ cup packed brown sugar on medium speed until light and fluffy. Stir in ½ cup chopped walnuts. Cover and refrigerate no longer than 48 hours. About 1 hour before serving, remove from refrigerator and let stand at room temperature. About 1¼ cups.

Spiced Tea

½ *cup unsweetened lemon-flavored instant iced tea*
¼ *cup sugar*
¼ *cup orange-flavored instant breakfast drink*
¼ *teaspoon ground cinnamon*
¼ *teaspoon ground cloves*
⅛ *teaspoon ground ginger*
12 *cups boiling water*

Mix all ingredients except boiling water; store in tightly covered container at room temperature no longer than 1 week.

Pour boiling water over tea mixture; stir until dissolved. Garnish with lemon or orange slices if desired. 16 servings (about ¾ cup each).

A Cold Morning Starter

1 day before buffet:
☐ Prepare Oven French Toast for baking; refrigerate.

About 20 minutes before serving:
☐ Bake Oven French Toast.
☐ Prepare Sausage with Peaches.
☐ Prepare Tomato Pow or Hot Cocoa.

Oven French Toast

$1/3$ cup margarine or butter, melted
$2/3$ cup orange juice
3 tablespoons honey
5 eggs
16 slices French bread, each 1 inch thick

Divide margarine between jelly roll pan, $15\frac{1}{2} \times 10\frac{1}{2} \times 1$ inch, and rectangular pan, $13 \times 9 \times 2$ inches. Beat orange juice, honey and eggs with hand beater until foamy. Dip bread into egg mixture; place in pans. Drizzle any remaining egg mixture over bread. Cover and refrigerate no longer than 24 hours.

Heat oven to 450°. Bake uncovered until bottoms are golden brown, about 10 minutes; turn bread. Bake until bottoms are golden brown, 6 to 8 minutes longer. Serve with powdered sugar and maple syrup if desired.

Sausage with Peaches

2 pounds fully cooked kielbasa or Polish sausage, cut into 1-inch slices
1 can (29 ounces) sliced peaches, drained

Cook sausage in 12-inch skillet over medium-high heat, turning occasionally, until brown, about 10 minutes. Add peaches; reduce heat. Cover and heat over low heat until peaches are hot, about 5 minutes.

Tomato Pow

3 cans ($10\frac{1}{2}$ ounces each) condensed beef broth
2 cups tomato juice
1 cup water
2 teaspoons prepared horseradish
$1/2$ teaspoon dried dill weed

Heat all ingredients just to boiling; serve hot.

Hot Cocoa

$1/3$ cup sugar
$1/3$ cup cocoa
$1/4$ teaspoon salt
$1\frac{1}{2}$ cups water
$4\frac{1}{2}$ cups milk
$1/4$ teaspoon vanilla

Mix sugar, cocoa and salt in 3-quart saucepan; add water. Heat to boiling, stirring constantly. Boil and stir 2 minutes. Stir in milk and vanilla; heat until hot (do not boil). Just before serving, beat with hand beater until foamy.

A Hearty Midwestern Breakfast

Menu

10 servings

Hash Brown Casserole*

Breakfast Steaks*

Fresh Applesauce*

Sour Cream Coffee Cake*

Coffee

***Recipe included**

---

1 day before buffet:
- ☐ Prepare Hash Brown Casserole for baking; refrigerate.
- ☐ Bake Sour Cream Coffee Cake; store at room temperature.
- ☐ Prepare Fresh Applesauce; refrigerate.

About 45 minutes before serving:
- ☐ Bake Hash Brown Casserole.

About 25 minutes before:
- ☐ Heat Sour Cream Coffee Cake.
- ☐ Prepare Breakfast Steaks.
- ☐ Prepare Coffee.

Hash Brown Casserole

2 packages (about 6 ounces each) hash brown
   potatoes with onion
¼ cup margarine or butter, melted
1 teaspoon salt
½ teaspoon paprika
1 medium green pepper, chopped (about 1 cup)
1 medium onion, chopped (about ½ cup)
¼ cup margarine or butter
12 eggs
¾ cup milk
1 teaspoon salt
¼ teaspoon pepper

Cover potatoes with boiling water; let stand 5 minutes. Drain thoroughly. Toss potatoes with ¼ cup melted margarine, 1 teaspoon salt and the paprika. Cook and stir green pepper and onion in ¼ cup margarine in 10-inch skillet until tender. Beat eggs, milk, 1 teaspoon salt and the pepper; pour egg mixture into skillet. Cook over low heat, stirring gently. Before eggs are completely set, spoon into ungreased rectangular pan, 13 × 9 × 2 inches. Spoon potato mixture evenly over eggs. Cover and refrigerate no longer than 24 hours.

Bake covered in 350° oven 20 minutes. Uncover and bake until potatoes are tender and hot, about 20 minutes.

Breakfast Steaks

Tenderize 2 pounds beef boneless bottom or top round steak (about ¾ inch thick) with unseasoned tenderizer as directed on package. Cut beef into 10 pieces. Heat 2 tablespoons vegetable oil in 12-inch skillet. Cook beef uncovered over medium heat until brown; turn. Cook until desired doneness, about 10 minutes longer for medium doneness. Sprinkle with salt and pepper.

Sour Cream Coffee Cake

Walnut Filling (right)
1½ cups sugar
¾ cup margarine or butter, softened
1½ teaspoons vanilla
3 eggs
3 cups all-purpose flour
1½ teaspoons baking powder
1½ teaspoons baking soda
¾ teaspoon salt
1½ cups dairy sour cream

Heat oven to 350°. Grease 12-cup bundt cake pan or tube pan, 10 × 4 inches. Prepare Walnut Filling. Beat sugar, margarine, vanilla and eggs in large bowl on medium speed, scraping bowl occasionally, 2 minutes. Beat in flour, baking powder, baking soda and salt alternately with sour cream on low speed. Spread ⅓ of the batter (about 1¾ cups) in pan and sprinkle with ⅓ of the Walnut Filling (about 6 tablespoons); repeat 2 times.

Bake until wooden pick inserted near center comes out clean, about 1 hour. Cool slightly; remove from pan. Cool completely; wrap in aluminum foil and store at room temperature no longer than 24 hours.

Heat wrapped coffee cake in 350° oven until warm, about 20 minutes. Sprinkle with powdered sugar if desired.

Walnut Filling

Mix ½ cup packed brown sugar, ½ cup finely chopped walnuts and 1½ teaspoons ground cinnamon.

Fresh Applesauce

4 large eating apples
½ cup light corn syrup
¼ cup lemon juce
1 tablespoon sugar
¼ teaspoon salt

Remove cores from apples; cut up apples. Place half of the apples and the remaining ingredients in blender container. Cover and blend on high speed until smooth, about 30 seconds. Add remaining apples. Blend on high speed until smooth, about 30 seconds longer. Cover and refrigerate no longer than 24 hours. About 3 cups applesauce.

Sour Cream Coffee Cake and Fresh Applesauce

A Mexican Breakfast

The unique character of Mexican food is the result of the blending of many cultures. Plan to serve this hearty Mexican meal of Eggs with Chilies when you want to start your morning in a festive mood. Buñuelos, which are crisp fried pastries, are considered to be a tradition-al part of Christmas Eve celebrations and are customarily served with mugs of Mexican Hot Chocolate. The hot chocolate is traditionally beaten with a wooden beater called a molinello but a hand beater gives the same result.

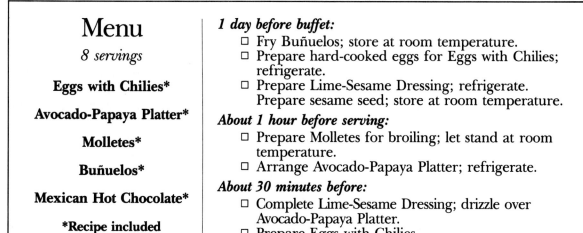

Menu

8 servings

Eggs with Chilies*

Avocado-Papaya Platter*

Molletes*

Buñuelos*

Mexican Hot Chocolate*

*Recipe included

1 day before buffet:
- ☐ Fry Buñuelos; store at room temperature.
- ☐ Prepare hard-cooked eggs for Eggs with Chilies; refrigerate.
- ☐ Prepare Lime-Sesame Dressing; refrigerate. Prepare sesame seed; store at room temperature.

About 1 hour before serving:
- ☐ Prepare Molletes for broiling; let stand at room temperature.
- ☐ Arrange Avocado-Papaya Platter; refrigerate.

About 30 minutes before:
- ☐ Complete Lime-Sesame Dressing; drizzle over Avocado-Papaya Platter.
- ☐ Prepare Eggs with Chilies.
- ☐ Broil Molletes.

At dessert time:
- ☐ Prepare Mexican Hot Chocolate; serve with Buñuelos.

Eggs with Chilies

12 hard-cooked eggs
 1 can (4 ounces) chopped green chilies, drained
¼ cup mayonnaise or salad dressing
½ teaspoon salt
 1 can (10¾ ounces) condensed cream of chicken soup
1½ cups milk
 1 package (10 ounces) frozen green peas
 2 tablespoons snipped parsley
½ cup sliced ripe olives

Cut peeled eggs lengthwise into halves. Slip out yolks; mash yolks with fork. Stir in chilies, mayonnaise and salt. Fill whites with egg yolk mixture, heaping lightly. Cover and refrigerate no longer than 24 hours.

Heat soup and milk to boiling, stirring occasionally. Rinse peas under running cold water to separate; drain. Stir peas into soup mixture. Heat to boiling; reduce heat. Cook uncovered, stirring occasionally, until peas are tender, about 5 minutes. Stir in parsley. Pour over eggs; sprinkle with olives.

Avocado-Papaya Platter

Lime-Sesame Dressing (below)
2 *large avocados*
2 *large papayas*
1 *lime*
Lettuce leaves
8 *lime wedges*

Prepare Lime-Sesame Dressing. Cut avocados and papayas lengthwise into halves. Cut each half lengthwise into 4 slices. Squeeze juice from lime evenly over slices. Arrange avocado and papaya slices on lettuce leaves; drizzle with Lime-Sesame Dressing. Garnish with lime wedges.

Lime-Sesame Dressing

⅓ *cup vegetable oil*
2 *tablespoons lime juice*
1 *tablespoon honey*
½ *teaspoon salt*
1 *clove garlic, crushed*
2 *tablespoons sesame seed*

Shake oil, lime juice, honey, salt and garlic in tightly covered container. Refrigerate at least 1 hour. Cook and stir sesame seed over medium heat until golden brown; cool. Add sesame seed to dressing; shake.

Molletes

4 *French rolls*
1 *can (16 ounces) refried beans*
½ *cup shredded cheese (2 ounces)*

Cut each roll lengthwise into halves. Set oven control to broil and/or 550°. Broil halves until golden brown. Spread each half with about 3 tablespoons refried beans. Sprinkle each half with 1 tablespoon cheese. Broil with tops 2 to 3 inches from heat until cheese is melted, about 1½ minutes.

Buñuelos

½ *cup water*
2 *tablespoons packed brown sugar*
1 *egg, slightly beaten*
2 *tablespoons margarine or butter*
2 *cups all-purpose flour*
½ *teaspoon baking powder*
¼ *teaspoon salt*
Vegetable oil
Honey

Heat water and brown sugar to boiling in 1-quart saucepan. Boil 2 minutes; cool. Stir in egg. Cut margarine into flour, baking powder and salt until mixture resembles fine crumbs; stir in egg mixture. Turn dough onto lightly floured surface. Knead until elastic, 5 minutes. Shape dough into roll, 20 inches long. Cover and let rest 1 hour.

Heat oil (1 inch) to 365°. Cut dough into 1-inch slices. Roll each slice on lightly floured surface into 5-inch circle. Fry circles, turning once, until golden brown, about 2 minutes; drain. Cover loosely and store at room temperature no longer than 24 hours.

Serve with honey. 20 buñuelos.

Mexican Hot Chocolate

4 *ounces sweet chocolate*
1 *cup water*
1 *teaspoon ground cinnamon*
¼ *teaspoon salt*
5 *cups milk*
½ *teaspoon almond extract*

Cut chocolate into pieces. Heat chocolate, water, cinnamon and salt in 3-quart saucepan over low heat, stirring constantly, until chocolate is melted and mixture is smooth. Heat to boiling; reduce heat. Stir in milk; heat through. Add almond extract; beat with hand beater until foamy. Serve immediately; garnish with stick cinnamon if desired.

Index

The following recipes are found in other Betty Crocker Cookbooks: